HOW POLITICIANS POLARIZE

CHICAGO STUDIES IN AMERICAN POLITICS

A series edited by Susan Herbst, Lawrence R. Jacobs, Adam J. Berinsky, and Frances Lee; Benjamin I. Page, editor emeritus

ALSO IN THE SERIES:

False Front: The Failed Promise of Presidential Power in a Polarized Age by Kenneth Lowande

Moral Issues: How Public Opinion on Abortion and Gay Rights Affects American Religion and Politics by Paul Goren and Christopher Chapp

The Roots of Polarization: From the Racial Realignment to the Culture Wars by Neil A. O'Brian

Some White Folks: The Interracial Politics of Sympathy, Suffering, and Solidarity by Jennifer Chudy

Through the Grapevine: Socially Transmitted Information and Distorted Democracy by Taylor N. Carlson

America's New Racial Battle Lines: Protect versus Repair by Rogers M. Smith and Desmond King

Partisan Hostility and American Democracy by James N. Druckman, Samara Klar, Yanna Krupnikov, Matthew Levendusky, and John Barry Ryan

Respect and Loathing in American Democracy: Polarization, Moralization, and the Undermining of Equality by Jeff Spinner-Halev and Elizabeth Theiss-Morse

Countermobilization: Policy Feedback and Backlash in a Polarized Age by Eric M. Patashnik

Race, Rights, and Rifles: The Origins of the NRA and Contemporary Gun Culture by Alexandra Filindra

Accountability in State Legislatures by Steven Rogers

Our Common Bonds: Using What Americans Share to Help Bridge the Partisan Divide by Matthew Levendusky

Dynamic Democracy: Public Opinion, Elections, and Policymaking in the American States by Devin Caughey and Christopher Warshaw

Persuasion in Parallel: How Information Changes Minds about Politics by Alexander Coppock

Radical American Partisanship: Mapping Violent Hostility, Its Causes, and the Consequences for Democracy by Nathan P. Kalmoe and Lilliana Mason

The Obligation Mosaic: Race and Social Norms in US Political Participation by Allison P. Anoll

A Troubled Birth: The 1930s and American Public Opinion by Susan Herbst

Power Shifts: Congress and Presidential Representation by John A. Dearborn

Additional series titles follow index

HOW POLITICIANS POLARIZE

POLITICAL REPRESENTATION IN AN
AGE OF NEGATIVE PARTISANSHIP

MIA COSTA

The University of Chicago Press
Chicago and London

The University of Chicago Press, Chicago 60637
The University of Chicago Press, Ltd., London
© 2025 by The University of Chicago
All rights reserved. No part of this book may be used or reproduced in any manner whatsoever without written permission, except in the case of brief quotations in critical articles and reviews. For more information, contact the University of Chicago Press, 1427 E. 60th St., Chicago, IL 60637.
Published 2025
Printed in the United States of America

34 33 32 31 30 29 28 27 26 25   1 2 3 4 5

ISBN-13: 978-0-226-83426-9 (cloth)
ISBN-13: 978-0-226-83894-6 (paper)
ISBN-13: 978-0-226-83893-9 (e-book)
DOI: https://doi.org/10.7208/chicago/9780226838939.001.0001

Library of Congress Cataloging-in-Publication Data

Names: Costa, Mia, author.
Title: How politicians polarize : political representation in an age of negative partisanship / Mia Costa.
Other titles: Chicago studies in American politics.
Description: Chicago ; London : The University of Chicago Press, 2025. | Series: Chicago studies in American politics | Includes bibliographical references and index.
Identifiers: LCCN 2024032854 | ISBN 9780226834269 (cloth) | ISBN 9780226838946 (paperback) | ISBN 9780226838939 (ebook)
Subjects: LCSH: Representative government and representation—United States. | Polarization (Social sciences)—United States. | Political culture—United States. | United States—Politics and government.
Classification: LCC JK1021 .C69 2025 | DDC 306.20973—dc23/eng/20240813
LC record available at https://lccn.loc.gov/2024032854

♾ This paper meets the requirements of ANSI/NISO Z39.48-1992 (Permanence of Paper).

CONTENTS

CHAPTER 1. How Politicians Polarize *1*

CHAPTER 2. Reinterpreting Representation for an "Us versus Them" Politics *17*

CHAPTER 3. Partisanship and Policy in Elite Communication *41*

CHAPTER 4. How Negative Representation Diminishes Substantive Representation *67*

CHAPTER 5. Negative Partisanship as an Electoral Strategy *81*

CHAPTER 6. The Hidden Layer of Polarization: Elite Animosity *114*

CHAPTER 7. Reaping the Rewards: Media, Money, and Influence *132*

CHAPTER 8. Americans Don't Like Negative Representation *151*

CHAPTER 9. Selective Tolerance: The Subgroups That Turn a Blind Eye *171*

CHAPTER 10. The Perception Gap *196*

CHAPTER 11. The Race to the Bottom (and the Way Back Up) *210*

Acknowledgments *219*

Appendixes

    Appendix to Chapter 3 *223*

    Appendix to Chapter 4 *227*

    Appendix to Chapter 7 *231*

    Appendix to Chapter 8 *235*

    Appendix to Chapter 9 *237*

Notes *243*

References *247*

Index *267*

1. HOW POLITICIANS POLARIZE

In 1832, Rep. William Stanbery became the first member of the House to be formally censured by his colleagues in Congress. His crime? "And let me say that I have heard the remark frequently made, that the eyes of the Speaker are too frequently turned from the chair you occupy toward the White House."[1] More plainly, he implied that the Speaker of the House, Andrew Stevenson, was too focused on trying to become president. A large majority, including members of Stanbery's own party, agreed that such "improper" and "disorderly" words amounted to unparliamentary language and deserved to be punished on the formal record for the first time in congressional history. Unfortunately, this did not set a precedent for more civility in politics. In the decades that followed, Congress saw many other instances of misconduct, sometimes including literal and physical attacks amongst members. Nonetheless, it was the first time in United States history a member was institutionally rebuked, which shows the extent to which hostile language was considered a grave disruption of the official duties of elected representatives.

That such a milquetoast statement was taken as so antithetical to good representation is quaint by today's standards. As of February 2024, only twenty-seven other censures have been issued since Stanbery's (ten since 1900, four of which occurred after 2021), but it would be impossible to count how many times politicians have said much, much worse about the people and groups with whom they disagree. As a point of comparison, one of the most recent censures in the House was of Rep. Adam Schiff (D-CA) in June 2023 for his role in congressional investigations of former President Donald Trump.[2] Addressing his Republican colleagues about his censure on the House floor, Schiff said "you honor me with your enmity," and ended with "today, I wear this partisan vote as a badge of honor." The preceding censure was of Rep. Paul Gosar (R-AZ) in 2021. In that case, the censure was for Gosar's act of sharing a photoshopped video on Twitter that depicted himself and other Republican lawmakers literally murdering Democrats.

The difference between what was considered normal politician behavior in Stanbery's time and what passes for such in the contemporary era is, obviously, stark. Stanbery's level of infraction has become so common that if Congress were to move to censure every instance of a partisan insult, they would get nothing else done. Not only are such attacks un-censorable by today's standards; they are an *expected* part of politician behavior, almost to the point of being mundane. If partisan attacks cut into actual legislative duties, then so be it. Rep. Marjorie Taylor Greene (R-GA) was stripped of her House committee assignments in February 2021 for similar incendiary remarks, such as endorsing violence against Democratic lawmakers. In theory, being removed from committees is meant to deprive a lawmaker of one of their fundamental representational powers. Yet, in a press conference, Rep. Greene said, "I'm fine with being kicked off my committees because it'd be a waste of my time," adding that she can now "talk to a whole lot more people all over this country" and that "[her] district is thrilled with [her]." For her, promoting partisan division through rhetoric was, in a way, more key to representation than having *actual* legislative influence in the House.

Given increasing political polarization, many scholars, pundits, voters, and even politicians themselves have come to believe an "us versus them" dynamic is central to the culture of contemporary political representation. Still, political scientists study political representation with regard to the "us" only. Traditionally, the diagnostic tools used to understand representation center around the interests of constituent groups, the people who make up the *represented*: for example, their policy preferences, service needs, or descriptive characteristics such as race, class, or gender. By definition, political representation is something that is done by representatives (agents) in relation to the people they were hired to represent (principals). If *re-presentation* means to literally and etymologically "make present again," as the theorist Hannah Pitkin argued in her groundbreaking work on the concept of representation, then it would seem nonsensical to undertake representation by "othering" a specific group, by making them present again only for the purpose of disassociating from them.

Political representation is conceived of as something that happens *for* people. This book is about what happens when representation is something that happens *against* people. I introduce a theory of representation that extends beyond classic conceptions to fit a context of political polarization and, specifically, negative partisanship. If negative partisanship is partisanship centered on the other side rather than one's own, then "negative representation," a concept introduced in this book, is representation centered on the other side rather than one's own. Social-psychological theories of identity suggest that who one is not (their negational identity) is sometimes just as, or even more, important than who one is (their affirmational identity)

How Politicians Polarize 3

(Zhong, Galinsky, and Unzueta 2008). At the same time, American political behavior is increasingly driven by out-group affect and hostility rather than in-group attachment or loyalty (Abramowitz and Webster 2018; Bankert 2020). Political identities are as much negational as they are affirmational. An opportunity therefore exists for representatives to serve the interests of constituents based on who they are *not*, rather than who they *are*.

This book is called *How Politicians Polarize* because I argue that a negative "us versus them" representational style that emphasizes out-groups is an act of political division. I focus on partisan identities because, as partisanship aligns with social identities, affective polarization has come to characterize much of American politics. Historically, social identities comprised characteristics like race, gender, class, and religion. Today, partisanship is likewise viewed and internally felt to be a crucial component of who we are. As a result, supporters of both major parties are drawn together by an intense hatred of the other party. In the study of political representation, we are most often concerned with how elected officials serve the public's policy interests. Yet as partisanship increases in importance, a growing body of research challenges the importance of policy congruence and substantive representation for mass political behavior. Negative partisan identities and out-party loathing are argued by some to be more motivating than loyalty to one's own party, and therefore this loathing may take precedence over policy or electoral victories (Abramowitz and Webster 2016; Iyengar, Sood, and Lelkes 2012; Iyengar and Krupenkin 2018; Mason 2018b). To be clear, political disagreement is an expected and even necessary part of any healthy functioning democracy. People with different views compete, deliberate, and negotiate with one another to make progress on shared concerns. But the shift in focus from *in-groups* to *out-groups* and from *policy* to *partisanship* requires a reinterpretation of representation for a polarized age.

Negative representation does not always have to be about partisanship, nor are all negational identities political. For example, the first time I went to a college football game at the University of Georgia, my husband (a UGA alum) taught me the fight song for the Bulldogs:

Glory glory to old Georgia
Glory glory to old Georgia
Glory glory to old Georgia
And to hell with Georgia Tech!

We scream-sang it from the crowded stands, barking (literally) at our opponents. Never mind that our opponents that evening were the Alabama Crimson Tide; to hell with Georgia Tech anyway. At large universities with massive football programs, one of the first things you learn is not just which

4 CHAPTER ONE

team you are supposed to root for, but which team you are supposed to root against. Chants, songs, and rituals that are meant to represent the fandom of these communities do so by calling attention to what they stand against, in addition to what they stand for. It is about not just the positive identification with the in-group, but also the negative othering of an out-group. As this example illustrates, not all negative identities are partisan in nature. But the context of *affective partisan* polarization gives new language and focus to this symbolic behavior from politicians. If your politics are defined, even somewhat, by being against what the other party stands for, then a politician who represents specifically by opposing the other party is representing your *negational* interests. As the parties polarize, politics reflects the qualities of a sports rivalry (and to hell with the opponent). Rep. Steven Palazzo (R-MS) sent a newsletter to his constituents in May 2018 with the subject line: "Tired of winning? Neither am I." Palazzo went on to use the words "win," "won," or "victorious" thirteen times in the newsletter, which was, in total, about as long as this paragraph. If we are the fans watching from the stands, politicians are now as much the cheerleaders on the sidelines as they are the players on the field.

WHAT THIS BOOK SHOWS

This book answers several interrelated questions raised by this contemporary political reality. What does representation look like when focused on out-groups rather than in-groups? Why do political elites (candidates and officeholders) use this negative representation style? How do voters react to such representation? What are the consequences? Is policy responsiveness still the cornerstone of American representative democracy when negative partisanship motivates political attitudes? Throughout the chapters, I empirically demonstrate how partisan negative representation operates in the American context. The findings challenge current understandings of affective polarization and political behavior. The research reveals several striking insights about the nature of political representation in an age of negative partisanship in the United States:

1. **The Prevalence of Negative Representation**: Politicians frequently engage in negative representation. While policy discourse dominates congressional newsletters, social media platforms like Twitter are rife with negative out-party language. Bipartisan language has also steadily increased over the last two decades, complicating the narrative of monolithic polarization.
2. **Electoral Safety and Competition**: Legislators from noncompetitive districts are more likely to engage in out-party appeals. The security of

their electoral position affords them the latitude to make partisan attacks without significant electoral repercussions. One implication of minimal turnover in Congress is that there is little incentive for politicians to adjust their behavior if the penalty for negative representation is not large enough to threaten their incumbency.

3. **Trade-offs with Substantive Representation**: Both ideological voting and ineffective lawmaking co-occur with negative representation. The politicians who talk about the out-party the most demonstrate lower efficacy in policymaking, suggesting that negative rhetoric undermines substantive representation. Partisan rancor detracts from the principal legislative responsibilities of elected representatives, thereby compromising the quality and effectiveness of lawmaking.

4. **Rethinking Electoral Rewards**: The research dispels the notion that negative representation directly leads to electoral gains. Neither observational analysis of election returns, nor survey data on elite perceptions, nor conjoint experiments on political candidates and officeholders shows significant electoral benefits for politicians employing negative rhetoric. This result challenges theories suggesting that politicians use negativity solely to court voters, and in so doing reveals a striking misalignment between what elites think voters want and what they tend to do anyway.

5. **Elite-Driven Negative Partisanship**: Political elites are inclined toward partisan antipathy. Despite recognizing that such negativity may not be electorally beneficial, elites perceive it as acceptable, particularly when both sides engage in it. This suggests that affective polarization is not just a grassroots phenomenon, but is equally fueled by the elites.

6. **Media and Fundraising Incentives**: Negative partisan language on social media platforms not only attracts more likes, retweets, and coverage in partisan television news media, but also boosts campaign donations, especially from out-of-state contributors. Engaging in negative representation enhances a politician's national profile.

7. **Citizen Preferences for Substantive Representation**: The findings challenge the prevailing view that citizens are motivated more by negative partisanship than by policy-based representation. Conjoint experiments demonstrate that Americans value substantive representation and would rather be governed by politicians who focus on issues rather than on partisan animosity.

8. **Limited Penalties for Negative Representation**: While negative representation is not favored even among highly polarized groups, it is not heavily penalized either, as long as policy alignment exists. This offers political elites ample room to employ negative tactics without facing electoral backlash.

9. **Perception Gaps and Negative Representation**: Misperceptions about the preferences of the opposite party perpetuate the cycle of negative representation. People do not desire negative representation themselves, but they erroneously believe that the opposite party does, creating a self-fulfilling prophecy that reinforces negative representation.

Collectively, these findings illuminate the complex dynamics of negative representation and challenge existing theories about its root causes and societal impacts. For example, even though Americans do *not* favor elite expressions of partisan animosity, and political elites do *not* think voters reward such rhetoric, the broader context of affective polarization makes the use of negative representational styles all too common. The research uncovers the intricacies of representation in an era characterized by both policy-focused and negative, affective styles.

DEFINING NEGATIVE REPRESENTATION

Before getting to the rest of the book, which walks through each of these analyses in turn, it is important to articulate exactly what I mean by "negative representation." Hannah Pitkin argues that most people use the concept of *political representation* but do not define it, instead taking a "you know it when you see it" approach. She stresses the importance of defining and elucidating the concept in different ways since it is so central to the study of politics; everyone wants to be represented and every government claims to represent. She likens the concept to "a rather complicated, convoluted, three-dimensional structure in the middle of a dark enclosure." Political theorists provide "flash-bulb photographs of the structure taken from different angles" (Pitkin 1967, 10). I offer yet another snapshot by highlighting the role of out-groups and polarization. It is not new to suggest that politicians denigrate and divide, but it is new to consider this behavior as another form of *representation*, and it can help us understand this behavior in a more systematic way.

Negative representation is a style of representation focused on out-groups rather than in-groups. This contrasts with "positive representation," which is focused on in-groups and encompasses most treatments of representation in the literature. Representatives make constituents present by acting on behalf of them, standing for them, making known their claims and interests. Elected officials can represent their constituents in a variety of ways, by focusing on policy concerns, allocating resources to their district, or providing service responsiveness. When using a negative representational style, representatives instead draw on negational identities by "othering" a different set of constituents. In practice, this takes the form of partisan (or in-group) cheerleading or emphasizing opposition to the other party (or out-group). As negational identities become more profound and crystallized, the opportunity arises for negative representation. If one of the key components of your identity is to *not* be something else, then othering and distancing *that* thing that you are not is itself a form of representation.

Importantly, I use the term "negative" in a directional sense to indicate something that is oppositional or negational, rather than to ascribe affective value. Lau and Pomper define negative campaigning in the same way: "in effect, the directional meaning of negative—statements in opposition to a person or program—is too often equated with the evaluative meaning—statements that are normatively disvalued" (2002, 48). There is an entire body of research within political science that is devoted to the study of "negativity" as it relates to civility (see, e.g., Geer 2008). This research has been crucial in shedding light on when, why, and how negativity as incivility happens, and what the consequences are. Naturally, this research influences my theory and study of negative representation. But it is important to note that not all group-based "othering" is necessarily uncivil; politicians can reference an out-group to draw attention to a "them" different from an "us" without explicitly using emotional or inflammatory language. Of course, many times, when politicians talk about the other side, they do so in an uncivil way. What distinguishes negative representation from mere hostility is the explicit invocation of the other side as a group. When Donald Trump tweeted that Rep. Justin Amash is "one of the dumbest & most disloyal men in Congress" and "a total loser!" (July 4, 2019), he used uncivil language, but he was not denigrating a group as a whole. When Trump tweeted "The Dems are vicious" (May 16, 2020) or "This is the NEW and very sick Democratic Party" (September 2, 2020), he was referencing the other party as a whole, *and* one might also consider "very sick" and "vicious" to be examples of incivility. When Trump tweeted, "Democrats are so obviously rooting against us in our negotiations with North Korea" (May 25, 2018), he was referring to the Democrats as a group, but was not using particularly uncivil language. Negative representatives are those who use rhetoric not necessarily against their individual opponents, but against the other party in general.

Using uncivil language against an out-party is one way partisan identities could manifest in negative styles of representation. While a certain level of negativity has always been common in campaigns, hostile discourse among elites has become more salient in the digital age (Gainous and Wagner 2014; Geer 2008; Prior 2013; Russell 2021). Some research suggests that more hostile and uncivil campaign environments contribute to the growing affective gap between partisans (Iyengar, Sood, and Lelkes 2012; Iyengar et al.

2019). When legislators use *affective* forms of representation, they may rely on emotional appeals that refer to the personal qualities of partisan groups.

Distinct from pure affective partisan rhetoric is rhetoric based on winning and losing elections. Representatives focus on out-group electoral loss (or in-group victory), without particular use of incivility. By emphasizing victory in an election, partisans are pitted against one another as if in a spectator sport. For example, Rep. David Price (D-NC) wrote a newsletter to his constituents in May 2022 with an electoral focus: "The troubles in the Congress are political, and so the answer is simply to win an election. I'm not saying Democrats are all virtuous or anything like that. But some of the most satisfying, coherent operations I've seen here have been in the years where there was unified party control, and it was Democratic control. Especially given the turn the Republican Party's taken and the threat of Donald Trump coming back, I feel very strongly we need to win these next elections." In this quote, Rep. Price used both a *positive* (by mentioning the in-group, Democrats) and a *negative* (by mentioning the out-group, Republicans) representational style focused on elections. This differs sharply from representational styles that are more affective in nature, like those used in Speaker Nancy Pelosi's newsletter in July 2013: "Americans needed Congress to work together so they wouldn't have to worry about going to bed hungry. Instead, Republicans decided to jeopardize the certainty and stability of America's rural communities, and risk taking food out of the mouths of those who need it most. It is shameful, disgraceful, and wrong—wrong for our families, wrong for our communities, and wrong for our country."

To be clear, while this book focuses on partisanship, the theory of negative representation can apply to any out-group. Social identity theories have long predicted that how individuals define themselves as members of groups helps to explain their attitudes and behavior (Tajfel 1982). In political science, these theories have been used to better understand party affiliation (Campbell et al. 1960; Green, Palmquist, and Schickler 2004), group conflict (Elkins and de Figueiredo 2003), and policy preferences (Burns and Gimpel 2000). Social identity and group theory have so far not been used to investigate forms of representation based on who a representative's constituents are not, even though politicians often publicly express disdain for "the other side." Defining "the other" is, empirically, a question of measurement. Immigrants, the wealthy, Black Americans, Muslim Americans, and LGBTQ+ individuals, among others, are all groups politicians frequently make out to be a "them" in their rhetoric and their legislative actions. Existing research has offered many insights about othering with regard to social, economic, racial, ethnic, gender, and other groups. In this book, I focus on explicit language about the other *party* specifically. While ample research exists on language from politicians about identity groups (e.g., Gervais and

Wilson 2017; Haines, Mendelberg, and Butler 2019; Tillery 2019) and electoral opponents in campaigns (e.g., Ansolabehere et al. 1994), and on the use of incivility and emotional rhetoric in electoral politics (e.g., Brooks and Geer 2007; Geer 2008; Webster 2020), the field does not yet have an adequate understanding of group-based partisan appeals from politicians, especially in relation to policy-oriented appeals, and of the consequences for representative democracy.

Finally, note that I am referring to negative representation as a "style" of representation. Eulau et al. (1959) distinguished between representational style and focus. The "focus" of representation deals with categorizing the constituency group—for example, people residing in the official's district, party voters, all citizens in the nation, and so on. "Style" refers to how representatives see their role—as delegates or trustees—which governs their behavior in office. I talk about representational styles focused on negative partisanship compared to policy, for example, because these are ways legislators approach and talk about their job.

THEORETICAL AND EMPIRICAL INNOVATIONS

Theoretically, this book engages with a new way of thinking about representation. In her book *Making Constituencies*, the democratic theorist Lisa Disch (2021) offers an interpretation of representation that adopts a "constructivist" perspective: constituents do not simply delegate their will to representatives; representatives actively construct constituencies. She challenges the assumption in much theoretical and empirical research that "responsiveness" to the public is or should be the goal of political representation. Rather than *responding* to deeply divided camps of partisans who stand in opposition to one another, Disch argues that representatives *forge* these camps themselves. In other words, scholars who argue that affective polarization is born out of voters assigning themselves a social identity tied to their partisan affiliation get it wrong. She writes (2021, 13): "The constructivist alternative, which builds on Fiorina's work, turns this model around. Rather than explain sorting as an affective divide rooted in the dynamics of social identity, this approach posits a political divide emerging in response to increasing polarization among political elites. They theorize acts of political representation *making* the social as opposed to *reflecting* it" (emphasis in original). In this book, I empirically demonstrate what Disch theorizes. Understanding elites' rhetoric about the other side as a form of representation flips standard theories on their head and shows how such rhetoric can *make* the polarized social order instead of just reflecting it. Understanding the causes and consequences of political communication is important for understanding the rhetoric that characterizes today's political landscape.

Empirically, I test the causal foundations and effects of negative partisanship at both the mass public and the politician level in ways that have not yet been done. In doing so, the book fills important gaps across two academic literatures. First, scholarship on political representation has not explicitly defined a form of legislator behavior based on out-group identities, something that is more and more pressing in an age when partisanship is more negative (or based in distance from the other side) than it is positive (or based in closeness toward the same side). Understanding political representation from an "us versus them" perspective is crucial for the modern political climate. Second, research on affective polarization focuses almost exclusively on negative and positive partisanship in the public. Scholars have not yet systematically studied how out-party affect operates at the politician level, nor what the consequences might be for representative democracy in the United States. Do politicians feel as negatively about the out-party as the American public does? Do they think attacking the other party is a good way to represent their constituents and win elections? The findings in this book contribute to and challenge existing theories held by scholars, voters, and pundits alike about mass and elite political behavior in an era of heightened affective polarization.

Importantly, the book challenges some of the doom-and-gloom conclusions about polarization in American politics. I do not claim that politicians polarize because all they focus on in their communications is partisan division. I also do not claim that politicians polarize because they are responding to voters' partisan vices. Rather, I show how politicians polarize *despite* these things. Politicians polarize *despite* the fact that they focus on policy more than partisanship. Politicians polarize *despite* the fact that most people desire representation based on policy agreement. Politicians polarize *despite* the fact that they think negative partisanship is a bad electoral strategy and think ideological representation is more important. While that is not necessarily a sunny conclusion about the health of American representative democracy, it is also not quite as bleak as some other research suggests— and it potentially offers a way out.

In the introduction of *Why We're Polarized*, Ezra Klein includes a sort of disclaimer: "Let me be clear from the beginning: This is not a book about people. This is a book about systems." While the topics of our respective books are similar (they both address polarization in American politics), I could say essentially the opposite. From a political science perspective, this not a book about systems. This is a book about people. As a behavioral social scientist, I believe that studying people is at the core of understanding political and social phenomena. Of course, both are important. How institutions function is shaped by the people within them, and how people behave is shaped by the institutions in which they act. This is especially true for legislative representation—which bills are put on the agenda, which laws are passed, how those laws are enacted through the bureaucracy, and ultimately how they do or do not serve the public interest. How politicians speak and symbolize on behalf of constituents, however, is the makeup of negative representation. I therefore use a behavioral approach to make generalizable descriptive and causal inferences by using large-scale quantitative communications datasets, surveys, and experiments. There are several ways I take institutions and certain temporal contexts into account in the analyses in this book. But the findings are ultimately about how people and politicians behave in the contemporary American political system.

Klein departed from the standard journalistic practice of focusing on specific political actors in favor of a more systematic analysis, so the two of us ultimately end up with similar conclusions. Klein catalogs the logic of polarization as the following cycle: "To appeal to a more polarized public, political institutions and political actors behave in more polarized ways. As political institutions and actors become more polarized, they further polarize the public. This sets off a feedback cycle: to appeal to a yet more polarized public, institutions must polarize further; when faced with yet more polarized institutions, the public polarized further, and so on." I illuminate this logic in a different way, with new and original data, through the lens of representatives' individual rhetoric and voters' reactions to that rhetoric. I do this to center one important part of the story, which is politicians' communication about the other party. Almost all political scientists so far have studied negative partisanship from the side of voters—how voters feel about the other party compared to their own party. We do not yet have an account of negative partisanship from the side of politicians themselves. How do politicians speak about the parties? How do they feel about the parties? What are the downstream effects of their rhetoric about the parties on voters' attitudes and perceptions about politics? These are questions about people, so I center people in the research in this book. I hope future research will examine more closely the relationship between these individual-level behaviors and the systems of polarization as institutions.

OUTLINE OF THE BOOK

Chapter 2 provides more background on the book's theoretical framework. I discuss current and historical patterns of political representation and polarization, and the important role group identity plays in political attitudes and behaviors. How negative representation is both related to and distinct from other classic forms of positive representation (substantive, descriptive, and symbolic) is also considered. I describe the potential mechanisms tested throughout the book by which politicians might engage in negative forms of representation—is it driven by voters, elites themselves, or external incentives to increase exposure? Finally, I outline the consequences for American representative democracy. If you are interested in refining your understanding of negative representation as a concept, chapter 2 is a good one to read.

I then turn to the empirical analyses, which are plentiful. In the first part of the book (chapters 3–7), I examine political representation in an age of negative partisanship from the side of politicians. How often does it occur? How is it related to substantive representation on policy? Are political elites as affectively polarized as the public? How is negative representation treated by the media, and how does it influence campaign fundraising? In the second part (chapters 8–10), I study the effects from the side of citizens. How do Americans react to partisan attacks by elites? How do people weigh partisan rhetoric versus policy rhetoric? What are their attitudes about negative representation?

Chapter 3 lays some important groundwork with qualitative and quantitative evidence of how politicians use a negative style of political representation. It provides important proof of concept for the theoretical construct of negative and positive partisan communication styles. Using text analysis of large-scale datasets of congressional newsletters and social media posts, I examine the nature of representational styles centered on affective, group-oriented motivations rather than substantive, policy-based concerns. What does congressional communication look like when it is focused on (partisan) out-groups rather than in-groups? First, the chapter shows that rhetoric about policy is much more common than partisan rhetoric. However, while policy-oriented language appears in almost every congressional newsletter, it appears much less on social media: only about one-third of all tweets analyzed contain policy-coded words. Representatives consistently invoke negative out-party language more frequently after their party loses control of Congress, but the use of bipartisan language has (perhaps surprisingly) slowly but steadily increased over time. And the language members of Congress use to tweet about the out-party has become increasingly negative in sentiment during this same period.

Chapter 4 examines which legislators are most likely to use out-party appeals and what this means for representation on policy. Congress members elected to noncompetitive districts use negative representation more than do members elected to competitive districts. Electoral safety offers leeway to gain from making partisan attacks without having to worry about reelection, which has implications for politicians' legislative activity. Members of Congress who are more ideological in their voting patterns tend to talk more about the other party, but not about policy issues that are in the interest of voters. Moreover, the politicians who talk more about the other party are less effective at actual policymaking. Overall, negative out-partisan rhetoric has meaningful, and dire, implications for substantive representation.

Chapter 5 tests the first of the book's hypotheses regarding why politicians use a negative representational style. Do politicians think voters reward negative partisanship? First, I examine how language is associated with Congress members' vote share in the next election and find no statistically significant relationship between the use of out-party rhetoric and how many votes a representative receives. Second, an original survey of politicians shows that elected officials who insult the other party are perceived to *lose* support among both undecided voters and core supporters. Finally, I use a conjoint experiment to isolate the effect of out-party animus, in-party cheerleading, and ideological congruence on politicians' perceptions of electoral viability. I again find little support for the voter-driven hypothesis. Politicians and candidates think negative partisan rhetoric harms candidates' electoral chances. Talking about issues is believed to be a better electoral strategy than talking about partisanship, and specifically better than attacking the other side. The findings generate a puzzle tackled in chapters 6 and 7: if garnering support from voters does not drive this behavior, then what does?

Not much research has examined affective polarization at the level of candidates or politicians, but this is crucial for understanding how elites represent during a polarized era. Contrary to the idea that politicians are always rational, strategic decision-makers unlikely to admit genuine attitudes, chapter 6 shows that they are all too willing to denigrate the opposite party when asked in a survey. Political elites have high levels of partisan antipathy toward the out-party themselves, and they also perceive increased negativity in politics. At the same time, they think negative partisan rhetoric does not necessarily lose elections when both candidates use it. In campaigns that are characterized by negativity, attacking the out-party is viewed as fair game. Therefore, elite-driven negative partisanship is part of the vicious cycle of affective polarization and provides intrinsic incentives to engage in negative representation.

There are external incentives as well. The increasing number of safe districts means that politicians may have opportunities to indulge in their partisan proclivities, even if doing so does not win support in the aggregate. Chapter 7 documents the role of social media, traditional cable news, and campaign finance. First, I find that congressional tweets that contain out-party appeals garner significantly more attention than tweets about the in-party, policy, or compromise. Second, partisan television news media disproportionately highlight stories about partisan attacks by members of Congress that are communicated via Twitter. Finally, the cost of political campaigns has escalated, increasing the importance of fundraising. Research indicates that social media posts by politicians that receive more attention enhance a candidate's visibility, leading to increased financial contributions. Congressional tweets that contain polarizing language in particular increase both the amount of money raised and the number of donors. Is negative representation associated with an increase in fundraising, particularly from out-of-state donors? I find that negative partisan language in tweets, but not necessarily in newsletters, is associated with a rise in overall fundraising and out-of-state donations. This is consistent with what has so far been learned about negative representation in newsletters versus social media: newsletters are targeted at constituents within the politician's district, whereas tweets reach a broader audience. Social media posts that criticize the opposing party are more likely to be liked and retweeted, reaching potential donors in various locations. The empirical patterns of this chapter suggest that engaging in negative representation serves to enhance a legislator's national profile and influence.

Chapter 8 begins the section of the book investigating negative representation from the side of citizens. How do citizens want to be represented by elected officials in an age of negative partisanship? The title of the chapter pretty much gives it away: "Americans don't like negative representation." Contemporary narratives about American politics argue that people embrace elite expressions of negative partisanship, above and beyond representation on policy. Across three conjoint experiments, I examine how individuals weigh the relative value of substantive representation on issues, constituency service, and expressions of partisan affect. The findings challenge the notion that Americans are primarily motivated by their affective, partisan identities and demonstrate the value of substantive representation. In fact, people evaluate elected officials in ways we would expect them to in a healthy, functioning representative democracy, rather than one characterized by partisan animus. Even if polarization is driven by "affect, not ideology," as some scholars suggest, citizens prioritize representational styles centered around the issues that matter to them.

Chapter 9 further explores Americans' reactions to negative representation. Even if voters in the aggregate penalize negative representation, are there certain subsets of the electorate (like political donors, primary voters, or Trump supporters) who respond favorably to partisan attacks? Are there conditions under which voters are willing to tolerate negative representation? I show that even though many groups report above-average levels of negative partisan affect, they do not generally support negative partisan rhetoric from representatives. These findings highlight how persistent, widespread, and robust unfavorable reactions to negative representation really are. That said, while certain groups do not *favor* negative representation, they do not necessarily *penalize* it either. Moreover, when a representative aligns with voters on policy, their rhetoric is not a discriminating factor in how voters evaluate them. Constituents are willing to turn a blind eye to incongruent policy representation, as long as their representative avoids negative partisanship. This suggests that ample opportunities for leeway exist for elites to attack the other side without repercussions from voters, and provides important nuance to understanding the relationship between negative and substantive representation.

One takeaway from these analyses so far is that perceptions about polarization feed into representational styles that capitalize on negativity. Chapter 10 investigates this argument a step further by measuring what is known in psychology as a "perception gap," the distance between people's judgments about others' social-political attitudes and the reality of those attitudes. I use another original survey experiment to examine how people think members of the other party perceive partisan attacks. Partisans themselves do not want negative representation, but they think people in the opposite party do. Beliefs about negative representation and affective polarization are part of a self-fulfilling prophecy. We do not get the kind of representation we want from our elected officials; instead, we get the kind of representation we believe everyone else wants.

The book concludes with a chapter discussing the implications for representation and democracy. The first implication is that representatives sometimes respond to incentives that are antithetical to quality substantive representation and that encourage citizens' feelings of distrust and disillusionment with politics. It is notable that legislators engage in negative representation even when they understand that ideological congruence is more important to voters. Much classic research on representation suggests that elected officials' lawmaking behavior is responsive to constituent preferences (Erikson, MacKuen, and Stimson 2002; Erikson 2013; Tausanovitch and Warshaw 2014). Other research shows, on the other hand, that many representatives misperceive what their constituents want and therefore do not act according to these preferences (Arnold 1990; Broockman and Skovron 2018; Butler and Dynes 2016; Miler 2010). In this case, politicians know what voters want but choose to act differently because of other benefits or pressures. This mismatch between lawmakers' actions and constituents' desires diminishes the quality of substantive representation. A further implication is that we must take seriously the electoral setting and structural forces that play a key role in allowing legislators to act this way without repercussions. Lawmakers from strongly partisan, noncompetitive districts have leeway to use more negative rhetoric, warranting future research on how affective polarization may influence candidate emergence. On the other hand, there are reasons to be optimistic: most people prioritize representational styles centered around important issue areas, and representatives are aware of this, which may offer a way back up from the race to the bottom. I close by discussing considerations for how we might break the cycle of negative representation, which include keeping in mind the benefits of partisanship and polarization, identifying interventions to reduce mass-level partisan animosity, and addressing the attention economy and negativity biases.

2. REINTERPRETING REPRESENTATION FOR AN "US VERSUS THEM" POLITICS

The congressman conveys a sense of identification with his constituents. Contextually and verbally he gives them the impression that "I am one of you."

RICHARD FENNO, "US House Members in Their Constituencies: An Exploration"

Our current leadership believes the way you win elections is that you don't stand for anything, you don't have an agenda, you don't have a plan. Instead, that the only thing you stand up and say is "Well, I'm not a Democrat. So vote for me."

SEN. TED CRUZ (R-TX), November 15, 2002

Everyone seems to be worried about increasing partisan polarization. The division between Democrats and Republicans has caused tension and mistrust in American society, leading to a decline in faith in political institutions and the federal government. According to recent surveys from Gallup, trust in government remains low, many Americans have little faith in democracy, a majority do not believe in the ability of the government to solve problems and address the needs of its citizens, and people today are as likely to mention the functioning of government as a top critical issue for the country as they are to mention things like the economy and immigration.[1] In order to understand the theoretical framework for analyzing negative representation, let's start with a simple question: How did we get to this point?

HOW THE PARTIES HAVE POLARIZED

To document how Congress has polarized, political scientists have examined the voting patterns of its members. Poole and Rosenthal (1984) developed a methodology to attribute an ideological score, called DW-

NOMINATE, to each member of Congress based on roll call votes. Figure 2.1 shows the median DW-NOMINATE score for members of each party. Both Democrats and Republicans have increasingly voted along ideological lines over time. This trend began in the Senate in the 1950s, and the House followed about two decades later. While Democrats vote more liberally and Republicans vote more conservatively than they did in the past, the shift has been more pronounced among Republicans. Republicans consistently vote in more ideologically extreme ways than do Democrats, increasing the distance between the parties to its greatest point since the Civil War (McCarty 2019).

Of course, ideological distance measured by roll call voting is just one aspect of legislative behavior and is limited by what votes get called to the floor in the first place. The level of bipartisan cosponsorship of bills has declined over time, but this decline has been much less pronounced than the drop in bipartisan roll call voting (Harbridge 2015). Party leaders' agenda-setting powers inflate levels of polarization while also providing evidence of a legislature engaged in partisan conflict. Indeed, the institutional rules and procedures of Congress appear to exacerbate partisan politics. It is easy to forget now that Democrats held overwhelming control of both chambers of Congress for the better part of the entire twentieth century. This one-party dominance of Congress created a situation that was ripe for bipartisan compromise; after all, Republicans saw little chance of controlling Congress during this time, so the only way to influence policy was to compromise with Democrats. But starting in the 1980s, when the Democrats lost control of

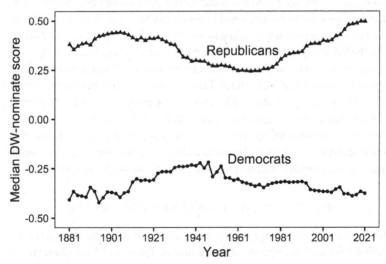

Figure 2.1. Polarization in the US Congress
Note: Median DW-nominate score 1881–2021. Source: voteview.

the Senate, and increasingly since 1995, when they also lost control of the House, elections have been closely contested in the aggregate pretty much at every turn. This means both sides are intently focused on the next election, where control of Congress is always up for grabs. The insecure status of the party in power leads them to emphasize partisan agenda-setting to try to score points for the next election, while the minority party is incentivized to wait it out instead of compromising, hoping to advance its own agenda if and when it regains majority status in the next election, rather than to hand the majority bipartisan legislative victories (Lee 2016; Gelman 2019, 2020).

In her book *Beyond Ideology* (2009), the political scientist Frances Lee shows how party leaders are incentivized to compete for institutional power and embarrass the other side. Lee argues that much of what has been cast as purely ideological polarization between the parties in Congress is instead the natural result of the logic of partisanship. Even in the Senate, a legislative body where we should be least likely to observe partisan behavior due to the individual power possessed by each senator, members band together for electoral as much as ideological reasons. High levels of partisan voting exist on what can even be considered non-ideological issues, such as those dealing with Senate procedure or ethics. Through partisan behavior, members can create long-lasting legislative blocs, avoid the risks of potentially controversial actions, and develop partisan brands on which to campaign. Even when parties generally agree on an issue, they amplify conflict to gain advantage over their opponents. For instance, for years there has been bipartisan support for immigration reform in Congress, yet party leaders consistently keep these compromise proposals from gaining serious traction, choosing instead to try to use the issue to score points in the next election campaign. At the same time, the issues on which the parties do not agree are the most likely to be given the most attention. When party leaders exercise agenda-setting power more frequently and in ways that serve to undermine the opposition, bills that might receive bipartisan support (and thus reduce observed levels of ideological voting in Congress) stay off the floor (Theriault 2008, 2013).

Also contributing to the increasing polarization in Congress was a significant realignment in the South during the latter part of the twentieth century. Before the 1960s, Democratic legislators from the former confederate states were a large contingent, almost a third, of the Democratic Party. Those representatives were considerably more conservative than their Democratic counterparts in the North, particularly on racial issues and civil rights. They continued to affiliate with the Democratic Party because the South largely lacked an active Republican Party. The landscape began to change with the civil rights movement and the subsequent passage of the Voting Rights Act in 1965. This landmark legislation sought to eliminate racial discrimination in voting, a policy that was at odds with the racial conservatism prevalent among many southern Democrats at the time. The tensions within the Democratic Party led to a reevaluation of political affiliations. Over time, the Republican Party gained more traction in the South, and conservative politicians began running as Republicans rather than Democrats. As a result, the southern states elected fewer Democratic representatives, and those they did elect were more liberal. Now, the much smaller contingent of Democrats representing southern states do not clearly differ along ideological lines compared to Democrats in the North. At the same time, more representatives in the Republican Party today are from the South than they were fifty years ago, and southern Republicans in particular have become even more conservative in their voting patterns.

Issue-based polarization in the public can be thought of in the same way as ideological polarization in Congress: in terms of the distance between the average issue positions of Republican and Democratic citizens. According to a large Pew survey, the percentage of Americans who held "consistently liberal" or "consistently conservative" positions increased from 10 to 21 percent between 1994 and 2014. The median Republican is more conservative than at least 94 percent of Democrats, compared to 70 percent two decades ago. During the same period, the median Democrat moved from being more liberal than 64 percent of Republicans to being more liberal than 92 percent of Republicans. In other words, more Democrats are liberal and more Republicans are conservative than before. But ideological *consistency* is not quite the same as ideological *polarization*. The political science research on whether Democrats and Republicans have actually taken more *extreme* issue positions has been hotly debated. One camp, pioneered by Fiorina, Abrams, Pope, and Levendusky (Fiorina and Abrams 2008, 2012; Fiorina, Abrams, and Pope 2005, 2008; Levendusky 2009a, 2009b), contends that most citizens are moderate. Polarization, they argue, is an epiphenomenon of people sorting into the appropriate parties (liberals into the Democratic Party and conservatives into the Republican Party), but actual issue positions have remained unchanged and relatively centrist. The other camp, led mostly by Abramowitz and Saunders (Abramowitz 2010; Abramowitz and Saunders 2005, 2008), claims that the ideological consistency and division of Democrats and Republicans in the mass public has grown over time. At the very least, we know that people have regrouped into parties along ideological lines, even if their issue positions have not become more extreme—a conclusion that is backed up by studies that use newer methods and data (e.g., Hill and Tausanovitch 2015). In short, voters are more ideologically aligned with the parties. When mass-level constituencies are sorted in line with the party's preferences, members are not pulled in opposite directions and are able to cede more power to party leaders, which can further amplify polarization (Theriault 2008).

NEGATIVE PARTISANSHIP AND "US VERSUS THEM" POLARIZATION

Of course, when people talk about "polarization" these days, they often mean more than just the measured distance between specific policy views. They mean the conflict, division, and distrust that seems to permeate American politics, leading to a breakdown of dialogue and understanding between different political groups. This type of division between partisans has contributed to a decline in social cohesion and a rise in party teamsmanship, as individuals become more entrenched in their political beliefs and less willing to engage with those who hold opposing views. *Affective polarization* is the distance between how individuals feel about their own party (positive partisanship) and how they feel about the opposite party (negative partisanship). Both external factors—such as the changing media environment (Lelkes, Sood, and Iyengar 2017; Iyengar et al. 2019; Boxell, Gentzkow, and Shapiro 2017), social sorting (Mason 2016, 2018a, 2018b), and electoral institutions (Abramowitz and Webster 2016; Gidron, Adams, and Horne 2020)—and internal factors—like partisanship as a social identity (Green, Palmquist, and Schickler 2004), emotional reactions (Huddy, Mason, and Aarøe 2015), partisan stereotyping (Ahler and Sood 2018; Levendusky and Malhotra 2016a), and psychological traits (Simas, Clifford, and Kirkland 2020; Luttig 2017)—can contribute to growing affective polarization. The extent to which ideological polarization drives affective polarization is an open debate among scholars. Some argue that feelings about the other party are not consistently grounded in policy attitudes (e.g., Iyengar, Sood, and Lelkes 2012). Other evidence shows that affective polarization is closely connected to and reinforced by ideological polarization (Dias and Lelkes 2022; Lelkes 2021; Rogowski and Sutherland 2017; Webster and Abramowitz 2017). While it is not *only* sorted partisans who are affectively polarized (Lelkes 2018), people who have more extreme and ideologically constrained policy attitudes tend to dislike the other party the most (Bougher 2017).

There are several ways to measure affective polarization and negative or positive partisanship (see Druckman and Levendusky 2019; Iyengar et al. 2019 for overviews). The first and most straightforward is the use of feeling thermometers in surveys. Feeling thermometers are a type of survey question that asks individuals to rate their feelings toward a specific person, group, or issue on a 0 (cold or very unfavorable) to 100 (warm or very favorable) scale. Figure 2.2 shows the average feeling thermometer ratings American adults have given their own party and the opposite party from 1978 to 2020 according to the American National Election Studies (ANES). In 1980, people rated their own party on average just above 70 on the 0 to 100-point scale. By 2020, their ratings had not changed much—they still

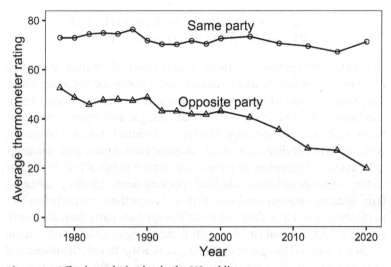

Figure 2.2. Affective polarization in the US public
Note: Average thermometer rating 1980–2020. Source: American National Election Studies. Sampling weights applied.

registered right around the 70 mark. Ratings of the opposite party, however, have dramatically decreased. In 1980, the average thermometer rating of the other party was about 50, meaning that, on average, partisans were fairly neutral in how they rated the other party. In that year, just 7 percent of the partisans in the ANES sample gave the other party the lowest possible rating of 0. By 2020, these ratings dropped by over half to an average of 20—and 40 percent of respondents gave the other party the lowest possible rating of 0. Affective polarization (the average distance between in-party and out-party ratings) has increased from 20 to 50 points in the past forty years.

Other measures of affective polarization, negative partisanship, or partisan animosity try to capture similar negative attitudes about out-partisans and conclude that, along a number of different metrics, partisans in the mass public increasingly dislike and distrust one another. Studies using trait ratings find that people are increasingly likely to ascribe negative characteristics (e.g., unintelligent, selfish, and hypocritical) to out-partisans and positive characteristics (e.g., open-minded, intelligent, and generous) to in-partisans (Iyengar, Sood, and Lelkes 2012; Levendusky 2018; Levendusky and Malhotra 2016a). Iyengar and Westwood (2015) employed a version of an implicit association test (IAT), traditionally used to measure racial bias, to measure the strength of an individual's automatic associations between concepts (e.g., political parties) and evaluative dimensions (e.g., positive or negative) and found that implicit partisan bias is more common than implicit racial bias. Approximately 70 percent of Republicans and Democrats showed an unconscious bias against the other party compared to their own party. Shanto Iyengar, one of the coauthors of the study, was quoted in a *Vox* piece (Klein and Chang 2015) about this research: "Political identity is fair game for hatred. Racial identity is not. Gender identity is not. You cannot express negative sentiments about social groups in this day and age. But political identities are not protected by these constraints. A Republican is someone who chooses to be Republican, so I can say whatever I want about them." Partisan animus is so widely expressed at least partly because there are no social norms discouraging it. If anything, these sentiments are broadly encouraged by many political elites.

It is worth noting here that a lot of research has been conducted on feelings of negative partisanship among citizens, but very few studies, if any, have been published on feelings of negative partisanship among political elites. This is due in part to the difficulty of gathering this data. It is not easy to ask members of Congress to rate fellow and opposite partisans on feeling thermometer scales for comparison with the mass public. For this book, I was able to survey different kinds of political elites, including political candidates and current officeholders at mostly the state and local levels, for their feelings of negative partisanship and perceptions of negative representation (see chapter 6). The elites in my surveys gave even lower thermometer ratings of the opposite party than a large, nationally representative mass public sample. I also asked them to describe partisans in their own words; terms such as "liars," "evil," "dishonest," and "greedy" showed up the most when these elites were asked about the other party. These findings suggest that affective polarization and negative partisanship are not just public-level phenomena.

The consequences of affective polarization can be profound. "Social distance" measures the extent to which people wish to avoid interpersonal relations with others. In 1960, about 5 percent of partisans felt very upset at the idea of their child marrying someone of the other party. In 2008, that figure jumped to over 25 percent for Republicans and 20 percent for Democrats. By 2010, just two years later, the figure doubled to 50 percent for Republicans and exceeded 30 percent for Democrats (Iyengar, Sood, and Lelkes 2012). Research by Klar, Krupnikov, and Ryan (2018) provides an important caveat to these findings by showing that this reflects a general aversion to partisan politics more than partisan animosity per se. Using a similar survey instrument about a child marrying a same- or other-partisan, they found that the results were moderated by the extent to which the hypothetical spouse was said to discuss politics. People expressed much less opposition to their child marrying someone from the other party when the person rarely talked about politics, and they also expressed *more* opposition to their child marrying someone from the same party when the person was said to frequently talk about politics. In their book *The Other Divide*, Krupnikov and

Ryan (2022) argue that the real divide in America is between people who are deeply engaged and interested in politics and people who are not. They find that only 15 to 20 percent of Americans follow politics closely. This group of partisans has different policy priorities than people who do not follow politics; they are also the people who drive affective polarization and feel most negative about the out-party.

Two conclusions from this large and growing body of existing work are important for understanding representation in a polarized era. First, people who identify with a party have increasingly hostile and negative feelings toward the other party on average, and perceptions of policy disagreement exacerbate negative affect. Second, most people do not want to engage in partisan warfare; there is a large portion of the public that is disillusioned by partisan politics. Taken together, these conclusions form the basis of the logic of how affective polarization distorts the representational relationship. Many people do care about policy in and of itself and prefer bipartisanship over "us versus them" polarization. At the same time, negative partisanship is all around us, whether we ourselves engage in it or not. This raises the stakes of electoral competition. People who have strong negational partisan identities are more likely to reject bipartisan action (Bankert 2021) and feel stronger emotions when their party is threatened (Huddy, Mason, and Aarøe 2015). As Ward and Tavits (2019, 7–8) put it, those with strong partisan feelings are "more likely to view politics as high stakes competition, where ideological polarization is rampant, participation is crucial, and electoral outcomes are highly consequential." Thus, in an era of negative partisanship and affective polarization, an "us versus them" style of representation is more salient, which in turn reduces the importance of actual policy in service of beating the other side.

The empirical analyses that follow in this book examine how representatives engage in group-based partisan bickering (not necessarily against individual members of the other party, but against the other party as a whole) not because this is what voters want, and not because they are under the impression that this will directly result in electoral victories. Rather, even though the data show that representatives on average talk about policy significantly *more* than they talk about the parties, partisan warfare is amplified by the media, receives more attention online, rakes in more money, and creates the downstream widespread perception that this just "how it is."

NEGATIVE REPRESENTATION AS SUBSTANTIVE, DESCRIPTIVE, AND SYMBOLIC

The literature on representation generally breaks the concept into several broad types, such as substantive, descriptive, and symbolic, which can all loosely be considered forms of *positive* representation using this book's framework. Again originating with Hanna Pitkin, these different views of representation lend themselves to different mechanisms for understanding representatives' behavior, evaluating representation, and holding representatives accountable. In this section, I explain how my concept of negative representation intersects with each.

Substantive Representation

When most people think of what elected officials do, they think of substantive representation. Substantive representation occurs when an elected official promotes constituents' interests via the official's legislative activities. Much research has been devoted to studying whether policy outcomes or representatives' voting records reflect the public's interests and preferences. Theoretically, in the median voter model articulated by Downs (1957), voters choose the candidate that is ideologically closest to them, and since candidates care about being elected, their preferences converge with the median voter's preferences. The electorally motivated candidate, on issues where the public cares, is incentivized to move toward the ideological middle. How this is borne out in practice once representatives are in office is a different, and more complicated, empirical question. Early and influential research on representation (Mayhew 1974; Fenno 1978; Miller and Stokes 1963) laid the groundwork for studying how legislators work toward substantive goals and represent voters. Many studies contribute to the debate on whether lawmakers are (or should be) delegates in the tradition of James Madison, following voters' preferences as mandates, or Burkean trustees, making independent decisions on behalf of constituents that are not necessarily always in line with voters' preferences. Research generally agrees that policy usually follows the delegation of public opinion to some extent, but that voters' lack of information and engagement limits the influence of public opinion on policy.

Miller and Stokes (1963), in essentially the first quantitative analysis of congressional substantive representation, argued that the extent to which Congress members vote in line with their constituents' preferences ultimately depends on the issue area. In the area of civil rights, they find evidence of the informed delegate model, in which roll call votes are determined by region regardless of party. On social issues, members vote as trustees along party lines. Finally, neither the trustee nor the delegate model held on foreign affairs, as both parties deferred to the president. Of course, as members' roll call votes have polarized and sorted along partisan lines in more recent decades, these exact conclusions about particular issue areas have evolved along with more recent research (e.g., Bartels 2016;

Clinton 2006; Tausanovitch and Warshaw 2013; Stimson, MacKuen, and Erikson 1995; Page and Shapiro 1983; Rigby and Wright 2013; Swers 2002; Wlezien 2004). It is also worth noting that some theorists have critiqued the approach of measuring policy responsiveness in such a narrow way and situating policy as the cornerstone of representative democracy (e.g., Sabl 2015). Nonetheless, it is useful as a framework for studying how responsive legislators are to constituents' desires and/or needs.

Legislative responsiveness often refers to the degree to which legislators' policy positions follow the preferences of their constituents. However, some scholars have also studied how legislators literally "respond" to constituents through emails and letters or in handling casework (e.g., Butler and Broockman 2011; Costa 2017; Eulau and Karps 1977). Constituent service responsiveness is taken seriously by public officials. In 2016, the Senate received more than 6.4 million letters via postal mail, not counting the increasing numbers of emails that are received on a daily basis (Goldschmidt 2011), and nearly all people who write to members of Congress indicate that they expect a response (Goldschmidt and Ochreiter 2008). According to the 2020 Cooperative Election Study, 21 percent of American adults reported that they had contacted a public official during the previous year. Answering requests is a clear way that representatives can act on behalf of their constituents' interests without actually advancing policy goals in the legislature. Harden (2015) shows the conditions under which policy-based versus service-based substantive representation occurs. The wealthy prioritize policy-based representation from their elected officials, while people who are more economically disadvantaged care more about constituent services and resource allocation. This is reflected in legislators' behavior, with those who represent wealthy, predominantly white districts focusing more on policy, while those representing economically disadvantaged and racially diverse districts tend to prioritize constituent services and resource allocation.

Mayhew (1974) offered another influential framework to study substantive representation. He defined three kinds of electorally useful behaviors that characterize lawmakers' substantive activities: advertising, position-taking, and credit-claiming. None of the three actually requires representatives to advance and implement meaningful policy outcomes in the legislature for their constituents. Electoral payoffs are received for positions, not outcomes, and the policy outcomes representatives do focus on are those that involve small, particularistic benefits for which they can easily claim credit. Such particularistic policies distance representatives even further from acting in the universal best interest of their constituents. Richard Fenno's (1978) classic account of how members of Congress cultivate a "homestyle" also argues that the goal of reelection motivates legislators to primarily work to project the *image* to their constituents that they are doing things in Washington to advance constituents' substantive interests. A legislator's homestyle is their style of representation as portrayed to their districts, and dictates how the legislator cultivates constituents' trust to gain leeway to advance good policy (on their own terms) in Washington. Indeed, explaining one's policy-related activity in Washington is one of the main ingredients of Fenno's homestyle. The relationship between a representative and their constituency rests on how that representative rhetorically presents their legislative activities. The electoral incentive makes *explaining* substantive representation in Washington more important than substantive representation itself.

Negative representation, as a form of representation based on who constituents are not, could theoretically mean the advancement of policies that disadvantage an out-group. Many acts of representation might have worse outcomes for certain segments of the population while still fulfilling an ideological agenda: for example, bills that might remove immigrants from their jobs, homes, or families, or initiatives to slash the social safety net for the lower class. In this book, I don't consider that kind of substantive legislation as part of negative representation. It is true that some policies will disproportionately affect members of one party more than the other. Increasing taxes on the rich might be more likely to hurt Republicans, and reducing subsidies for health care might affect more Democrats. But these disproportionate effects are not necessarily the point of those policies—Republicans are not proposing to strip Democrats of their health care and Democrats are not proposing to raise taxes on Republicans. Instead I explore how much legislators talk about policy compared to how much they talk about the other party, and also whether the extent to which a legislator is good at substantive policymaking is related to how much they focus their rhetoric on attacking the other party. Of course, because the parties are so ideologically sorted at this point, people will likely infer issues from a mention of partisanship. If a politician says that the other party must be stopped because they are bad, one might infer that the other party is bad because of the policies it stands for. Thus, a legislator's reference to a political party is not entirely devoid of policy or substance. But the focus on broad partisan attacks rather than more specific ideological or issue-based critiques is an important distinction. With negative representation the substance is left implicit; it's much more about symbolism.

Descriptive Representation

While substantive representation occurs when representatives "act for" constituents, descriptive representatives "stand for" them to the extent that there are shared characteristics and identities, such as gender, race, occupation, veteran status, and so on. Many scholars study descriptive representation as a mechanism for reducing inequality. Having legislators who are traditionally underrepresented in government can help to break down stereotypes and give legitimacy to those communities. Descriptive representatives may also better understand and empathize with their constituents, building trust and improving communication (Mansbridge 1999). Naturally, this has implications for the extent to which those communities are *substantively* represented. In terms of substantive benefits, descriptive representation can lead to increased information flow from traditionally marginalized groups and enable legislators to more effectively advocate for their interests. These benefits can be particularly important for marginalized communities who may not have as much representation or influence in the policymaking process (e.g., Hayes and Hibbing 2017; Lowande, Ritchie, and Lauterbach 2019).

As partisanship becomes a salient identity in and of itself, researchers must begin to consider how "resembling" a constituency based on partisan affiliation alone intersects with descriptive representation. Scholarship on descriptive representation and race, for example, examines how African American elected officials advocate on behalf of and stand for African American constituents. The field of gender and representation asks how women behave in office compared to men. What does it mean to represent *as a partisan*? On one hand, it may mean voting the party line in Congress, or voting in line with what most party members in the general public want. On the other hand, partisanship is more than just an instrumental means to a substantive, policy-based end. Representing constituents based on partisan identities, whether affirmational or negational, may not come with actual substantive benefits and instead may serve to descriptively "stand for" a partisan constituency.

Symbolic Representation

One answer to the question "what does it mean to represent *as a partisan*?" is simply: as a symbol. Symbolic representation is a term that has been used by scholars in a variety of ways. It generally refers to the ways in which politicians engage in behavior outside of government, through activities such as communication and constituent service, and by using symbols, language, and gestures to evoke some meaning for the constituent. By using symbols and language to convey their messages and to demonstrate their commitment to certain values and causes, politicians can create a sense of connection and solidarity with the public and build trust. For example, President George W. Bush's cowboy hat and Texan persona have been studied as symbolic (re)presentations of certain mythic values of American leadership (Hoffman 2011).

Unlike substantive and descriptive representation, symbolic representation has no clear method for evaluation, so it is not clear whether or how people hold representatives accountable for their symbolic acts. Substantive representation can be evaluated by how well representatives advance constituents' best interests through activities in office. Descriptive representation can be evaluated by how well representatives resemble constituents along one or more dimensions. Several scholars have examined representatives' symbolic behavior, such as drawing on their identities as Black women (Brown and Gershon 2017) or constructing gender identity in policy discourses (Lombardo and Meier 2014). But as Pitkin notes, "it makes no sense to ask whether a symbol represents well, for there is no such thing as mis-symbolizing" (1967, 110). The key component of symbolic representation is that a leader is believed in and accepted by the constituents. "The concept of the political leader as essentially passive, standing for others symbolically, must thus be supplemented by the view that he is a symbol-maker, making himself into an accepted leader through his activity. . . . It is a kind of activity to foster belief, loyalty, satisfaction with their leaders, among the people" (Pitkin 1967, 107).

Even if less obviously identifiable than other forms of representation, how politicians connect with and build trust among constituents is central to the representational relationship. Politicians can stand for any number of values and bring them into the political process depending on what the political culture is at any given time, by the way they choose to act and speak and interact with the people they represent. Negative representation, which functions based on group identity, most clearly falls under the symbolic umbrella. Representing symbolically is a form of behavior that persuades, cultivates an image, and manufactures acceptance through discourse or imagery. When representatives invoke the other party through rhetoric, they are often symbolizing constituents' (and perhaps their own) negational partisan identities.

THE CAUSES OF NEGATIVE PARTISANSHIP
IN REPRESENTATION

Voter-Driven Hypothesis

The most straightforward, and commonly assumed, mechanism for negative representation is that it is driven by voters. Parties and legislators are motivated to win elections. People dislike the opposite party more than they have at any time since political scientists began collecting this data. If elites are under the impression that negative representation appeals to voters, then they might engage in this behavior to consolidate support. Accordingly, the *voter-driven hypothesis* simply states that politicians use partisan rhetoric because they think it is a successful way to appeal to voters.

A vast literature in legislative studies characterizes elite behavior as rational and strategic. Politicians and candidates who want to win elections must do what is popular with voters. Of course, legislators have their own agendas and beliefs, but to make those a reality, they first must win popular support. There is a lot of evidence to support this view of legislators as "single-minded seekers of reelection" (Mayhew 1974), both in research on how policy outputs roughly follow mass preferences (e.g., Erikson, MacKuen, and Stimson 2002; Canes-Wrone 2015; Page and Shapiro 1983; Stimson, MacKuen, and Erikson 1995; Tausanovitch and Warshaw 2013) and in work showing how candidates "pander" to the public in their campaign rhetoric (e.g., Hillygus and Shields 2009). When legislative behavior does *not* align with voters' preferences, it is often because politicians can be confident that their behavior is either private (for instance, when negotiating behind closed doors) because they can be sure that most voters will not actually be paying attention (as with their roll call votes on less salient issues), or because they do not actually know what their constituents want (Anderson, Butler, and Harbridge-Yong 2020; Broockman and Skovron 2018; Butler and Nickerson 2011; Kirkland and Harden 2022; Pereira 2021).

Voters make evaluations based on information that is accessible and salient (Iyengar and Kinder 1987; Zaller 1992), making rhetoric a powerful tool to shape voters' considerations (de Benedictis Kessner 2022; Grimmer 2013; Lowande, Ritchie, and Lauterbach 2019; Lipinski 2001; Westwood 2021). In an age of affective polarization and "identity politics," it is likely that politicians are aware that voters are driven by affective and group tendencies. What is important here is not whether voters are perceived by elites to be affectively polarized, but whether they are perceived by elites to *vote* based on those affective considerations. Research finds that negativity is more likely to be used when electoral tensions are high (Druckman, Kifer, and Parkin 2010) or in high-profile visible debates (Osnabrügge, Hobolt, and Rodon 2021). Moreover, House members are more likely to invoke notions of bipartisanship in floor speeches during presidential election cycles and less likely to do so during midterm election cycles. While this evidence is not causal, it suggests that elites talk less about bipartisanship when they need to appeal to their party's base. When they have to garner broad support from both parties, they claim to care about reaching across the aisle (Westwood 2021). This line of research suggests that politicians use certain types of rhetoric strategically to appeal to voters.

Dickson and Scheve (2006) offer a game theoretic model that defines a utility function for when politicians should use social identity appeals compared to policy appeals. They write: "The need for candidates to resort to group-based appeals can be expected to vary systematically depending on details of the strategic settings of given elections, such as the relative sizes of social groups; the policy preferences of group members; whether candidates care about policy and if they do, their preferred policies; and the extent to which individuals identify with groups" (Dickson and Scheve 2006, 31). In other words, use of a policy versus an identity representational style is a function of the legislator's estimation of the optimum strategy in any given election. If legislators think a large share of their constituents identify with a particular political party (and strongly dislike the other party), then they may choose to engage in negative representation in order to appeal to that identity.

The elites I survey for this book report that negative representation is likely to *lose* support among voters. At the same time, observational patterns of when negative out-partisan rhetoric occurs on Twitter and in congressional newsletters indicate that negative representation escalates after a party loses an election. When the opposite party controls either Congress or the presidency, members of the minority party resort to more partisan language that specifically targets the other party. This trend likely stems from the fact that the minority party, having less capacity to legislate than the majority, often adopts a stance of obstruction and attack with the goal of regaining control in future elections. This approach serves to coordinate an attack on the opposition, creating favorable media narratives and formulating the argument for recapturing power. In sum, there is only indirect evidence of the voter-driven hypothesis. Engaging in negative partisanship is not directly correlated with the vote share legislators receive in the next election, and politicians expressly report that citizens care more about policy than about affective partisan rhetoric. But the context of insecure majorities (Lee 2016) means that partisan attacks become a more viable strategy for members of Congress during certain shifts in party control, which are driven by elections.

Elite-Driven Hypothesis

Political scientists often view politicians as highly strategic actors, but it is worth remembering that they are also subject to the same identity-based emotions and biases that affect the broader public. It is also worth noting, then, that no research I know of at the time of writing this book has studied affective polarization among legislators. As I've described earlier in this chapter, ideological polarization is easy to document using roll call votes and other observable legislative behavior, but measuring affective polarization requires capturing individuals' feelings about the parties. We assume that affective polarization is a uniquely mass-level phenomenon, but if we could survey members of Congress, it is possible (even likely) that we would see high levels of affective partisanship at the elite level as well.

The *elite-driven hypothesis* states that politicians are drawn to using negative styles of representation partly because they themselves have a highly affective orientation toward the parties. We know that elites are more politically engaged and politically interested—the specific types of traits associated with expressing more negative feelings toward the out-party (e.g., Krupnikov and Ryan 2022). Of course, it is possible that because they are in contact more often with members of the other party, elites are inoculated against the feelings of social distance that pervade partisans in the mass public. To the contrary, the data show they are, at the end of the day, just like us. Through a variety of negative partisan measures, I find that political candidates and officeholders are all too willing to denigrate the other party in a survey. Elites may engage in this behavior because they themselves are intrinsically motivated by their negational, affective identities. That is, politicians may frequently speak negatively about the other party because it reflects how they truly feel. Some part of this behavior may not be a means unto an end, but an end itself.

Importantly, negative representation can be both voter-driven *and* elite-driven. Politicians can think it appeals to their base and also be affectively polarized themselves. The "false consensus effect" in psychology occurs when individuals overestimate the degree to which their own beliefs, attitudes, and behaviors are shared by others (Marks and Miller 1987; Ross, Green, and House 1977). Studies have shown that elites often misperceive the policy preferences of their constituents, in many cases by projecting their own views onto constituents (Broockman and Skovron 2018), and it is reasonable to believe that this tendency could extend to negative representation as well. Politicians who are highly affectively polarized may be prone to projecting this polarization onto their constituents. This can manifest as the false consensus effect, in which politicians assume that their constituents share their negative views of the opposing party and thus prioritize this out-group identity in their communication. Indeed, the experiments on political elites later in this book show that politicians who have the highest levels of negative partisanship themselves did not think expressions of negative partisanship were as harmful to a candidate's electoral viability as other, less polarized politicians did. This is not totally consistent with a false consensus bias, which would show that these polarized elites think partisan attacks are electorally beneficial. But disliking the other party does reduce the perceived electoral penalties for attacking the other party.

Overall, I find strong support for the idea that elites themselves perpetuate negative representation on their own. Even if politicians do not think expressing negative partisanship is a winning strategy that appeals to voters, they may be internally motivated to do so anyway if they have strong feelings against the out-party. This is especially true if there are *other* external incentives besides votes that drive legislators' behavior.

Exposure Hypothesis

The elite-driven hypothesis is derived from a theory about politicians' intrinsic motivations, while the voter-driven hypothesis posits that elections provide an extrinsic incentive to engage in negative representation. There are other extrinsic incentives that drive politicians' behavior. The *exposure hypothesis* states that negative affective appeals attract attention both on social media and in more traditional news outlets, boost politicians' national exposure, attract campaign donors, and consequently provide them with leverage and power in office. The extrinsic incentive to attack the other party, therefore, might not be the votes it is believed to win, but the media attention, increased fundraising power, and national notoriety it generates.

While members of Congress are often treated as single-mindedly focused on reelection, it has long been understood that their goals are far more diverse. Influence and power within the chamber are highly important to members of Congress. Receiving attention from the news media and donors from beyond one's jurisdiction both help members accrue power and influence (Cook 1989, 1998; Hess 1986; Jacobs and Shapiro 2000). Legislators are certainly seeking reelection, but many are also seeking much more, including a prominent national profile. In the "post-broadcast democracy" world (Prior 2007), one clear path to such prominence is by engaging in rhetorical attacks to capture attention from partisan media outlets and ultimately go viral (Berry and Sobieraj 2013), thus raking in more money from donors across the country (Ballard et al. 2022).

There is evidence to suggest that politicians use social media and traditional media outlets to gain national exposure and shape their public image. While negativity in campaigns is not new, hostile discourse among elites has indeed increased in the digital age (Gainous and Wagner 2014; Geer 2008; Prior 2013; Russell 2018). The frequency of attack ads containing negative or ambiguous language has been increasing at rapid rates over the last few decades (Geer 2008; Tomz and Van Houweling 2009). Negativity stimulates attention and action on the part of voters and conveys important information about campaigns (Ansolabehere and Iyengar 1995; Druckman and McDermott 2008; Freedman and Goldstein 1999; Lau 1985; Marcus, Neuman, and MacKuen 2000). News media outlets often have a negativity bias, meaning that they are more likely to cover negative or controversial stories than positive ones. This can further reinforce the incentive for politicians to engage in divisive or extreme rhetoric to attract media attention. As John Geer explains about presidential campaigns and advertising, the news media plays a significant role in shaping campaigns, rather than simply reflecting them. The extensive coverage of advertising and negativity in the media can contribute to an increase in attacks and negative behavior, creating a reinforcing cycle. He writes: "The core idea is that the news media now cover negative ads so extensively that they have given candidates and their consultants extra incentive to produce and air them" (Geer 2012, 423).

The negativity bias also extends to the type of content most likely to receive engagement on social media. For example, Schöne, Parkinson, and Goldenberg (2021) study emotional language on Twitter regarding both predominantly negative and positive situations. Across several different events, including the 2016 elections, the Supreme Court approval of same-sex marriage, and the Ferguson protests, increased negativity predicted the spread of content, while positivity did not. The more negative language a tweet contained, the more likely it was to be retweeted, even controlling for whether the larger context of the situation was overall positive or negative. Numerous other studies support the general pattern that negativity is more likely to capture attention and increase engagement on social media compared to positivity (Brady, Gantman, and Van Bavel 2020; Meffert et al. 2006; Rozin and Royzman 2001). In a particularly relevant study analyzing tweets by US senators, Fine and Hunt (2023) find that "messages that contain attacks and those that are negative in sentiment are significantly more likely to be retweeted than those without attacks and messages with positive sentiment. . . . The policy content of these messages, however, has no effect, underscoring that the tone of messages matters more than the substance." Other research shows that the downstream effects of viral social media posts include other benefits as well. Legislators who use polarizing language online receive more attention (Ballard et al. 2022; Rathje, Van Bavel, and Van Der Linden 2021), which in turn brings in more campaign donations (Kowal 2023).

My findings are consistent with prior research, providing strong support for the exposure hypothesis. Negative representation on social media receives far more "likes" and shares than positive representation. Moreover, partisan television news media cover congressional tweets more in the context of partisan attacks than in the context of partisan compromise. That is, when members of Congress tweet about their more traditional duties having to do with actual representation, such as legislative compromise, this is not newsworthy. But outlets report more on congressional tweets when they are negative and contain attacks. In general, partisan news channels also cover the opposition party more frequently when the party they lean toward is in power. Fox News increased its coverage of Democrats after Trump's inauguration, while MSNBC showed the opposite pattern, focusing more on Republicans when they were out of power and then shifting focus to Democrats in 2019–2020. This again highlights the importance of shifts in party control and how the news media perpetuates a focus on partisan division.

I also find that negative representation helps with national exposure in terms of campaign fundraising. Out-partisan rhetoric in tweets is associated with an increase in total fundraising dollars as well as out-of-state donations. Negative partisan rhetoric in newsletters, however, is negatively associated with overall fundraising, meaning that legislators who use more out-party mentions in their newsletters raise less money. Out-party mentions in newsletters have no significant association with out-of-state donations. This is consistent with the exposure hypothesis. Newsletters are narrowcast communications, typically sent to constituents within the members' district or state. Social media, on the other hand, reaches potential donors in other districts and states, suggesting that negative representation is a reputation-building activity. Politicians are driven by the quest for fame and influence. Since there are conditions under which voters tolerate negative representation, politicians can reap the benefits, especially when they are in noncompetitive districts and do not have to worry about losing their seat (something I also test and find empirical evidence for in chapter 4).

* * *

Overall, then, there are three broad reasons why politicians use negative representation: to appeal to voters (for which I find little and only indirect support), to satisfy their own intrinsic desire to engage in partisan negativity, and to gain national attention and notoriety. These explanations are not mutually exclusive—it is possible that all of these might be at play. As the evidence in this book will ultimately make clear, however, we cannot properly understand negative representation if we think it is happening only because voters are demanding it.

THE CONSEQUENCES OF NEGATIVE PARTISANSHIP IN REPRESENTATION

Just as with substantive, descriptive, and symbolic representation, negative representation and other types of representational behavior are not mutually exclusive. It is also true that there are sometimes trade-offs, perceived or actual, that occur when one type of representation is more salient or emphasized than others. The most pressing question is whether negative representation in rhetoric comes at the expense of substantive representation through actual policy action. If a politician spends a lot of effort cultivating an image as a partisan warrior, this may take the place of actual substantive action. There is some evidence to suggest that elites vary in how they think voters prioritize "identity politics" compared to policy concerns and that this has implications for how much time they spend on substantive representation. Specifically, when politicians think voters care more about social identities than about policy, they spend more hours communicating with constituents and less time studying and developing policy (Lucas, Sheffer, and Loewen 2022). In 2021, newly elected Rep. Madison Cawthorn (R-NC) told Republican colleagues in an email that he built his staff around "comm[unications] rather than legislation."[2] Pundits on the left were quick to criticize the move, while at the same time expressing resigned unsurprise that this is just how politicians govern in the "post-policy" world.[3] There is an expectation (whether based in evidence or not) that when politicians emphasize the symbolic parts of their job, especially when using an "us versus them" style, they do so at the expense of substantive representation. The observational analyses in chapter 4 of how negative representation is associated with ideological voting and legislative effectiveness suggest that this is precisely the case.

What are the consequences for political attitudes and behaviors in the mass public? The "folk theory of democracy" suggests that voters correctly reward and punish politicians, make choices based on policy preferences, and orient their decisions toward the future. In *Democracy for Realists*, Achen and Bartels (2017) argue that such a theory is a myth. Voters, even those who are politically knowledgeable, base their decisions on social identities and partisan loyalties rather than on political issues. As a result, the preferences of individual voters do not shape public policy and elites do not have to be accountable to voters' policy concerns. If policy considerations drove voters, politicians would be held accountable based on how well they substantively deliver in those areas. Yet in an era of negative partisanship, out-group animus drives voters, which would mean that politicians are evaluated based on how well they inflame those affective tendencies, which causes the logic of democratic representation to fall apart. This would mean that voters *are* getting what they want, but what they want results in increased polarization, partisan division, and decreased substantive representation on the issues that matter.

Scholars, pundits, and journalists suggest that this is exactly what is happening. For the hyperpolarized context, many claim that Americans will reward elected officials who cater to their affective partisan identities. Citizens' perceptions of representation and government rely in part on how representatives make them feel (Fenno 1977; Eulau and Karps 1977; Mansbridge 1999). If an affective, negative partisanship dominates how Americans view one another in the mass public, then surely it affects how Americans view politicians as well. Perceptions of representation are based on how politicians meet constituents' affective, partisan interests rather than their ideological interests.

It is a common perception that most Americans are highly partisan and deeply invested in the political ideologies of their preferred parties. However, this perception is not entirely accurate. While it is true that there are many Americans who are deeply committed to their political beliefs and actively dislike the other side, there are also many Americans who are turned off by partisan politics and the divisive nature of the current political climate (Krupnikov and Ryan 2022). The parties have become increasingly polarized, with each side viewing the other as the enemy rather than as opponents with whom they can find common ground. This can make it difficult for people to feel that their voices are being heard or that their concerns are being taken seriously by their elected representatives. Many Americans are frustrated by the lack of progress and cooperation in government and bemoan the state of polarization in the country. Partisan bickering and gridlock have become the norm in Congress, which is demoralizing for people who have genuine concerns about the challenges facing the country and want to see them addressed and overcome. Many Americans are disillusioned with the political parties themselves. Nearly 40 percent say they wish there were more political parties to choose from, and a majority say that both parties "too often make excuses for party members with hateful views" (Pew Research Center 2022).

Even the most extreme negative partisans themselves want representation based on substantive issues instead of "us versus them" partisanship. In other research, my coauthor and I use two experiments to examine how negative partisanship influences vote choice in primary elections (Albert and Costa 2024). We find that voters who rate high in negative partisanship care about winning elections and beating the other side more than do voters who rate lower in negative partisanship. This may suggest that at least some voters would be motivated by elite expressions of negative partisanship. But we also found that negative partisans are still highly motivated by being represented substantively on the issues and are not always willing to trade off substantive representation for beating the other side.

Across three original experiments in this book, people prefer representatives who share their policy views and provide quality service responsiveness to constituents. Negative representation makes legislators significantly less likely to be chosen as a preferred representative. Negative partisanship is penalized even if it is expressed by a politician from one's own party, and policy congruence has a significant positive impact on approval. Issue importance does not seem to play a significant role, as most respondents do not distinguish between issues that are more or less important to them personally, as long as policy is prioritized. I also find that people generally prefer in-party cheerleading over out-party rhetoric, and show more approval if legislators prioritize an electoral win for their party rather than a loss for the other party. But again, prioritizing an important issue increases approval even more than prioritizing an electoral win. At the same time, while most people do not favor negative partisanship, there are conditions under which it is tolerated. Specifically, negative representation does not lead to lower favorability ratings or support among individuals who have strong attachments to their party or high animosity toward the opposing party, are highly engaged partisans, or strongly approve of Donald Trump. Moreover, out-party rhetoric is especially tolerated when representatives also focus on issues and substantive representation. People are willing to ignore partisan warfare among elites, even though they do not typically favor this behavior, when those representatives also focus on advertising their policy views, even if these views are not entirely in line with what those constituents desire.

All in all, negative representation creates a feedback loop. It influences how people perceive the state of political culture and further feeds affective polarization. Soon after the presidential election of 2020, the Pew Research Center asked Americans what they would want voters on the other side to understand about them. A plurality shared their policy views and attitudes, indicating that they think out-partisans inaccurately believe they are more extreme than they really are. Over 10 percent of both Biden and Trump voters said they would want the other side to stop mischaracterizing their values and feeding into partisan stereotypes (for example, "racists and bigots" for Trump voters and "soy latte-drinking godless hippie elites" for Biden voters). A woman in her seventies wrote, "being a supporter of Donald Trump does not make me evil." Another woman of the same age wrote, "it's hard for me to answer this because I don't think Trump supporters are interested in understanding me." At the same time, several expressed themes of unity and called attention to the idea that there are probably more similarities between camps than differences. A young Biden voter said, "we want the same things: security, happiness, prosperity. We also probably like similar things: sports, movies, music, etc. In the end, we're pretty similar. . . . In fact, we have more in common than we don't." That these sentiments were expressed as the *single* thing they would want those on the opposing side to understand better is telling. While the false consensus effect occurs when individuals overestimate the extent to which others agree with their own beliefs and attitudes, a false uniqueness effect occurs when people underestimate the extent to which others agree with their own beliefs and attitudes (Pope 2013). People may bemoan an "us versus them" style of representation themselves, while also thinking that the other side is fanning the flame.

Indeed, later in the book I explore people's metaperceptions of the desire for negative representation in Congress, estimating both their own preferences and their views of opposing partisans' preferences. Although only about a quarter of both Democrats and Republicans expressed a desire for members of Congress to focus on talking about the other party rather than policy issues, people drastically overestimated the other party's desire for this negative representation, with a perception gap of 33 percentage points across all partisans. This gap was even larger than the perception gap in ideological polarization noted in previous research (that is, the gap between how extreme liberals think conservatives are and how extreme conservatives actually are, and vice versa). This gap persisted across various segments of the population, including different education levels, news consumption habits, and voting patterns. The substantial overestimation of the other side's preference for partisanship over policy is a widespread and deep-seated misperception, present even among those who do not desire negative representation themselves. A breakdown in understanding between opponents leads to more interpersonal conflict and a lack of willingness to engage with the other side. Negative representation matters not necessarily because it is what people want, but because they think that it is what other people want and that it is all that is available anyway.

A Market for (Political) Lemons

In February of 2019, a series of right-wing rumors circulated through the web that Rep. Alexandria Ocasio-Cortez (D-NY) had a bad credit score, two past evictions, and a series of closed checking accounts. Multiple figures on the right cited these false claims as evidence that she is unqualified to work on economic issues. Ocasio-Cortez responded by posting on Twitter: "This stuff is really sad. The GOP is so intellectually bankrupt that they no longer engage to debate issues in good faith, but instead seek to lie, distort, name-call, target, & destroy people/communities w[ith] any means possible. It's a virus and a race to the bottom" (February 9, 2019). The post was liked over 51,700 times and retweeted over 9,300 times. It is not clear that any of Ocasio-Cortez's Republican colleagues did in fact spread the rumors about her at all, but that did not stop her from calling out "the GOP" in its entirety.

Two features of Ocasio-Cortez's tweet are notable. First, her out-party attack did not occur in a vacuum: it was a *response* to attacks first launched at her from the other side. Second, even while taking part in partisan rhetorical warfare herself, she calls it out explicitly, and in so doing correctly diagnoses the problem by using a concept that is the crux of this book's argument. A "race to the bottom" refers to when competitors, in an effort to undercut one another, resort to behaviors that result in a worse outcome for stakeholders. For instance, in an article that won him the Nobel Prize in Economics, George Akerlof described how this phenomenon plays out in markets with asymmetric information, using used cars as an example. He documented "a market for lemons," in which buyers cannot distinguish good cars from "lemons" (or bad cars), so they are only willing to pay a price that averages the value of both. Since sellers with good cars know they will not receive what their car is worth, they decide selling is not worth it and exit the market. Eventually, lemons are all that are left, further reducing what buyers are willing to pay for used cars. This race to the bottom results in more and more high-quality products exiting the market, worse and worse products being left, and a lower and lower average willingness to pay, ultimately leading to market collapse.

With negative representation, a "race to the bottom" occurs when competitors (politicians), to undercut one another (gain power), resort to behaviors (negative partisan attacks) that result in a worse quality outcome for stakeholders (citizens in a democracy). If negative representation is a "lemon," the more the political environment breeds negativity and encourages the perception that lemons are all that are available, the more sour politics seems—and the more sour it actually becomes. No one *wants* negative partisanship as a viable form of political representation, just as no one wants to buy a junk car. Politicians themselves do not think that voters prefer negative partisanship as representation over policy representation—just like car salespeople do not think buyers prefer lemons—but the market ecosystem fuels this behavior anyway.

The more people expressively loathe the out-party, the more they see out-partisan attacks by opponents, and the more politicians communicate using negative partisanship themselves, the more this performance captures our attention, turns into belief, and reinforces the cycle of polarization. Just as sellers of good cars exit the market when they cannot receive a fair price, politicians who prioritize policy over partisanship may find themselves pushed out of the political landscape. Indeed, other research has documented how moderate candidates opt out of the field as partisan polarization increases (Hall 2019; Thomsen 2017). At the least, politicians who do not engage in negative representation receive comparatively less attention in the media and fewer fundraising dollars. And the more politicians focus on negative partisanship, the less actual legislation they sponsor and pass in Congress. Politicians who talk a lot about the other party, often in negative terms, are the same legislators who are less effective at their more central policy-focused representative duties. The result is a prevalence of lemons—a political environment dominated by negative partisanship rather than substantive policy engagement. The market collapse that occurs in this scenario is the collapse of quality policy representation.

3. PARTISANSHIP AND POLICY IN ELITE COMMUNICATION

On January 26, 2022, Rep. Tom Cole (R-OK) sent an email newsletter to his constituents that began: "The first month back in Congress this year has been marked by Democrats failing to do any worthwhile work for the American people." He went on to reference "Democrats"—not individual politicians, but the party as a group—nineteen more times in the rest of the newsletter. He also shared news of his recent votes on the House floor, characterizing all of them as "against" the Democratic agenda, nothing "for." He mentioned his own party only three times in the entire letter.

Partisan attacks are not new in Congress, but political scientists have more traditionally focused on the nature of *individual* attacks against members of the other party or challengers in an election (Ansolabehere and Iyengar 1995; Lau et al. 1999; Lau, Sigelman, and Rovner 2007; Theriault 2013), rather than how elites invoke the other party altogether. Several decades ago, Americans did not feel as strongly about the parties themselves, so it made less sense for politicians to attack a party than it did for them to criticize other individual politicians. However, with increasing levels of affective polarization, politicians now make affective appeals to negative partisanship by denigrating the out-party as a group. How common is such partisan rhetoric? When are legislators most likely to use it? How does it compare to policy-based rhetoric?

In this chapter, I illustrate the nature of representational styles centered on affective, partisan communications over six congressional sessions across two different mediums through which lawmakers talk to voters: email newsletters and posts on Twitter (now rebranded as "X"). The findings contribute to existing knowledge about legislator communications while offering several new insights. First, I show that rhetoric about policy is much more common than partisan rhetoric. However, while policy-oriented language appears in almost every congressional newsletter, it appears much less on social media: only about one-third of all tweets analyzed contain policy-coded words. I also find that representatives consistently invoke negative out-party language more after their party loses control of Congress, but the use of bipartisan language has (perhaps surprisingly) slowly but steadily increased over time. Finally, the language members of Congress use to tweet about the out-party has become more negative in tone over time.

The data I present in this chapter serve two additional purposes. First, they provide necessary proof of concept for the theoretical construct of negative and positive partisan communication styles. Before I explore the causes and consequences of such communication styles, it is important that I establish how common this is in contemporary politics. Second, the analyses contribute to the growing focus within political science on quantitative description.[1] In doing so, they offer a form of context for understanding analyses that appear later in the book regarding why elites are motivated to use such rhetoric and how voters respond. I show that the invocation of certain language varies systemically across mode of communication, time period, and certain legislator traits, but the purpose is not to establish clear and definitive causal relationships between these factors. Rather, the findings document important patterns for understanding how rhetoric can polarize during an era in which the internet, social media, and negative partisanship have fundamentally altered the state of elite-constituent communication.

WHAT WE KNOW ABOUT ELITE RHETORIC

Scholars of political communication have long been interested in how politicians talk about their legislative activities in Washington. For example, Mayhew's (1974) classic study of the electoral connection suggested three behaviors legislators take part in if primarily focused on seeking reelection: advertising, position-taking, and credit-claiming. Even though these behaviors involve some form of symbolic action (i.e., not actual legislation), such as making speeches and giving interviews, Mayhew and other scholars using his framework study how they facilitate communicating with constituents about legislative activities. For example, examining senators' press releases from 2005 to 2007, Grimmer (2013) finds that aligned senators (those whose policy positions coincide with the position of their constituents) do more position-taking than credit-claiming, while marginal senators (those with more heterogenous political backing in the district) engage in more credit-claiming. In other words, when lawmakers anticipate agreement with their constituents, they talk more about their policy positions. In general, members of Congress strategically engage in tailoring their policy positions based on both the views of their constituents and stereotypes of party-owned issues (Arbour 2014; Grose, Malhotra, and Van Houweling 2015).

While talking about policy is clearly an important part of legislative speech, drawing on social identities also appeals to constituents. The relatively few studies that have examined how politicians talk about identity focus on rhetoric in the presidency and/or how politicians talk about racial in-groups and out-groups. For example, an analysis of President Trump's speeches demonstrated that he constructed in-group/out-group dynamics by his use of first-person plural pronouns ("we" instead of "I") to pitch white voters against immigrants and refugees ("they") (Matos and Miller 2021). President Obama, on the other hand, as the only Black general election presidential candidate, discussed race explicitly only once and implicitly only eight times in his first term. Augoustinos and De Garis (2012) argue that he instead emphasized the diversity of his other identities, such as being raised by a single mom. He promoted the concept that despite having different backgrounds, Americans share the same values. In doing so, he sought to coalesce a uniform social identity around American values as a way of widening the scope of who belongs to the in-group. While campaigning for president in 2016, Hillary Clinton famously called Trump supporters "a basket of deplorables." These cases show how politicians can construct both in-groups and out-groups, by either limiting or widening the definition of who is like "oneself."

Social identity has long been important to scholars of symbolic representation as a means of connecting constituents to representatives (Brown and Gershon 2016, 2017). Symbolic representation encompasses activities that politicians do outside of office, like delivering speeches and interacting with constituents, and is central to building trust and political power (Pitkin 1967). Elite communications that make group-based appeals can prime the salience of social identity. And voters' negational identities are as important as their affirmational identities, especially when it comes to partisanship (Bankert 2021; Zhong et al. 2008). The extent to which legislators communicate about the parties in terms of *in-groups* and *out-groups* is therefore an important form of symbolic representation. Elites invoke the opposing party as a group to make claims about how and whom they represent. By expressly "othering" the opposing party as a group, rather than just targeting an individual opponent, they stake a claim to represent whoever is motivated by their out-partisan identities. When Rep. Cole, quoted at the start of this chapter, used his newsletter to repeatedly criticize Democrats, he signaled that he will provide a voice for those in his district who strongly dislike Democrats more than he signaled that he will provide a voice for Republicans per se.

Both Democrats and Republicans engage in partisan rhetoric, but the extent to which they do so varies. In stump speeches by presidential candidates, party mentions used to be made almost exclusively by Democratic candidates, but over time (up until 2012 at least), Democrats have come to talk less about the parties (Rhodes and Albert 2017). This perhaps reflects the need for presidents to win over swing voters—particularly those turned off by partisan politics—in a large and diverse nation. In Congress, however, politicians on both sides are still considered to be partisan warriors, attacking political opponents on the other side and championing their party brand (Carson, Crespin, and Madonna 2014; Lee 2009; Russell 2018; Theriault 2013). Some research suggests that members of the minority party are especially likely to mention the opposite party to draw attention to the failings of the out-group and find alternative agenda-setting opportunities (Green-Pedersen and Mortensen 2010; Morris 2001; Russell 2020).

At the same time, politicians make appeals to *bipartisanship* to appeal to broader swaths of voters (Rhodes and Albert 2017; Trubowitz and Mellow 2005; Rottinghaus and Tedin 2012). From 1992 to 2018, references to bipartisanship by both parties increased in House floor speeches, and voters respond generally favorably to the idea of legislators working across the aisle (Westwood 2021). Citizens view those who reference bipartisanship and work with members on the other side as more moderate, which especially makes the use of bipartisan rhetoric useful for representatives in competitive districts. Just as politicians tailor policy-based rhetoric to align with constituents' positions, they may strategically signal bipartisanship to garner voter support.

While it may seem counterintuitive, it is important to note that legislators may engage in partisan rhetoric while *also* paying lip service to bipartisanship. One reason for this is that while most Americans dislike the out-party, they also frequently express a desire for bipartisan policymaking. But the catch is that when Americans think about bipartisanship, what they typically have in mind is the out-party compromising to support proposals made by the party they support (Tyson 2019). For this reason, scholars repeatedly find that while Americans like the *idea* of bipartisan compromise, they place greater weight on their partisan loyalties (Harbridge, Malhotra, and Harrison 2014). For this reason, politicians may very well see the logic in talking about their desire for bipartisanship while also often criticizing the out-party.

USING COMMUNICATIONS DATA TO UNDERSTAND CONGRESSIONAL RHETORIC

To examine how members of Congress invoke policy, party in-groups and out-groups, and bipartisanship in their communications, I conduct text analysis on large datasets of congressional email newsletters and tweets from 2009 to 2020. Newsletters are a long-standing and important way members of Congress communicate directly with their constituents. Most scholars examining communication styles in congressional newsletters have focused on how legislators talk about policy or constituent service. Overall, researchers argue that members use newsletters to explain roll call votes to constituents and claim credit for particularized projects (Clarke, Jenkins, and Micatka 2020; Cormack 2016a, 2016b; Lipinski 2001; Yiannakis 1982). Much less attention, if any, has been paid to how members of Congress use their newsletters to talk about partisanship.

Twitter, on the other hand, is more commonly associated with the reward system of the social media ecosystem, in which partisan vitriol easily makes its way into bite-sized, pithy headlines. For this reason, several analyses exist of partisan or polarizing rhetoric from members of Congress on Twitter and its associated effects (e.g., Russell 2021). This research demonstrates that members of Congress tweet more about the parties, and use more hostile and polarizing language, when their party is not in power in the White House. For example, Republican senators tweeted more partisan messages in 2013 and 2015, but in 2017 Democratic senators used much more partisan language (Russell 2020). The trend is similar when considering "polarizing" language, which specifically affirms in-groups by subverting out-groups. From 2009 to 2020, almost 20 percent of tweets posted by members of Congress were considered polarizing, and patterns over time followed those of party mentions: Republicans posted more polarizing tweets than Democrats until 2017, after which this trend reversed (Ballard et al. 2022).

The data I draw on are not meant to be exhaustive or to provide a full picture of all types of elite communication. They are only two examples of media in which negative representational styles can be employed. Other scholars can (and should) examine how negative representation shows up in other communications data: campaign ads, floor speeches, town halls, party platforms, and so on. Since I am primarily interested in the act of representation rather than campaigning, and since I am interested in how politicians talk to voters rather than to each other (e.g., on the House floor), I chronicle rhetoric on two different, though archetypal, platforms that are commonly used during a politician's tenure in office: one a long-form method of speaking to donors, supporters, and residents in a representative's jurisdiction (newsletters), and the other a near polar opposite, short-form social media content for a wider public audience (Twitter posts).

Congressional Newsletter Data

I examine email newsletters sent by members of Congress collected and provided by the DCInbox project (for more information, see Cormack 2017). The dataset contains every email a member of Congress has sent to their district from 2009 to 2020, amounting to 130,332 newsletters in total. Email newsletters are used by nearly every member of Congress, though how frequently legislators send these newsletters can vary considerably. During the 116th Congress, the median legislator sent roughly two newsletters each month to constituents (forty-five total over the two-year period). However, some representatives sent just one per year, while others sent one per week.

I cleaned and processed the data to merge them with unique identifiers and metadata such as gender, party, and DW-nominate scores for each member of Congress.[2] I then disaggregated the newsletter corpus of text to the word-, email-, and legislator level. After stopwords and other irrelevant words are removed, over 37 million words are left in the corpus. Each word is associated with a congress and a legislator so I can examine associations between the language used and characteristics of when and by whom it was used. There are 939 unique members of Congress for whom newsletter data is available; 47 percent of legislators in the dataset are Democrats and 52 percent are Republican (1 percent are Independent), though more newsletters are sent from Republicans than from Democrats overall. The volume of newsletters increased significantly over time. In the 111th Congress, the earliest for which the newsletter data are available, 7,928 email newsletters were sent. This number increases to 30,189 in the 116th Congress, reflecting how members of Congress shifted their newsletters from postal mail to email over time.

Congressional Tweet Data

I explore partisan and policy rhetoric used by members of Congress on Twitter for the same time period. Tweets by members of Congress who served in the 116th Congress, going back in time through the 111th Congress, were scraped from the web using Twitter's API (up to 3,200 tweets per member, the maximum permitted by Twitter).[3] This totals over 1.35 million tweets. Using the same methods to process the data at the word-, tweet-, and legislator level results in about 16.6 million words. Again, 48 percent of legislators in the dataset are Democrats and 52 percent are Republican; unlike newsletters, though, slightly more tweets were made by Democrats than by Republicans. Note that while the newsletter data contain observations for every member of Congress who served from 2010 through 2020, tweets were only collected for members who served in the 116th Congress, representing a slightly different sample. In some ways, this provides a cleaner test: any patterns observed over time are not a result of different people being elected to office. These are the same 509 legislators (all House members and senators who had Twitter) throughout the time they were in office; any change in the frequency and quality of communication represents a change in those exact individuals' behavior.

MEASURING PARTISAN AND POLICY APPEALS

To measure negational partisan rhetoric, I code for whether a legislator mentioned one of the two major parties or its members (as an indicator variable) and the number of times mentioned (as a count variable). Appeals were only considered to be a partisan mention if the party or its members were explicitly mentioned by name as a group (e.g., "Democrat," "Republican," or "GOP"). For instance, Republican members of Congress who talk about "Democrats" are given a value of 1 for out-party; if they also talked about "Republicans," they are given a value of 1 for in-party. My measurement of in-partisan and out-partisan rhetoric is relatively strict. Some scholars cast their net wider and define partisan language as mentions of individual politicians by name (such as Pelosi, Trump, etc.) or ideological terms (liberal, conservative, socialist, etc.), even if the party as a whole is not mentioned. Yet my interest is in how elites talk about the parties as a *group*. If a Republican mentioned Nancy Pelosi, for example, but did not talk about the "Democratic Party" or "Democrats" as a group, they would be given a 0 for mentioning the out-party, because they are not invoking partisanship as a social identity as it is constructed affectively. While this measure is consistent with the relevant theoretical framework outlined in chapter 1, it naturally undercounts how much legislators signal the parties in their communications in a more implicit, vague way. Below, I estimate the magnitude of this undercounting by comparing an extended measure of other ideological terms in tweets, devised by Rogers and Jones (2021) and Rathje, Van Bavel, and Van Der Linden (2021), to my measure of out-/in-party mentions.

Bipartisanship, election, and policy mentions were coded the same way (as indicator and count variables). For bipartisanship mentions, I specifically look for explicit uses of "bipartisan" and "compromise." While other phrases and words may signal notions of bipartisanship (such as "unity" or "working across the aisle"), officials use the term "bipartisan" in 99 percent of communications about the general concept.[4] Indeed, in prior research on bipartisan content in elite rhetoric, scholars only search for the single term (Westwood 2021). As discussed in chapter 2, one component of negative representation is focusing on out-group electoral loss without necessarily denigrating the out-group using other affect-based statements. For this reason I also code for whether and how many times representatives refer to an "election." While not a major focus of this chapter, this variable helps to establish how much out-party rhetoric is centered around winning and losing. For policy mentions, I created a custom dictionary of terms relating to legislative activity generally (e.g., policy, bill, legislation, etc.) as well as more specific policy areas and issue areas (e.g., abortion, guns, healthcare, education, etc.). See the appendix to this chapter for the list of policy terms. None of these categories are mutually exclusive. For example, if a tweet by a Democratic member of Congress uses the word "Republicans," it is counted as an out-party mention. If the tweet also refers to "Democrats," it is additionally coded as mentioning the in-party, and so on.

POLICY AND PARTY IN CONGRESSIONAL NEWSLETTERS AND TWEETS

What do lawmakers talk about in newsletters and tweets generally? Figure 3.1 shows the words used most in both modes of communication. Even though Twitter is a fundamentally different platform with a different audience, several of the top words used are shared across mediums. Many of the most frequently used words have to do with the act of legislating, especially in newsletters: act, bill, legislation, tax, issues, committee, policy, program, law, and service. While a few of these words are also among the most frequently used in tweets, other popularly tweeted words place less emphasis on policy and are more group-based or affective in nature: families, proud, protect, women, bipartisan, community, and join. Notably absent from tweets are some policy terms that appear frequently in newsletters: legislation, policy, committee, issues, program, law, and service. Clearly there is a greater emphasis on policy in newsletters than there is on social media. There are no clear differences between the top words used by Democrats and those used by Republicans.

Figure 3.2 shows the percentage of newsletters and tweets that mention policy, bipartisanship, the in-party and out-party, and elections across all congresses. Policy is talked about in 97 percent of newsletters, yet in only 35.5 percent of tweets. What *do* tweets mention, if not policy? The remaining tweets that are not picked up by my coding methods generally touch on current events that are not explicitly issue-based, such as more localized events in a legislator's jurisdiction or natural disasters and tragedies. There are also many moments of "advertising" à la Mayhew (1974)—stories about visits to a district or business, events with the representative, speeches, interviews, ceremonies, and the like. Donald Trump's multiple impeachments were also a major topic on Twitter. Impeachment is, of course, an official legislative action, but I do not consider it policy-relevant in the same way issue-based legislation is.

Bipartisanship is referenced in 26 percent of newsletters, and less than 3 percent of tweets. Among newsletters, 20.5 percent mention the out-party, and 18 percent mention the in-party. Of course, newsletters are significantly

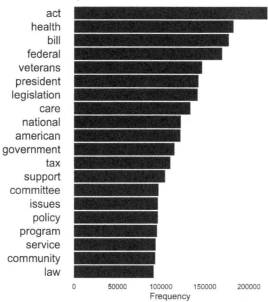
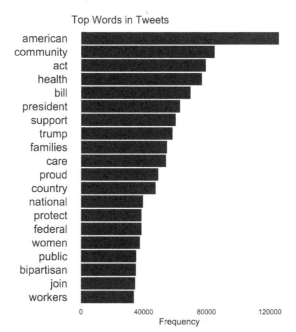

Figure 3.1. Words used most frequently in newsletters and tweets
Note: Number of words in newsletters = 37,015,742. Number of words in tweets = 16,590,438.

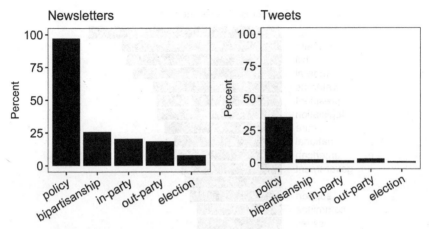

Figure 3.2. Prevalence of partisan and policy rhetoric

Note: Percentage of newsletters (*left*) and Twitter posts (*right*) by members of Congress 2009–2020 that contain rhetoric about policy issues, bipartisanship and compromise, the legislator's own party, the legislator's opposite party, and elections. Number of newsletters = 130,332. Number of tweets = 1,358,680.

Table 3.1. Average Counts per Legislator

	AVG. TOTAL IN NEWSLETTERS	AVG. TOTAL IN TWEETS
Out-party	17.1	35.6
In-party	16.1	19.0
Policy	770.3	570.8
Bipartisan	21.0	28.7
Election	7.5	12.6

Note: Average total mentions of the opposite party, same party, policy, bipartisanship/compromise, and elections per legislator in congressional newsletters and tweets.

longer than tweets, so all concepts are more likely to be mentioned in a single newsletter than in a single tweet. At the same time, most legislators tweet more often than they send newsletters. Table 3.1 therefore shows the average number of times those concepts are mentioned per legislator in one congress.[5] The average legislator mentioned the out-party 17 times in their newsletters during a given congress, the in-party 16 times, and policy 770 times. On Twitter, the overall patterns are mostly similar, with one notable exception: legislators on average reference the other party more than twice as frequently on Twitter in a given congress as they do in their newsletters. Legislators tweet about the other party over 35 times on average and about their own party 19 times, and they use policy-oriented terms an average of 570 times. This is our first indication about how legislators may use these platforms in different ways.

Of course, as mentioned above, my measure of partisan language is relatively narrow. If members used more vague or implicit language about the other side, such as ideological terms or the name of a high-ranking member from the other party but not the other party explicitly, that is not counted here. Other scholars interested in political terms more generally (Rathje, Van Bavel, and Van Der Linden 2021; Rogers and Jones 2021) provide a measure for the Twitter data that includes ideological, in addition to party, terms. For example, for Democrats, the terms "liberal," "socialist," "leftist," "communist," "progressive," and "left-wing" are included. For Republicans, the terms "conservative," "alt-right," "right-wing," and "far right" are included. While I focus on the party-explicit language in the rest of this chapter and book, this "extended" version of my measure (plotted in this chapter's appendix) can give us a picture of just how much other general, ideological terms are used in an out-group and in-group way. While only just over 3 percent of legislator tweets contain an explicit mention of the other party, these broader ideological terms appear in almost 11 percent of legislator tweets. In-party mentions (using my narrower measure) appear in less than 2 percent of tweets, but the extended measure for in-group ideological mentions appears in up to 15.9 percent of legislator tweets. Clearly, members of Congress are more likely to invoke ideological terms like "liberal" and "conservative" (and their more extreme counterparts, like "socialist" and "alt-right") than the explicitly partisan terms "Democrats" and "Republicans," but the meaning behind these terms is up for further interpretation. "Liberal," for example, can used when discussing a policy agenda rather than necessarily a set of people in an out-group. Indeed, policy language is still more prevalent even compared to this broader set of ideological terms.

The relative magnitude of policy language in both newsletters and tweets is not surprising given the broader dictionary of terms compared to the other, much narrower measures. Nonetheless, it demonstrates that legislators often communicate about issues. A central question in the literature on affective polarization is whether policy views undergird partisan affect. If legislators mostly invoke partisanship only when discussing issues, that may suggest that the two concepts are inexorably linked—that is, partisanship is only relevant in legislator communication as it relates to policy debates. However, if representatives often communicate about parties and partisans in the absence of discussions about policy, then it would suggest that a significant amount of that communication is related solely to identity-based rhetoric without a clear issue focus.

How much does partisan language co-occur with policy language? The overlap is shown in the top two diagrams in figure 3.3. Since policy language appears in almost all newsletters, almost all instances of out-partisan rhetoric appear in newsletters that also discuss policy. Sometimes this reflects a genuine connection of out-partisan rhetoric on a policy debate. For example, in his May 2018 newsletter Congressman Michael Capuano (D-MA) discusses a Republican threat to end a government-run consumer complaint database and notes that "Republicans may talk about transparency and accountability in government but don't do much about it." This is a clear example of attacking Republicans in relation to a policy debate.

There are a significant number of tweets that reference the other party that do not mention any policy terms at all (plot A). In fact, almost half (49.3 percent) of tweets that talk about the other party make no mention of policy. Given the number of words in the policy dictionary compared to the number of words in the out-partisan dictionary, the frequency of non-policy out-partisan tweets is noteworthy. Members of Congress tweet about the other party even without any explicit reference to policymaking or issue-based concerns. One example comes from Rep. Steny Hoyer (D-MD), who tweeted, "I am outraged the GOP continues to spread hate and falsehoods. This ad is a despicable example of the politics of hate and division and misleads the American public. I call on every GOP leader to condemn and disassociate themselves from this hateful, divisive, inaccurate ad." A similar tweet from Rep. Dan Meuser (R-PA) stated, "I strongly oppose Democrat leadership's latest effort to harass @realDonaldTrump. For years, he and his supporters have been subjected to baseless attacks. Such slander is a disservice to our nation and the American people, and I am tired of it." Note that both tweets, perhaps ironically, denounce partisan attacks by the other party while themselves denouncing the other party (by using words such as "despicable" and calling out the entire party instead of individuals). As an additional example, consider an October 2018 newsletter from Rep. John Shimkus (R-IL), who cites threats of violence against his Republican colleagues and places the blame on Democrats for encouraging those attacks. He writes:

> The threats and the violence have not let up and instead of seeing my Democrat colleagues calling for an end, there have been calls for their supporters to keep going, to do even more to threaten Republicans. . . . If this is going to stop, it must start with Democratic leaders, who need to condemn, rather than promote these dangerous calls to action. . . . While it's clear many Democrats refuse to accept the election of President Trump, if they want change, they need to convince people with their ideas and actually win elections, rather than call for violent resistance, harassment, and mob rule.

This is a common theme with many of the out-party mentions in congressional communications, especially those that are not policy-focused, and it illustrates the vicious cycle I previewed in chapter 2. Specifically, out-partisan appeals are often framed as a response to transgressions the other side has already been committing. In each of these examples, the member of Congress makes clear that they are justified in attacking the other side because their side has already been subjected to attacks. In later chapters, I present evidence of this vicious cycle and how it affects the behavior of both politicians and the public around the proliferation of partisan rhetoric.

That said, many out-partisan mentions are also *only* about the other side, and are not included with discussions about both parties in general (plot B). Almost 87 percent of tweets (and 41 percent of newsletters) that talk about the other party do not mention the legislator's in-party, and 76 percent of tweets (and 47 percent of newsletters) that talk about the legislator's in-party do not mention the other party. The same goes for mentions of bipartisanship and compromise (plot C). That is, more legislators tweet things like "Democrats have a simple message for the American people: You don't matter. Democrats are only creating a constitutional crisis for pure political gain" (Rep. Kevin Brady [R-TX], September 24, 2019) than things like "ICYMI: Last night a bipartisan group of congressional leaders announced an agreement on comprehensive legislation to combat the opioid crisis. I applaud the leaders for their work and look forward to passing this vital piece of legislation" (Rep. Robert Aderholt [R-AL], September 26, 2018). It is even more common to singularly attack the out-party in a tweet than to make affective attacks that invoke both the in-group and the out-group, such as "the difference couldn't be clearer. Democrats are #ForThePeople. Republicans are for millionaire and billionaire donors, wealthy corporations and every well-funded special interest group that swarms around Washington" (Rep. John Sarbanes [D-MD], October 2, 2018). In line with conceptualizations of negative partisanship as either electorally focused or affectively driven, the bottom two diagrams show the overlap between newsletters and tweets that invoke partisanship and *elections* (plots D and E). There is some overlap, but a majority of references to the parties in both newsletters and tweets are not strictly about winning or losing an election.

One striking pattern emerges from the graphs in figure 3.3. On Twitter there is much less overlap between negative partisan rhetoric (mentions of the out-party) and other related rhetoric than there is in newsletters. With fewer characters to work with, legislators are more likely to invoke the other side as a sole appeal on its own. Later in the book, I show the impact of partisan-only rhetoric on things like voters' evaluations of representatives and perceptions of what the other side wants. I also show how talking about the other party increases social media engagement and fuels a positive

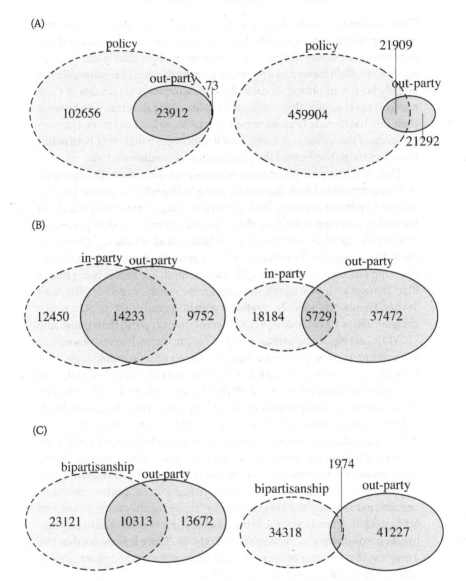

Figure 3.3. Overlap of rhetoric in newsletters (*left*) and tweets (*right*): (A) Policy versus out-party; (B) In-party versus out-party; (C) Bipartisanship versus out-party; (D) Election versus out-party; (E) Election versus in-party

(D)

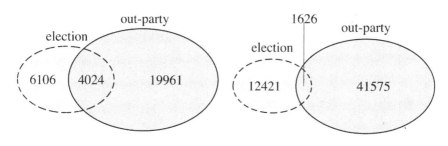

(E)

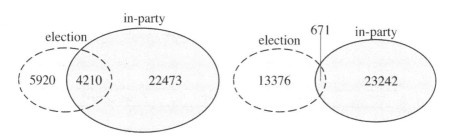

feedback loop for continued negative styles of representation. Since many representatives do in fact mention the other party in a vacuum, and not always alongside topics that might temper negative representation (regarding policy issues or bipartisanship), that feedback loop is further reinforced.

TRENDS OVER TIME

The above analyses help to contextualize the book's main concepts relative to one another within elite communications. Also important is how these communications have changed over time, especially considering arguments about the influence of majority and minority control. For example, the historical shift in party competition leads members in both parties to engage in activities that advance their own party's reputation and undermine that of the opposing party (Lee 2016). When parties are in the minority, they have greater incentive to focus on denigrating the other party rhetorically than to try to advance their own agenda, which may be dead-on-arrival. Figure 3.4 shows the percentage of congressional newsletters (the two plots on the top) and tweets (the two plots on the bottom) that invoke policy compared

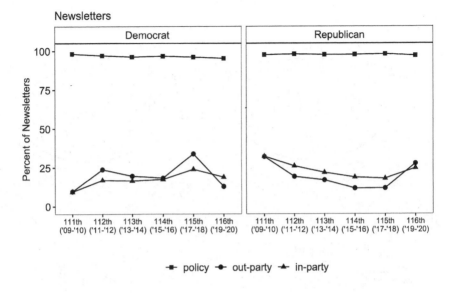
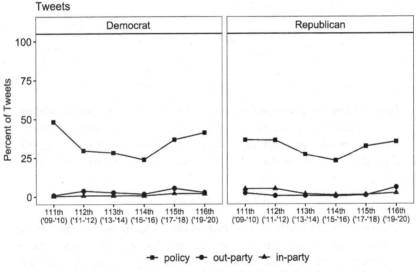

Figure 3.4. Policy, out-party, in-party over time by party in newsletters and tweets

Note: Percentage of newsletters (*top*) and Twitter posts (*bottom*) by members of Congress over time that contain rhetoric about policy issues, the out-party, and the in-party. 2009–2020.

to those that invoke the out-party and in-party over time (see the appendix to this chapter for the average number of mentions per legislator over time as well as the Twitter data shown with retweets removed—the overall patterns remain the same). Almost all newsletters invoke policy in some way, but not nearly as many tweets mentioned policy. While over a third of tweets on average mention policy in some way, in some years this is as low as 23 percent. In each year, the percentage of newsletters that invoke policy remains above 96 percent. After Republicans took back control of Congress in 2011, the Twitter focus on policy decreased for Democrats. Both Democrats and Republicans tweeted about policy the least in the final two years of the Obama presidency, and during the 114th Congress (in which the 2016 presidential election took place) mentions of policy were at their lowest, appearing in only a quarter of tweets.

Following Republicans' assumption of control of Congress in 2011, Democrats increased their out-partisan focus on Twitter and in newsletters, and Republicans decreased their out-partisan focus. Conversely, after Democrats took control of Congress in 2018, Republicans talked about the other side more. For example, it was rare for Republicans to talk about the Democratic Party on Twitter before 2018; less than 1 percent of tweets by Republicans mentioned the out-party. But this jumped to 6 percent in the 116th Congress, when Democrats became the majority.

After Donald Trump took office, Democrats invoked the out-party in 35 percent of newsletters in 2017 to 2018. This dropped to 12 percent after Democrats took control of Congress in the 2018 midterm elections. Republicans used out-partisan language in 12 percent of newsletters after Trump took office, and this increased to 29 percent after they lost the House and Senate in 2018. Democrats' use of in-party appeals remained relatively low on Twitter from 2009 to 2020, moving from only 1 percent of tweets to 2.5 percent in 2019 and 2020. Republicans mentioned their own party as a group in 5 percent of tweets in Obama's first term, after which the percentage decreased.

In sum, out-partisan mentions increase in both mediums after a party loses an election. Is partisan rhetoric by members of Congress driven by winning and losing elections? In general, we know that the minority party legislates less than the majority party. Instead, they tend to obstruct the majority party's legislative agenda and launch attacks with the aim of winning back control in the next election. The trends demonstrated here clearly flow from elections, regardless of whether it is strategic at the individual member level or more procedural based on what is happening in the chamber and which party has more legislative control. Later in the book (chapter 5), I investigate whether out-party language by legislators during a congressional session is associated with an increased share of the two-party vote in the next election. The results here suggest that members of Congress may be responding to overall gains and losses in previous elections. Once the other party is in control of Congress or the presidency, members in the minority party use more partisan language, especially language that invokes the other party rather than their own. A minority party needs to develop a coordinated line of attack on the opposition in order to drive favorable media narratives and develop its argument for retaking power.

Even if partisan language increases in congressional communications after losing an election, it is possible that *bipartisan* language increases as well. If members of Congress are likely to talk about the other side after they lose power, maybe they are making calls for unity, compromise, and bipartisanship. To examine this possibility, I also estimate the percentage of newsletters and tweets that invoke "bipartisanship" or "compromise" overlayed on mentions of the out-party for a clear comparison (see figure 3.5). Across both mediums and parties, discussions of bipartisanship have increased over time. For example, Democrats and Republicans in the 111th Congress use bipartisan rhetoric in 15 percent and 17 percent of newsletters, respectively, and this increases to 26 percent and 30 percent by the 116th Congress. Similar patterns appear in congressional tweets. Very few Democrats and Republicans made calls for bipartisanship on Twitter at the start of the time period, but by 2020 they did so in about 4 percent of tweets on average. Unlike mentions of the parties, which rise and fall after a change in power, there is no clear pattern over time for bipartisanship other than a slight and steady increase.

Of course, it is hard to discuss the prevalence of negative out-group rhetoric without mentioning one of the most notorious purveyors of this craft—Donald Trump. The rhetoric of Trump has been a major focus of the examination of negative partisanship and incivility in politics. His style of communication was often characterized by its confrontational and divisive nature, and he frequently used inflammatory language in public statements and tweets (Gross and Johnson 2016). Many other politicians, particularly those in the Republican Party, adopted similar rhetoric and tactics in their own public statements and campaigns. The rise in the national prominence of people like Reps. Paul Gosar, Lauren Boebert, Marjorie Taylor Greene, and Ron Johnson demonstrates the attractiveness and endurance of Trumpism. Of course, some of these people (and other Trump supporters) underperformed in relation to electoral benchmarks, but Trump's influence on political rhetoric has nonetheless been notable. Many politicians who *oppose* Trump also felt the need to respond to his rhetoric and tactics, which seemingly led to a further escalation of political hostility. For example, during the height of the 2018 midterm election campaign, Hillary Clinton said: "You cannot be civil with a political party that wants to destroy what you stand

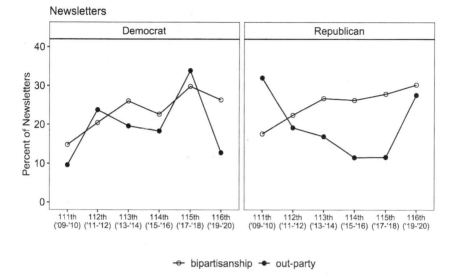

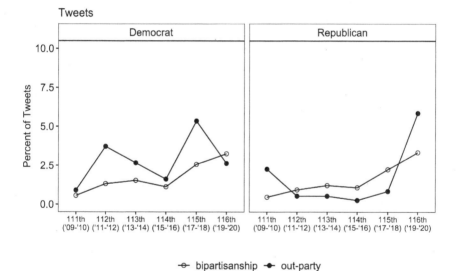

Figure 3.5. Bipartisanship, out-party over time by party in newsletters and tweets

Note: Percentage of newsletters (*top*) and Twitter posts (*bottom*) by members of Congress over time that contain rhetoric about bipartisanship and the out-party. 2009-2020.

for, what you care about. That's why I believe, if we are fortunate enough to win back the House and/or the Senate, that's when civility can start again. But until then, the only thing that the Republicans seem to recognize and respect is strength" (Ventresca 2018). As with many other instances of negative representation, Clinton here is justifying incivility by pointing to uncivil behavior from the other side.

Exactly how much Trump's political rhetoric during his time in office contributed to a more divisive "us versus them" political climate, or whether it was just a symptom of such a climate, is an empirical question. In that same interview, Clinton pointed to attacks she faced from Republicans while serving as First Lady in the 1990s, long before Trump was a political presence. Also up for debate is whether his style of communication has had lasting effects on the way politicians engage in public discourse. The prevalence of hate crimes against marginalized groups, violence against protesters, and hateful language online has led some to suggest that Trump's rhetoric has had a direct influence on increasing intergroup conflict at the mass level (Feinberg, Branton, and Martinez-Ebers 2022; Nithyanand, Schaffner, and Hill 2017). Scholars using experimental methods have found that being exposed to prejudiced rhetoric from politicians, whether Trump or others, increases expressions of prejudice among voters (Newman et al. 2021; Schaffner 2020). Likewise, there is evidence that when people see politicians engaging in uncivil discussions they also become less civil in their own discussions of politics (Cappella and Jamieson 1997; Gervais 2014, 2015; Mutz 2006).

It is certainly the case that Americans think Trump has had an adverse influence on political discussions. A 2019 Pew survey found that a majority of Americans thought that Trump had changed the tone of political debate in the US for the worse. Little scholarship has been conducted on the direct effects of Trump on elite-level discourse, but journalists have written about how Trump "proved that incivility works" (Bump 2018). Did Trump's rhetoric elucidate for politicians the playbook for using explicit polarizing language? Research in comparative politics finds that populist political leaders do not singlehandedly produce regime change, but preexisting institutional features and the normalization of demagoguery in public discourse provide conditions for such leaders to come to power (e.g., Hawkins and Littvay 2019). As the historian of political rhetoric Jennifer Mercieca said, "he took advantage of preexisting distrust and polarization and frustration, and he used rhetorical strategies that were designed to make all of those things worse."[6]

Overall, Trump likely accelerated a process that was already well underway before he rose to political prominence during the Obama administration. The broader context is that partisan-based rhetoric has become increasingly viable for politicians as the public has become more affectively polarized and as the nature of closely contested national elections incentivizes party leaders to engage in more posturing for the next campaign. But even as this context has made negative representation a more viable possibility for politicians, the adoption of that representational style is by no means predetermined, nor is it universal.

NEGATIVITY AND OUT-PARTISAN RHETORIC

So far, I have largely assumed that when legislators mention the out-party they do so in a negative way. But to what extent is this actually the case? To examine *how* the out-party is being invoked by legislators, I conduct a sentiment analysis using the Hu and Liu (2004) lexicon coding of words into "positive" or "negative" categories. Merging the text data with the sentiment lexicon enables me to associate each word with a positive, negative, or neutral tone.[7] I then apply a measure of negativity I created by taking the ratio of the number of negative words to the number of positive words in each newsletter or tweet. A score of 1 means the text had an equal number of negative and positive words and can therefore be considered neutral in tone. Negativity scores below 1 indicate a text that is more positive than negative, and scores above 1 indicate the opposite.[8]

Figure 3.6 shows the negativity of newsletters and tweets that invoke the out-party. To ensure that these patterns are not just a function of the rate of negativity across the platforms in general, I compare this score to the scores of all the other newsletters and tweets that do not mention the out-party at all. In 2009, out-party newsletters were more negative than positive, with a negativity score of 1.25, meaning that negative words were used 25 percent more than positive words in newsletters that mentioned the other party. Over time, newsletters became less negative and more positive. Newsletters that did not invoke the out-party were generally consistent in sentiment over time, with a drop of negativity in 2017 and a return to more neutral levels in 2019. It is important to note, however, that newsletters are long documents often with several distinct sections, so it is possible that a newsletter could mention the opposite party in a negative way but then offset that with positive language in other parts of the newsletter.

Notably, tweets tell a different story. Tweets that did not mention the out-party were relatively consistent over time in sentiment, but tweets that mention the out-party increasingly use more negative words. In fact, the shift in the tone of out-party tweets from the 111th to the 116th Congress represents about a 20 percent increase in negativity when tweeting about the out-party. Unlike newsletters, tweets are so brief that we can be quite confident that when out-party tweets use negative terms, the negativity is

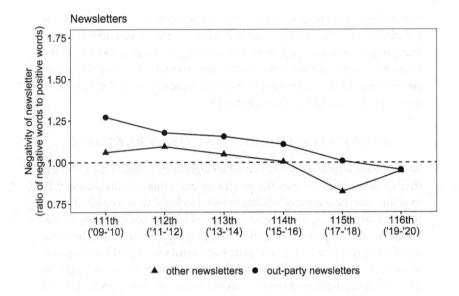

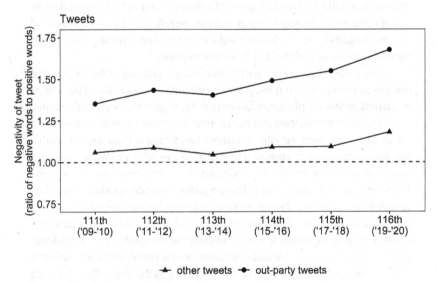

Figure 3.6. Negativity over time in newsletters and tweets
Note: Ratio of negative words to positive words in newsletters (*top*) and Twitter posts (*bottom*) by members of Congress. Circles show negativity in newsletters and tweets that contain out-partisan rhetoric. Triangles show all other newsletters and tweets. 2009-2020.

actually being directed toward the out-party. While most tweets mentioning the out-party included just 1 or 2 negative words, there were hundreds of tweets in the 116th Congress alone that included 5 or more negative words. Rep. Bill Pascrell (D-NJ) set the bar by using 18 negative words in a single tweet, which read:

> Thoughts and prayers to the republicans who've excused every
> atrocity
> corruption
> crime
> cruelty
> deception
> defamation
> disgrace
> felony
> fraud
> guilty plea
> hypocrisy
> impeachment
> indignity
> insult
> lie
> libel
> scandal
> slander
> slur
> theft
> treachery.
>
> They own all of it.

Overall, newsletters, which provide a platform for communicating at length, have become slightly more positive over time, while tweets that specifically make out-partisan appeals have become significantly more negative over time. Recall that legislators also disproportionately mention the out-party in their tweets in a way that is less prevalent in newsletters. Are there partisan asymmetries in sentiment? Figure 3.7 shows that from 2009 to 2016, Democrats were more positive than Republicans in both newsletters and tweets. From 2017 to 2020, after Trump won the presidency and took office, the trend reverses and Republicans become more positive than Democrats. Taken together, the findings suggest that, after losing an election, members of Congress referenced the other party more and were more

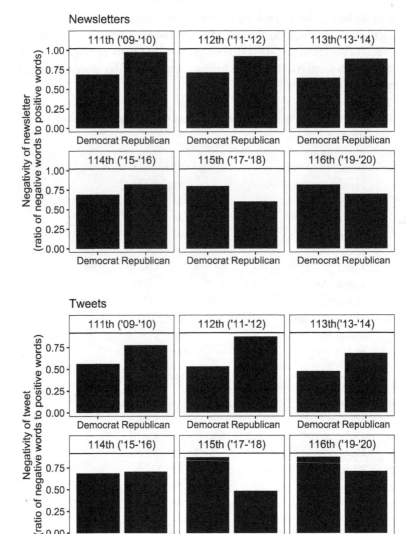

Figure 3.7. Negativity over time in newsletters and tweets by party

Note: Ratio of negative words to positive words in newsletters (*top*) and Twitter posts (*bottom*) by Democratic (grey) and Republican (black) members of Congress.

negative on social media when they did so. Legislators appear to react to big election losses by lashing out at the party who has just triumphed.

Studies on political advertisements show that negativity plays an important role in campaigning. Negative ads often provide voters with crucial information about salient issues, rather than simply attacking personal characteristics of an opponent (Geer 2008). Negative ads also sometimes have a mobilizing effect on voters. Attack ads are more attention-grabbing and memorable, stimulating voters to recall relevant information and be interested enough to engage (Meffert et al. 2006; Newhagen and Reeves 2013). Negativity in campaigns also activates emotions like anxiety and anger to induce engagement (Gervais 2017; Marcus, Neuman, and MacKuen 2000; Valentino et al. 2011). But I again find that the difference in audience is important. Newsletters are going to a member's primary constituency of core supporters in the district. Tweets are seen by a much broader audience. Why would members speak in more positive terms to their electoral base and in more negative terms for the whole world to see? The findings in the next few chapters provide an answer to this question. I find that elites do not think core supporters will support out-party language. At the same time, negativity on Twitter goes more viral than positivity; tweets that mention the out-party attract far more likes and retweets. Additionally, negative partisan rhetoric on Twitter is associated with an increase in fundraising, while negative partisan rhetoric in newsletters (and positive partisan rhetoric on Twitter) is not. The incentives to engage in negative representation therefore line up with the findings shown here.

CONCLUSION

The analyses so far lead to two overarching conclusions. First, the audience matters. There are more tweets that contain partisan language without language pertaining to policy or bipartisanship, while that is much less common in newsletters. In recent years, newsletters are much less negative in sentiment than tweets, and tweets that reference the out-party have become increasingly negative over time. Second, while there are significant differences between the two methods of communication, there are also similarities. Policy language still dominates on both mediums, even if this is less the case on Twitter. Representatives focus on the opposing party more after their own party loses power. At the same time, calls for bipartisanship and compromise have increased over time in both newsletters and tweets.

These conclusions set the stage for understanding the analyses in the rest of the book. Negative styles of representation matter because they symbolize what people value in politics and because they represent a trade-off in representational behaviors. When elites engage with constituents by giving voice to who they are *not*—to out-groups—it emphasizes what divides us rather than what unites us. When people consume messages about division over and over again, negational identities become more central to political behavior. This intensifies antipathy toward one's opponents and at the same time causes others to disengage. On the elite side, the implications for substantive representation are profound. Prior research argues that by using motivating group-based rhetoric, politicians can talk less about other, more specific and substantive policy-oriented concerns (Dickson and Scheve 2006). While the empirical findings do not support the idea that group-based partisan appeals overshadow policy-based appeals on a strictly numerical basis, it does appear that these partisan appeals are becoming more common and more negative (at least on social media). This trend is not lost on the public; later in the book, I show that voters are under the impression that group-based partisan appeals are prioritized over policy, which has downstream effects for a healthy, functioning democracy. An information ecosystem that rewards vitriolic, partisan communication creates the perception that elites focus almost exclusively on partisanship and identity politics rather than substantive issues, even when this is clearly not the case. When legislators *do* focus on partisanship, however, are their constituents less likely to be represented substantively?

4. HOW NEGATIVE REPRESENTATION DIMINISHES SUBSTANTIVE REPRESENTATION

It is not uncommon for politicians to blame the other side for legislative gridlock. The refrain is simple: if only the other party would stop partisan hate-mongering, then we could pass legislation. This is different from criticizing the other party's policy agenda. Rather, the critique is that there *is* no policy agenda and that the other party is focused more on baseless attacks, political games, and partisan showmanship. In other words, affective polarization has overtaken substantive representation. Below are just a few recent examples.

> "At a time we could (and should) be passing trade deals, lessening the opioid crisis, securing our southern border, and keeping our economy roaring, Democrats are instead blinded by partisan hatred." —Rep. Matt Gaetz in a newsletter to constituents, December 7, 2019

> "It is more clear than ever that the Democrats are primarily interested in scoring political points by opposing the President at every turn, not working on behalf of the American people." —Rep. Andrew Ferguson in a newsletter to constituents, June 23, 2019

> "They have no interest in passing legislation." —Rep. Ayanna Pressley on Twitter, June 7, 2021

> "Their hyper-partisanship completely prohibits their ability to get to work for the American people." —Rep. Marjorie Taylor Greene in a newsletter to constituents, March 9, 2023

> "The continued policing and bullying by Liz and her crew of the WOC members of Congress is just proof that the GOP don't have a policy agenda for the American people. Instead they want to focus on a hate agenda that doesn't better our lives, but divides us more." —Rep. Rashida Tlaib on Twitter, June 20, 2019

Are they right? Does negative representation come at the expense of getting the real work done? One important part of this book's theoretical argument is that negative rhetorical styles do not necessarily take the place of focusing on policy, but they do have consequences for substantive representation. Legislators who focus more time and effort on trying to score points by demonizing the other party may have fewer resources to devote to lawmaking, or they may erode the bipartisan social capital needed to succeed in pushing legislation through Congress.

In the aggregate, there is mixed evidence about whether the contemporary era of negative representation is making it harder for Congress to get things done. Congress is passing fewer laws (and perhaps even fewer important laws) than it did during previous decades (Whyman 2019) and roll call votes are more partisan than they used to be. At the same time, however, there is reason to think things may not be as bad as they seem. For example, while there are fewer pieces of legislation being passed, it is also true that the laws that do pass include many more provisions, reflecting the fact that much current policymaking happens in broad, sweeping legislation rather than multiple smaller laws (Whyman 2019).

Furthermore, it seems that bipartisanship is hardly dead in the contemporary Congress. Curry and Lee (2020) find that the legislation that does pass Congress in the present day does so with just as much bipartisan support as laws that passed in earlier decades. To explain why this happens despite the increasing polarization of congressional roll call voting, the authors make a distinction between lawmaking and representation. An important part of representational activity is aimed not at policymaking, but at communicating differences between the parties and giving voice to the groups they represent in the partisan back-and-forth that defines our politics. Congress provides a public forum to have these debates and score points against the other side. But Curry and Lee argue that when it comes time to actually engage in policymaking, many legislators are able to put partisanship aside and craft bipartisan coalitions.

This is how things look in the aggregate, but the extent to which lawmaking and negative representation might actually be in conflict is less clear when we look at individual legislators. Chapter 3 shows that there is significant variation in when negative appeals are invoked in congressional communications. This raises the possibility that some legislators focus more on negative representation while others might emphasize the lawmaking part of their jobs more.

Here, I analyze whether certain legislator traits (being elected in a noncompetitive district, ideological extremity, and legislative effectiveness) are associated with using negative appeals. These associations can tell us about the observed relationship between focusing on the other party and substantive representation. First, legislators in safer seats are more likely to use out-party rhetoric than are legislators who occupy seats in more competitive districts. While not directly tied to legislative outcomes, this provides context for the type of district that enables negative representation. Legislators who worry less about getting reelected have leeway to attack the other side. Second, both ideological extremity and ineffective lawmaking co-occur with negative partisan language. Members of Congress who are more ideological in their voting patterns tend to talk more about the other party in their newsletters, but not about policy issues that are in the interest of their constituents. At the same time, as mentions of the other party increase, legislative effectiveness decreases. While Congress in the aggregate may still be able to balance lawmaking and negative representation, this balancing act does not appear to be as straightforward for individual legislators. For individual members of Congress, negative representation in rhetoric comes with trade-offs for substantive representation in actual legislation.

ELECTORAL SAFETY OFFERS LEEWAY

How is electoral competition related to partisan appeals? Legislators who represent districts that are mostly one-sided should have the leeway to make partisan appeals without having to worry about turning off the small number of constituents who affiliate with the other party. By contrast, when a member of Congress represents a competitive district, any partisan appeals are likely to alienate the large share of their constituents who are from the other side, making a negative representation strategy less rewarding.

I categorized districts as either "competitive" or "safe" based on the vote share in the previous election. A district was classified as competitive if the vote share was closely contested, falling between 45 and 55 percent, indicating a relatively even split between the two main candidates. Conversely, a district was labeled as safe if the vote share was less evenly distributed, with one candidate receiving less than 45 percent or more than 55 percent of the vote. This distinction allows me to examine how the safety or competitiveness of a district might influence legislators' behavior, particularly their propensity to reference the other party, engage in bipartisan rhetoric, or focus on policy in their communication.

Figure 4.1 illustrates the differences in out-party mentions by safety of the district. Legislators from competitive districts significantly referenced the other party in their tweets less than those in safe districts ($p <$ 0.001). The mean number of times legislators in safe districts tweeted about the out-party is over 66, while in competitive districts it was significantly lower, at about 31. Legislators from competitive districts significantly tweeted about bipartisanship or compromise more often compared to those

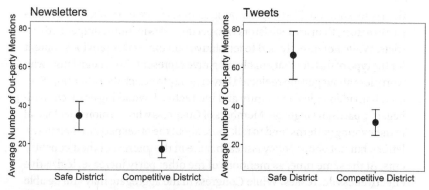

Figure 4.1. Out-party mentions by safety of district
Note: Vertical bars are 95 percent confidence intervals.

in safe districts ($p < 0.001$). Those in safe seats used bipartisan rhetoric an average of about 39 times. Those in competitive districts, on the other hand, used bipartisan rhetoric 20 more times (more than 59 times on average). Legislators in competitive districts also talked more about policy (832 times on average) than did legislators in safe seats (771 times on average), though this difference was not quite statistically significant. Thus, it is not that legislators in safe seats do not talk about policy at all; consistent with chapter 3, policy-focused language is still the most prominent type of rhetoric, well above and beyond partisan-focused language. But the fact that out-party appeals occur most frequently in electorally uncompetitive districts emphasizes that negative versus positive representation is a strategic choice. Legislators may find greater leeway to engage in partisan rhetoric when they do not have to worry about turning off voters.

The results for newsletters (using the same cohort of House members in the 116th Congress to compare to the Twitter analysis) follow the same pattern. Legislators in competitive districts referenced the other party in their newsletters significantly fewer times compared to those in safe districts ($p < 0.001$). The average number of times legislators in safe seats referenced the other party was about 35, while in competitive districts it was significantly lower, at around 17. Legislators from competitive districts, though, made significantly fewer references to their own party in their newsletters than did those in safe districts ($p < 0.01$). The average number of references to the in-party in safe seats was about 25, while in competitive districts it was 16. Again, legislators from safe districts significantly referenced bipartisanship less often compared to those in competitive districts ($p < 0.01$). Those in safe seats used bipartisan rhetoric an average of about 29 times, whereas those in competitive districts used bipartisan rhetoric an average of about

50 times in their newsletters. And there was again no significant difference in references to policy between legislators from competitive and safe districts ($p = 0.55$).

The findings reveal substantial differences in the behavior of legislators based on the competitiveness of their districts. Legislators from competitive districts seem to be more cautious in referencing the parties, possibly reflecting a strategic effort to appeal to a more diverse electorate. The increased emphasis on bipartisan language in competitive districts further supports this interpretation. This trend aligns with the broader transformation in the American political landscape characterized by the increasing number of safe districts. Elected officials may find themselves less concerned with securing votes for their next reelection campaign and more focused on building or maintaining their national influence. By focusing on the opposition, they not only resonate with their base but also position themselves as prominent figures within their party at the national level. To be sure, electoral safety is strongly correlated with party leadership in that members who hold high-ranking positions in the chamber are less likely to be in competitive districts. And party leaders are among the most prolific users of negative representation. After controlling for other relevant factors, party leaders mention the other party in their newsletters over 10 times more on average than do rank-and-file members, and a whopping 127 times more on average than rank-and-file members on Twitter (see the appendix to this chapter).

The dynamics of electoral competition appear to shape the prevalence of negative representational styles, which raises questions about the implications for policy representation. While attacking the other party may enhance a legislator's national profile, it may also contribute to a more adversarial and less collaborative legislative environment. This could hinder the ability to find common ground and compromise on key policy issues. This leads us to the next step: examining the relationship between how much a legislator references the other party and their legislative activity. Understanding this relationship provides deeper insights into how legislators' strategic communication choices impact substantive policy outcomes.

IDEOLOGUES TALK ABOUT THE OPPOSING PARTY, NOT POLICY

Talking about out-groups might be a proxy for focusing on legislation that drives polarization in the legislature. Some research demonstrates how ideology drives affective polarization (Bougher 2017; Orr and Huber 2020; Rogowski and Sutherland 2017; Webster and Abramowitz 2017). One hypothesis is that Congress members who are ideologically extreme are more likely to draw on partisan (negational or affirmational) identities. Do ideological extremists mention the parties more frequently than moderates? On one hand, if more extreme policy views underpin partisan affect, then pure ideologues may use more partisan language and less bipartisan language. On the other, more extreme legislators may also simultaneously use more *policy*-based language as well, since these are presumably policy purists who care most about their ideological agendas. If talking about the opposing party has a positive association with cross-party voting on legislation, then negative representation is simply a rhetorical tool that does not actually translate into how elites legislate. But if elites who talk about the out-party take more ideological positions, then negative representational styles undergird not only affective polarization, but ideological polarization as well.

I again analyze the average number of times a legislator invoked a concept across all their newsletters or tweets. While the graphs in these next sections plot the bivariate relationships between rhetoric and indicators of substantive representation, these relationships hold when controlling for other legislator traits (like race, gender, party leadership, and seniority) in a regression model, as shown in the appendix to this chapter.[1] First, I estimate the relationship between a legislator's DW-nominate score and how often they use partisan and policy-based rhetoric in their newsletters to constituents. A DW-nominate score is an estimate of a legislator's ideology based on how they vote on issues that come before Congress. These scores are used widely by political scientists to map the ideological distribution of legislators in each Congress during American history. Larger negative scores represent more liberal voting patterns, while larger positive scores represent more conservative voting patterns; scores near zero indicate more moderate members of Congress.

Figure 4.2 shows that as Democrats and Republicans become more liberal and conservative (respectively), they mention the opposing party more. This relationship is strong and statistically significant. Members near the center invoke the out-party in their newsletters fewer than 10 times per congressional session, while those on the extremes do so more than twice as much. Figure 4.3 shows that the patterns for mentioning the in-party are asymmetrical by partisan affiliation. Republicans who are more ideologically extreme also make more references to their own party, and this relationship is as strong and consistent as it was for out-party mentions. However, there is no clear relationship between the number of times a Democratic legislator invokes their own party and their ideology.

The plots in figures 4.4 and 4.5 show the average number of times a member of Congress talks about bipartisanship and policy across their DW-nominate score. As both Democratic and Republican legislators become more ideologically extreme, they talk about bipartisanship less often. This is

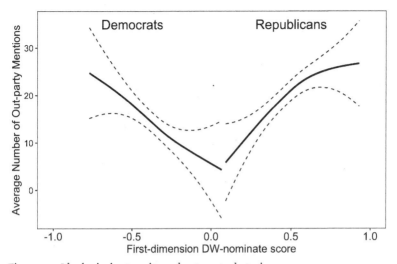

Figure 4.2. Ideological extremity and out-party rhetoric

Note: Plot shows average number of out-party mentions by Democrats and Republicans in newsletters across DW-nominate score. Areas between dotted lines represent 95 percent confidence intervals.

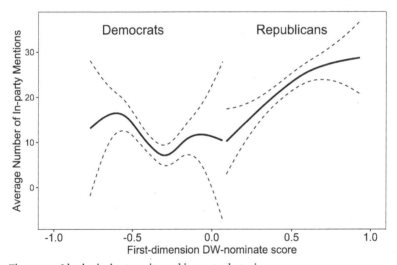

Figure 4.3. Ideological extremity and in-party rhetoric

Note: Plot shows average number of in-party mentions by Democrats and Republicans in newsletters across DW-nominate score. Areas between dotted lines represent 95 percent confidence intervals.

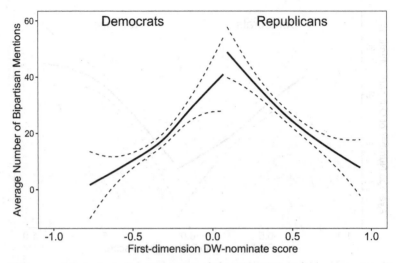

Figure 4.4. Ideological extremity and bipartisan rhetoric

Note: Plot shows average number of mentions of bipartisanship and compromise by Democrats and Republicans in newsletters across DW-nominate score. Areas between dotted lines represent 95 percent confidence intervals.

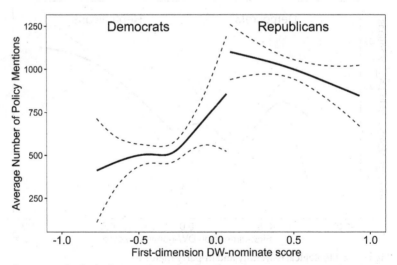

Figure 4.5. Ideological extremity and policy rhetoric

Note: Plot shows average number of policy mentions by Democrats and Republicans in newsletters across DW-nominate score. Areas between dotted lines represent 95 percent confidence intervals.

not surprising; legislators who are more ideologically extreme are less likely to talk about the value in compromising on legislation with members of the opposite party. What is more surprising, however, is that as ideological extremity increases, legislators also talk about *policy* less. Recall that I coded for a wide variety of policy-based terms, including specific issue areas but also general terms regarding the act of legislating. While all legislators talk about policy quite a bit, it is those in the ideological center who appear to be most focused on promoting their policy agendas in their constituent newsletters (though note that the most extreme Republicans are just as likely to mention policy as the most moderate Democrats).

This analysis provides important and somewhat surprising insights into the relationship between policy, ideology, and the use of partisan rhetoric. The ideological extremists in both parties are the most likely to invoke the out-party in their newsletters, presumably to critique their opponents. These extremists are also less likely to talk about bipartisanship, a pattern that makes sense given that their views on most issues are too distant from the other side's positions to make bipartisan compromise an attractive proposition. It is also notable that ideological extremists talk less about policy in their newsletters than more centrist legislators do. This may challenge our view of ideological extremists in Congress; perhaps they are not as motivated by purist policy agendas as they are by voting against the other party.

NEGATIVE PARTISAN WARRIORS ARE INEFFECTIVE LAWMAKERS

Plausibly, legislators could spend time criticizing the other party without having it affect the *actual quality* of substantive representation they provide to their constituents. After all, a member of Congress who rhetorically focuses on the opposite party could also spend time crafting important legislation and working to get those bills passed. However, there are also reasons to think that there may be at least some inherent trade-off between these two goals. First, legislators have limited time and resources, and whatever they allocate to crafting the newest attack on the other party may not go toward substantive legislative endeavors. Second, and perhaps more importantly, the act of criticizing the opposing party may be antithetical to effective lawmaking. After all, legislation is more likely to pass when it attracts support from members of both parties (Harbridge-Yong, Volden, and Wiseman 2020). Yet, such bipartisan support is less likely to be forthcoming on behalf of a legislator who spends a great deal of time alienating members of the other party.

Does such a trade-off exist? This section presents some evidence of the relationships between rhetoric and substantive representation that suggests it does. Legislators who spend more time criticizing the other party appear to be ineffective policymakers. For this analysis, I use legislative effectiveness scores from the Center for Effective Lawmaking. These scores are calculated using fifteen different indicators that "collectively capture the proven ability of a legislator to advance her agenda items through the legislative process and into law" and trace the bills through different stages of the lawmaking process across three levels of the significance of each bill.[2] The score takes into account the number of bills each member sponsored, how substantive and meaningful the content of each bill was, and where the bill ended up in the legislative process. Normalized to an average of 1 in each chamber, the scores are commonly used in legislative studies research (see Volden and Wiseman 2014, 2018).

The plots in figure 4.6 show the average number of times a member of Congress talks about the out-party and in-party across their legislative effectiveness score (with lower scores indicating lower effectiveness, and scores capped at 3 for the sake of visualization due to the few observations beyond that score). As legislative effectiveness increases, mentions of the out-party decrease. Legislators who talk about the opposite party the most, on average about twenty times per session, have an average legislative effectiveness score of 0, indicating they essentially have no impact on legislation in the chamber. The most effective lawmakers, on the other hand, talk about the opposite party about half as often as the least effective lawmakers. By contrast, the relationship between *in-party* mentions and legislative effectiveness is virtually a straight line.

Figure 4.7 shows the relationship between bipartisan and policy rhetoric and legislative effectiveness. As legislators become more effective at lawmaking, they talk about both bipartisanship/compromise and actual policy more. Again, while all legislators talk about policy in newsletters much more than they talk about the parties, those who talk about actual legislation and issues the most put their money where their mouth is by working to advance the most substantial and significant legislation.

While focusing on the other party in one's rhetoric is not mutually exclusive with other forms of representation, there are trade-offs between negative representation and substantive representation. To be sure, I cannot make any strong causal claims with these data; I am not arguing that talking about the other party more necessarily causes a legislator to be less effective (nor am I claiming that the opposite is true). What we do see clearly is that legislators who talk about the other party more often tend to be less effective at policymaking. The more time legislators take in their communications to constituents to discuss the other party, the less they advance legislation in the chamber and the more ideological their voting patterns are. As Volden and Wiseman (2014) discuss in their work, which develops the

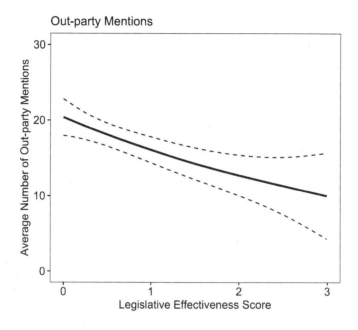

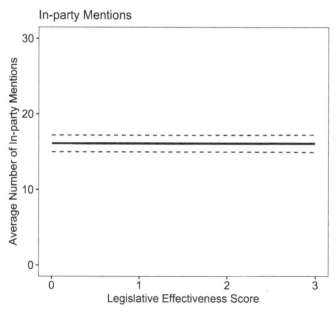

Figure 4.6. Legislative effectiveness and out-party/in-party rhetoric

Note: Plots show average number of out-party (*top*) and in-party (*bottom*) mentions in newsletters across legislative effectiveness score. Areas between dotted lines represent 95 percent confidence intervals.

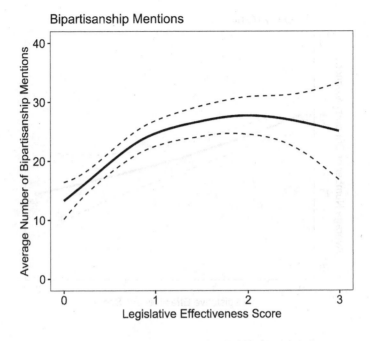
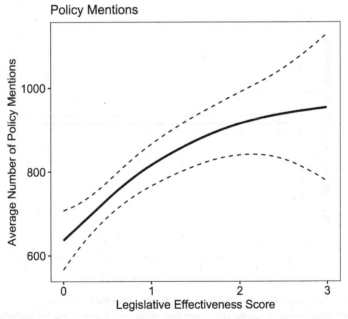

Figure 4.7. Legislative effectiveness and bipartisan/policy rhetoric

Note: Plots show average number bipartisanship (*top*) and policy (*bottom*) mentions in newsletters across legislative effectiveness score. Areas between dotted lines represent 95 percent confidence intervals.

construct of individual-level legislator effectiveness, these patterns have implications for the efficacy and organization of Congress as a whole. These effectiveness scores have been used to show how varying personal and institutional factors are correlated with individual Congress members' effectiveness at lawmaking (Hitt, Volden, and Wiseman 2017; Truel et al. 2022; Volden, Wiseman, and Wittmer 2013). The findings here make a new contribution in demonstrating that how legislators *talk* is also associated with what they *do* (or don't do), and consequently, how well the institution of Congress represents its people.

CONCLUSION

Together, these findings offer a compelling picture of how negative representation impacts legislative activity. Polarization increases as members vote along party lines. At the same time, as ideological voting increases, so does negative partisanship. Legislators who frequently engage in out-party rhetoric seem to sacrifice their efficacy in enacting meaningful laws. Consider the sharp rhetoric in the examples at the beginning of this chapter. Rep. Ferguson claimed in a newsletter that Democrats are solely interested in "scoring political points." Rep. Pressley tweeted that Republicans have "no interest in passing legislation." These instances are more than just anecdotal. They illustrate the very crux of the trade-off discussed in this chapter: while legislators are busy trading barbs, what substantive work is being achieved in the meantime?

The inability to enact substantial legislation not only impacts the reputation of the legislators but also hinders the ability of a democratic government to respond to pressing social issues. This echoes the findings of Binder (2003), who argues that legislative inefficiency, as evidenced by a high percentage of salient bills that fail to pass, correlates with low public approval of Congress. A legislature marked by ineffectiveness and focused on negative representation erodes public trust in democratic institutions. Indeed, increasing partisan polarization in Congress is negatively correlated with public trust in the federal government. Specifically, as ideological differences between parties in Congress grow, so does public distrust (Uslaner 2015). Importantly, the correlation between ideological extremity and legislative effectiveness is negative (-0.16, $p < 0.001$). This finding lends further support to the idea that ideologically extreme legislators are not merely more given to negative representation, but are also objectively less effective in legislative outcomes. This pattern suggests that the very legislators who are contributing to ideological polarization are also less effective at lawmaking, thereby reinforcing the cycle of public distrust, legislative gridlock, and polarization.

The divergence in rhetorical strategies between legislators from safe and competitive districts is not mere coincidence; it reveals underlying electoral calculations. Legislators from safe districts, as evidenced by their higher frequency of negative rhetoric, seem emboldened by the electoral insulation provided by their constituencies. These legislators are not just amplifying existing partisan tensions; they are also potentially sacrificing legislative effectiveness for the sake of intra-party standing and national prominence. Party leaders, often hailing from these safe districts, emerge as the most striking practitioners of negative representation—mentioning the opposition significantly more in their newsletters and tweets.

This highlights a problematic feedback loop: the safety of the electoral district could be indirectly contributing to legislative inefficiency by encouraging negative representation. This is disconcerting considering the necessity of cooperative legislation in a democracy. The data lay bare the trade-offs elected officials are willing to make, often prioritizing party loyalty and ideological voting over compromise. The mechanics of electoral competition—or the lack thereof—influence not just the tone but the very efficacy of political representation.

5. NEGATIVE PARTISANSHIP AS AN ELECTORAL STRATEGY

Behavior of an innovative sort can yield vote gains, but it can also bring disaster.

DAVID MAYHEW, *The Electoral Connection*

Drawing on the social and political identities of constituents (whether that is their partisanship, race, gender, occupation, or something else) is an important form of symbolic representation. That politicians draw on out-groups, instead of just in-groups, also reflects other trends in American political behavior. Constituents' negational identities (the identities they do not share, yet are important to who they are) are as important as their affirmational identities (the identities they do share), especially when it comes to partisanship. Politicians invoke negational identities to make claims about how and whom they represent. By expressly "othering" a particular group, they stake a claim in representing whoever positions themselves against that group. So far, I have distinguished between *positive representational styles*—communicating with constituents about their own party—and *negative representational styles*—communicating with constituents about the opposite party. Politicians engage in negative partisan representation in the years soon after their party loses power, and more discussion of the other party is associated with less discussion about policy issues and compromise. In a long-form medium like congressional newsletters, politicians have the room to talk about whatever they want. The more that newsletter space is devoted to talking about the other party, the less effective a lawmaker is at advancing significant agenda items through the legislative process. Clearly, negative representation in rhetoric has important implications for substantive representation.

This chapter tests the first of the book's hypotheses regarding *why* politicians use a negative representational style in the context of partisanship. This hypothesis is bottom-up and fits with most rational choice theories of elite behavior. It states that candidates and public officials think negative representation will garner support from voters. Another hypothesis (tested in chapter 6) is top-down and posits that negative representation is expressive on the part of political elites. It states that even though they think it is not necessarily a winning strategy, politicians engage in this behavior because they themselves are motivated by their negational, affective identities. The third hypothesis (tested in chapter 7) suggests that negative representation is driven by the media, fundraising, and the need for exposure.

In the voter-driven framework, candidates and elected officials strategically invoke in-group and out-group identities because they are under the impression that this is what voters want. Indeed, the literature on elite behavior in the US has documented at length how public officials respond to the electoral incentive. While the incentive does not always *exclusively* motivate politicians, it is a strong predictor of both policy and non-policy elite behavior. Candidates take positions on legislative issues, either by working to enact popular preferences via policy or by simply grandstanding in speeches and symbolic cosponsorships, to get credit for substantive representation (Anderson, Butler, and Harbridge-Yong 2020; Butler and Nickerson 2011; Grimmer 2013; Mayhew 1974; Pereira 2020; Pitkin 1967). Seeking election manifests in non-policy forms of behavior as well. Fenno's "homestyle" is developed by each legislator based on how they perceive their constituents' interests. The main goal of any homestyle is to gain constituents' trust. This is done by using certain communication styles and cultivating a personal image based on character traits that constituents value in representatives. While more informal and symbolic than lawmaking, this form of behavior is just as instrumental in service of getting (re)elected (Fenno 1978; Grimmer 2013; Grimmer, Messing, and Westwood 2012; Westwood 2021).

Homestyles used to be based around things like constituency service, explaining one's voting record or policy activities, and allocation of resources to one's district. But as affective polarization increases, it is suggested that voters' interests revolve around their partisan identities rather than their substantive policy interests (Iyengar, Sood, and Lelkes 2012; Huddy, Mason, and Aarøe 2015). Negativity against the out-party has increased dramatically over the past two decades (Abramowitz and Webster 2018; Iyengar and Krupenkin 2018; Iyengar et al. 2019). The parties have sorted along lines of race, class, gender, and religion (Abramowitz and Webster 2016; Barker and Carman 2012; Grossmann and Hopkins 2016; Mason 2018). Since partisanship is increasingly tied up in other social identities, one's partisan affiliation is viewed as a crucial component of who they are (Ahler and Sood 2018). These trends not only make partisanship a useful heuristic for identifying out-groups, but also help drive elite behavior. For example, Iyengar and Krupenkin (2018, 212) explain:

When citizens are motivated to support a candidate or party because of some admired attribute of the candidate, their continued support is predicated on the candidate's (or party's) ability to deliver on the attribute in question, be it the implementation of some policy agenda or the delivery of psychological rents. The logic of positive motivations holds candidates accountable—if they fail to deliver, citizens will no longer support them. However, when citizens' support for a candidate stems primarily from their strong dislike for the opposing candidate, they are less subject to the logic of accountability. Their psychic satisfaction comes more from defeating and humiliating the outgroup, and less from any performance or policy benefits that might accrue from the victory of the in-party. For this group of voters, candidates have every incentive to inflame partisan negativity, further entrenching affective polarization.

As this quote demonstrates, scholars clearly allege that elites believe such a voter-driven incentive ("to inflame partisan negativity") exists. On its face, this narrative is tempting. Several examples exist of politicians engaging in negative partisanship and seemingly garnering support from voters. Former President Trump, who is one of the most frequent, enthusiastic, high-profile proponents of expressing out-group animus, provides perhaps the best example. Trump maintains high approval ratings among members of his party and his negative, affective rhetoric seems to resonate with some voters.[1] Other politicians continue to denigrate their opposition with name-calling and party-polarizing language on social media (Russell 2018, 2021). If voters did not support this behavior, then why would politicians engage in it?

On the other hand, just as many examples exist of politicians being condemned for incivility or partisan affect. While Trump maintains a high approval rating among members of his own party, it is still lower overall than other former presidents.[2] His ratings also often decreased during his presidency after news appearances and press conferences (e.g., Martin and Haberman 2020), suggesting that his rhetorical style hurts him with voters. Indeed, some voters have explicitly indicated discomfort when he "attacks the other side" (PBS/NPR 2017), and he has been called out by members of both parties for particularly inflammatory remarks (e.g., Romney 2016; Andrews and Bender 2019; Winberg 2017). Not to mention the obvious: he lost his second term when running for reelection, which is not a common occurrence for incumbent presidents.

All in all, it is impossible to know for sure whether affective partisan appeals help or hurt elected officials purely from anecdotal evidence. Did Trump win in 2016 because of his use of negative partisanship, or in spite of it? Would the same candidate have fared even better without an inflammatory rhetorical style? Of course, it is difficult to answer these questions without observing the counterfactual. While many scholars and analysts have taken politicians' continued use of negative partisanship as evidence that voters endorse affective appeals, we lack generalizable empirical evidence. What we do know is that partisans and vying social groups in the mass public increasingly loathe one another, and that elites use negativity and other group-oriented appeals in campaigns. Does the latter stem from the former? Do elites actually believe they will be held accountable by voters based on whether they "defeat and humiliate the outgroup" (Iyengar and Krupenkin 2018, 212)?

INVESTIGATING THE ELECTORAL INCENTIVE

This chapter presents several tests to answer these questions. Previous chapters documented how negative representation is used in congressional newsletters and tweets, and that ideological voting and legislative ineffectiveness is associated with increased mentions of the out-party and decreased policy and bipartisan language. In this chapter, I first examine how Congress members' language is associated with their vote shares in the next election. I find no statistically significant relationship between the use of out-party rhetoric and how many votes a representative receives. This analysis is a good starting point for understanding negative representation as an electoral strategy, but is limited in its ability to support strong causal inferences.

To more systematically test the relationship between negative/positive partisan rhetoric and (perceptions of) voter support, I designed two survey experiments fielded on unique samples of elected officials and political candidates. First, I survey local politicians about the electoral consequences of engaging in negative partisanship. It is possible that politicians think it is a winning strategy for some types of voters but not others. I randomize whether respondents evaluate the effects of negative partisanship for core supporters or undecided voters. Respondents reported that elected officials who insult the other party are likely to *lose* support among both undecided voters and core supporters.

Second, I use a conjoint experiment to examine multidimensional perceptions of electoral viability more rigorously. By isolating the effect of out-party animus, in-party cheerleading, and ideological congruence between candidates and voters, I can estimate the relative importance of each of these characteristics on perceived electoral success in a primary election versus a general election. I again find little support for the voter-driven hypothesis. Elites think that negative affective rhetoric harms candidates' electoral chances. This is the case even in primary elections where negative partisanship has been treated in the literature as especially powerful.

Rather, representation based on ideological congruence with voters is perceived as more important.

Altogether, this chapter is the first test of the causal foundations of the book's theoretical framework. The observational analysis does not support the voter-driven hypothesis: politicians who talk about the other party more do not receive more support in elections. The experimental findings demonstrate that political elites think talking about issues is a better electoral strategy than talking about partisanship, and specifically that it is better than attacking the other party. This result has meaningful implications for representative democracy. Elites think negative representation will turn off voters in an election, but negative representation and partisan attacks persist nevertheless. We are also still left with the puzzle: if garnering support from voters does not drive negative representation, then what does? I propose some answers to this question in the conclusion and then test those possibilities in the chapters that follow.

DOES PARTISAN RHETORIC WIN VOTES?

To determine whether politicians use negative partisan rhetoric strategically to win votes, we need to know what they *think* about negative partisan rhetoric. But a first step is to simply see how a representative's vote share changes the more they talk about the parties. To analyze how elite communication influences voter support, I estimate regression models to predict how language in newsletters and tweets in a prior congressional session is associated with a change in an incumbent House member's vote share in the following general election. The models contain a full set of control variables including vote share in the last election, seniority, leadership status, race, party, DW-nominate score, and age, and also control for other types of rhetoric that appear in the tweet or newsletter (see the appendix to this chapter for the full models). For example, the figures below show the relationship between the number of times a representative talks about the other party (figure 5.1) and their vote share in the following election, *controlling for* the number of times they also talk about their own party, policy, and bipartisanship.

The results show that the number of times a member of Congress talks about the other party does not have a meaningful effect on how many votes they win in the next election. This is the case for communication both in newsletters and on Twitter. The effect of out-party mentions in an incumbent's tweets or newsletters on their vote share is effectively zero. This is also the case for how much they talk about their own party as well as about policy. As a robustness test, I examined whether the results significantly differed by party affiliation, competitiveness of district, seniority, and gender

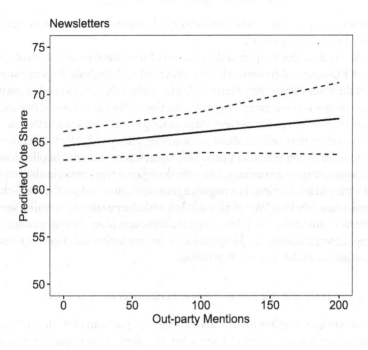
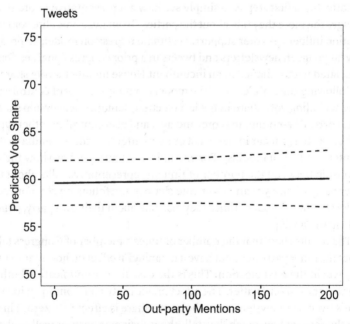

Figure 5.1. Negative partisan mentions have no effect on House members' vote share

Note: Plot shows relationship between number of times an incumbent member of the House of Representatives mentions the other party in their congressional newsletters (*top*) or on Twitter (*bottom*) and their predicted vote share in the next election. Estimates from ordinary least squares regression with controls. Dotted lines show 95 percent confidence intervals.

Negative Partisanship as an Electoral Strategy   87

and found that across the board, negative representation has a negligible effect on vote share.

On the other hand, with each increase in the number of times a legislator tweets about bipartisanship or compromise, their vote share in the next election decreases by 0.07 percentage points (figure 5.2). For context, the average number of times a legislator talks about bipartisanship on Twitter is about 28, though some legislators tweet about bipartisanship over 100 times. This means that the average legislator who tweets about bipartisanship loses about 2 percentage points in the next election. The pattern for newsletters is similar, but the effect is slightly weaker. With each increase in the number of times a legislator uses bipartisan language in their newsletters, their vote share in the next election decreases by 0.034 percentage points. In other words, if a legislator makes a call for bipartisanship 33 times in their newsletters, their vote share decreases by 1 percentage point (the mean number of times bipartisanship is invoked in a newsletter on average per legislator is 21).

While the analysis finds minimal evidence to support the hypothesis that negative representation significantly influences vote share in general elections, it is worth noting potential exceptions. For example, some high-profile cases such as Rep. Lauren Boebert (R-CO; who won reelection in 2022 by a mere 550 votes) raise the question of whether a threshold exists at which the frequency of negative representation could result in underperformance against electoral benchmarks. However, the models control for an incumbent's vote share in the previous election, which accounts for expected performance in their district. In summary, while there may be specific instances suggesting that high-profile or controversial negative representation could impact electoral performance, the overarching evidence indicates that this form of communication does not have a statistically significant influence on an incumbent's vote share in general elections, even when controlling for other important indicators about the legislator and election.

In many ways, these are surprising results. David Mayhew's pathbreaking work on the electoral connection in Congress detailed how incumbents are motivated by winning elections and how this might affect what they do and say (1974). One of the prototypical behaviors he said incumbents are likely to engage in was the public rhetorical explanation of their activities in Washington: "The congressman as position taker is a speaker rather than a doer. The electoral requirement is not that he make pleasing things happen but that he make pleasing judgmental statements. The position itself is the political commodity" (Mayhew 1974, 61–62). More recent studies have continued to explore this and Fenno's (1977) similar claim that since members are primarily concerned with seeking reelection, their communication with constituents is strategically oriented toward that goal. The conclusions

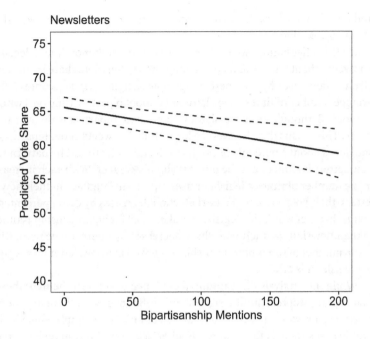
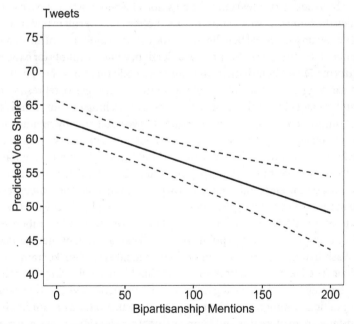

Figure 5.2. Bipartisan mentions have a negative effect on House members' vote share

Note: Plot shows relationship between number of times an incumbent member of the House of Representatives mentions bipartisanship or compromise in their congressional newsletters (*top*) or on Twitter (*bottom*) and their predicted vote share in the next election. Estimates from ordinary least squares regression with controls. Dotted lines show 95 percent confidence intervals.

from much of this research would suggest that, at the very least, politicians discuss policy and substantive issues in their communications because it increases support in their district. In an era defined by negative partisanship, we might also expect that engaging with constituents on the terms of their partisan identities would be associated with success in elections.

My findings run counter to these assumptions. Neither discussing policy nor partisanship has a meaningful effect on how many votes they receive. Even more surprisingly, discussing bipartisanship and compromise is actually associated with *less* success in elections. Notwithstanding negative partisanship and affective polarization, bipartisan discourse is popular among most voters (see, e.g., Anderson, Butler, and Harbridge-Yong 2020; Westwood 2018). Yet the politicians who invoke these concepts the most in their communications also receive the fewest votes. Of course, it is possible that the causal relationship flows in the reverse direction: marginal incumbents invoke bipartisanship *because* it resonates with voters and is most likely to garner support. It is possible that without using bipartisan rhetoric, these politicians would fare even worse in elections. While these analyses can neither establish a causal link between vote share and partisan rhetoric nor determine the direction of such a relationship, it is clear that attacking the other party is not strongly associated with electoral success.

PERCEPTIONS OF THE ELECTORAL IMPACT: ELITE EXPERIMENTS

The analysis above suggests that voters are not obviously nor consistently driving the demand for negative partisan representation. But there are drawbacks to deriving strong conclusions from these data. The standard cautions about making causal inferences from observational analyses apply. Moreover, if we want to know why elites engage in certain rhetorical styles, then we need to know what elites think. Even if out-partisan rhetoric were clearly and strongly associated with an increase in voter support, it would not tell us whether elites are aware of that association and whether it drives their behavior. It is therefore important to measure what political candidates and representatives perceive about negative partisanship and styles of communication. The prior analysis demonstrates that out-party rhetoric is not associated with a representative's vote share, while bipartisan rhetoric is negatively associated with how well they perform in the upcoming general election. What do elites think are the electoral impacts of these rhetorical choices? Do they think expressing negative (or positive) partisanship is a winning (or losing) electoral strategy? I use two surveys to directly measure political elites' perceptions about the electoral incentive in an age of affective polarization. The first survey exclusively recruited people currently in elected office at the county or municipal level. The second survey recruited people who have run for office at least once at any level of government and includes respondents who have served in office and who have never served. While the second survey comprises greater diversity in the types of elites interviewed, including several people who have run for federal office, the respondents are still mostly politicians at the state and local levels.

What can local or state politicians tell us about the incentive to use a negative representational style? The adage that "there is no Republican or Democratic way to fill a pothole" implies that the issues local governments deal with are inherently nonpartisan. Many local races do not allow partisan labels, even in some of the most populous cities in the US, like Los Angeles, Chicago, Phoenix, San Antonio, and Dallas. Officials elected to nonpartisan seats are often intentionally very hesitant to bring partisanship into their official duties. For example, quoted in the local newspaper in DeForest, Wisconsin, a then-candidate for town council, Rebecca Witherspoon, emphasized: "It's a nonpartisan position. It doesn't matter what my party is or isn't, I'm representing the people of our village."[3] If local elites think they need to purposely avoid the rhetoric of partisan politics, they would be less likely to report that negative partisanship would be a successful electoral strategy.

At the same time, the nationalization of local politics means that subnational politicians are just as tapped into trends of affective polarization as are members of Congress. The increasing alignment between partisanship and other social and cultural divisions has led to an increase in straight-ticket voting, even at the state and local level (Abramowitz and Webster 2018). Sub-national politicians thus also have an incentive to invoke voters' partisan identities. When local politicians campaign for office, they are just as likely to reference Barack Obama or Donald Trump as they are to reference localized issues (Hopkins 2018). Witherspoon, the Wisconsinite running for office who highlighted the nonpartisan nature of town council, had just a few weeks earlier enthusiastically shared an endorsement from a former town council member on her Facebook page: "Well, the progressive/socialists have complete control of the country now. . . . In DeForest, we have a board that is out of balance on the socialist side." Even though local officials may pay lip service to the importance of nonpartisanship, they still readily engage in negational campaigning.

When asked if people in their community have become more or less interested in talking with people they disagree with politically, 56 percent of local politicians in my survey answered that they have become less interested, only 21 percent answered more interested, and 18 percent said there had been no change (see figure 5.3). This suggests that local elected officials recognize that affective polarization manifests in "their community," and

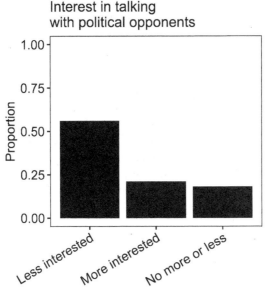

Figure 5.3. Perceptions of affective polarization among political elites

Note: Proportion of local and municipal politicians who think people in their community are less interested, more interested, or no more or less interested in talking to people with whom they disagree politically over time.

this would motivate elites to use a representational style based on negative partisanship if the voter-driven hypothesis is true.

It is therefore important to keep in mind that my theory is not *only* about political representation at the national level. While the data presented in chapters 3 and 4 were drawn from members of Congress, the theoretical framework applies to all levels of office. After all, candidates for congressional office often begin their careers by seeking and holding office at lower levels of government. High-profile politicians are probably less likely to admit to their partisan biases or to disclose that they think out-party attacks help win votes as they move up the political ladder. By contrast, state and local officials will be less guarded in their responses, and therefore are more likely to respond sincerely. Importantly, I ask respondents to recount not their *own* electoral strategies or communication styles, but what would generally be successful for any candidate in their area. In this way, I draw on sub-national politicians as elite "expert informants" to make judgments about how elites perceive negative representational styles, rather than assessing their own individual behavior as legislators (see, e.g., Maestas, Buttice, and Stone 2014).[4]

SURVEY 1: LOCAL AND MUNICIPAL POLITICIANS

The first survey was fielded in March-April of 2020 by CivicPulse, a nonpartisan, non-advocacy research group that conducts surveys on local government leaders across the United States (for other research that uses Civic-Pulse samples, see Lee, Landgrave, and Bansak 2023; Lee 2022; Sheffer and Loewen 2019; Malhotra, Monin, and Tomz 2019). Table 5.1 shows descriptive statistics for the 240 local-level public officials included in the survey. The sample is mixed when it comes to partisanship, with 43.8 percent identifying as or leaning toward Republican and 38 percent identifying as or leaning toward Democratic. More respondents identified as conservative rather than liberal or moderate, which aligns with what we know about ideological labels (see, e.g., Schiffer 2000).

Table 5.1. Descriptive Statistics of CivicPulse Sample

County official	11.7%
Municipal official	60.4%
Township official	27.9%
Republican	43.8%
Democrat	38.0%
Independent/other	13.4%
"Very" or "somewhat" liberal	30.0%
"Very" or "somewhat" conservative	41.9%
Moderate	27.9%
SUB-COUNTY OFFICIALS*	MEAN (STD. DEV.)
Proportion urban	0.668 (0.420)
Proportion college-educated	0.308 (0.162)
Population size	18,761 (54,246)
GOP vote share	0.505 (0.153)
COUNTY OFFICIALS	MEAN (STD. DEV.)
Proportion urban	0.483 (0.318)
Proportion college-educated	0.238 (0.105)
Population size	125,611 (219,456)
GOP vote share	0.594 (0.152)

* *Note*: This group includes officials from townships and municipalities.

The survey contained questions about general perceptions of representation, communication styles, and campaigns, as well as a simple A/B question-wording experiment. The prompt told respondents to imagine that an elected official insulted the opposite political party and asked, "Among [**their core supporters / undecided voters**], do you think this will make them lose support, gain support, or not make a difference either way?" (emphasis in original), with the words in brackets randomized. Respondents indicated whether the elected official would lose or gain support on a five-point scale (lose a lot of support, lose a little support, neither gain nor lose support, gain a little support, gain a lot of support). For the sake of comparison, respondents were also asked whether elected officials would gain or lose support if they insulted their challenger in an election, often talked about what's happening in the news, or sent a monthly newsletter to constituents. By asking about "an elected official" rather than about what would happen if they *themselves* used negative partisanship, the question creates distance between the strategy and the respondent. This approach is more likely to capture what they think is effective for politicians in general; asking about other people is commonly used to measure attitudes that are susceptible to socially desirable responding (Norwood and Lusk 2011; Schneider and Bos 2011, 2014).

Distinguishing between core supporters and everyone else, particularly undecided voters, is important for understanding elites' incentives to respond to their constituents. Elites may be motivated by some types of voters and not others and may engage in negative partisanship in order to court the electoral base. Even if they believe most constituents will be turned off by negative partisanship, perhaps they are in contact with a smaller, more engaged constituency that reacts positively to partisan cheerleading or hatred toward the opposition. Do elites think negative partisanship would appeal to their core supporters compared to all voters in general?

At the end of the survey, I asked an open-ended question: "Some of the previous questions asked you about your 'constituents.' When thinking about your constituents, which individuals or groups do you typically have in mind? For example, do you mainly think in terms of residents, voters, supporters, organized groups, or something else?" Most respondents indicated that they simply think of constituents in terms of "residents" or people who live in their county or city. Others took the question as an opportunity to express what it would mean to think of constituents as only those people who vote in elections or only those people who support them. For example, one respondent said: "I care not at all if someone has voted or even voted for someone else." Several others exclaimed that "[they] don't know who votes!" One interpretation of this is that the very idea of only considering *voters* as constituents is ridiculous; even if they wanted to represent supporters only, they couldn't because it is not clear who that is. At the same time, other public officials did say that they focus first on "voters" or "supporters." For example:

"I think about the individuals who vote in the local election every time. I then engage the voters who vote sometimes in the local elections."

"Voters that supported me or might support."

"I see it as two groups, first voters and then anybody that steps in my city."

Some, even while claiming to represent everyone in their district, expressed animosity toward constituents of the opposite party. For example, in one almost oxymoronic response, a public official wrote: "I cross both parties. I would never align with Republicans in our area because most of them are not impressive." Another said they would reach out to all constituents, even those from the other side of the aisle, if only those on the other side would invite them: "I regularly attend house district meetings and actually get invited. Have not received invites from the Republican house districts— even though we are nonpartisan and I am a citywide member." Many others listed even closer-knit groups, mentioning their family, relatives, friends, or neighbors. Therefore, understanding whether negative representation is perceived as beneficial for garnering support from an elite's inner circle is a first step in establishing the electoral incentive.

PARTISAN INSULTS LOSE SUPPORT, EVEN FROM THE BASE

According to the literature on affective polarization, elites should expect negative partisanship to appeal *at least* to their core supporters—the voters that make up their base. This would explain why they invoke partisan appeals in some circles and on some platforms more than others, as demonstrated in chapter 3. Central to my theory of identity-based styles, negative representation does not appeal to all voters all the time, and elites only invoke out-party rhetoric under certain circumstances. Data presented in chapter 4 suggest that while partisan rhetoric on social media is more intense in affect and tone than in other mediums, it happens more *frequently* in mediums where elites are talking to (what Fenno would call) their primary constituency, such as in newsletters to (presumed) constituent supporters. In this section, I analyze how elites think negative partisanship impacts voter support in general and also whether there is a perceived difference between the impact on core supporters and on undecided voters.

Figure 5.4 presents the mean response on the five-point scale with 95 percent confidence intervals. Values above 3 mean elected officials will gain support, and values below 3 mean elected officials will lose support. Overall, respondents reported that elected officials will lose support if they insult the out-party, regardless of which type of voter they were asked about ($p < 0.01$). The mean value when asked about core supporters was 2.4, and 2.1 when asked about undecided voters. The difference between these two groups is not statistically significant. In fact, just 16.5 percent of the elected officials in the survey said an elected official would gain support from insulting the opposite political party. Over 68 percent of respondents said the elected official would lose support.

Overall, I do not find support for the hypothesis that elites think out-party attacks will attract support from their base. Rather, these politicians perceive negative partisanship as electorally risky. One possible explanation for this result might be that the respondents are reacting to voters' disillusionment with politics in general. Some research has suggested that affective polarization stems from a distaste for government and partisan politics, rather than a distaste for the opposite party per se (Klar, Krupnikov, and Ryan 2018). Is insulting the opposite party just a proxy for talking about

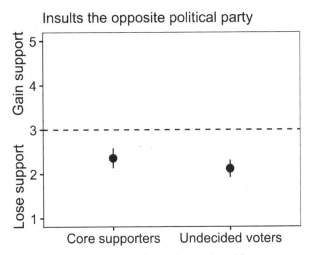

Figure 5.4. Perceived consequences of negative partisanship

Note: Figure shows mean response on a scale from 1 (lose a lot of support) to 5 (gain a lot of support). Horizontal dashed line at the midpoint indicates "neither lose nor gain support." Vertical bars represent 95 percent confidence intervals.

politics? If constituents do not want to hear about politics in general, then they would not want to hear their politician insulting the other party, which could explain the negative ratings. I thus also asked respondents how they think voters would react if they "often talked about what's happening in the news." Figure 5.5 shows that this is perceived to be an electorally *beneficial* type of behavior ($p < 0.01$), suggesting that losing support for negative partisanship is specifically about the out-party attack.

These findings begin to shed light on how politicians view elite expressions of partisan animosity. However, there are several limitations to this analysis. One drawback is that while I can measure the perceived effect for core supporters compared to undecided voters, the main finding that insulting the other party loses support is an observational one; I cannot identify the causal effect of partisan insults on voter support. We also don't know what the effects would be for expressing partisan cheerleading, a related but separate form of affective partisanship that is important to this book's theory about negational and affirmational representational styles. Many scholars assume that since out-party loathing has increased while in-party loyalty has decreased, elites will capitalize on negative, rather than positive, partisan appeals. Yet this has not been empirically demonstrated. Finally, on average, I find that elites think insulting the other party would "lose a little support." But it is possible they do not think it is enough to actually lose an election. If there are other incentives to engage in negative partisanship,

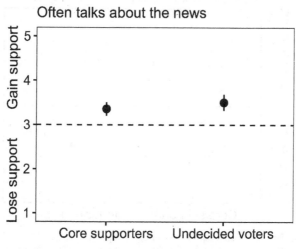

Figure 5.5. Perceived consequences of talking about politics in general

Note: Figure shows mean response on a scale from 1 (lose a lot of support) to 5 (gain a lot of support). Horizontal dashed line at the midpoint indicates "neither lose nor gain support." Vertical bars represent 95 percent confidence intervals.

a small erosion of support may be an acceptable cost to pay. In the next section, I experimentally manipulate elite partisan rhetoric to estimate the causal effects on evaluations of a candidate's electoral viability, and specifically whether expressions of negative partisanship are perceived to cost them an election.

SURVEY 2: CANDIDATES AND POLITICIANS AT THE LOCAL, STATE, AND FEDERAL LEVELS

The sample for this experiment includes a broader subject pool of both elected officials and political candidates in the United States. The survey was fielded in February 2021 and was administered by YouGov, a survey firm with a proprietary opt-in panel of respondents from all across the US. YouGov recruits individuals to be on their survey panel using a variety of methods to ensure diversity and representativeness in the panel population. Crucially, the Cooperative Congressional Election Study (CCES) is administered by YouGov.[5] The CCES is a large national stratified public opinion survey containing responses from at least 50,000 Americans, administered each year since 2006.

To identify political "elites" on their panel, YouGov used responses to a question on prior waves of the CCES. On the 2010, 2012, 2016, and 2020 CCES waves, respondents were asked if they ever ran for or held elective office at any level in the US. For my survey, YouGov specifically recruited people who indicated that they had in fact run for elective office at one point (regardless of whether they won or not). YouGov again separately confirmed that each respondent is or was a political candidate in the US, ensuring their eligibility for my survey. The resulting sample is 1,116 political candidates and/or elected officials. Responses were anonymous, and respondents were reminded of this several times throughout the survey to encourage honest responses.

After confirming that they were political candidates, survey respondents were asked about their political experience and other demographic characteristics. As seen in table 5.2, the sample is relatively diverse when it comes to political experience. Note that many respondents have run for more than one type of office. For example, many respondents indicated they served locally on a board or commission as well as at the state level. A majority of respondents (63 percent) reported that they have held or currently hold office, and 37 percent reported that they have never won an election. The sample is again mixed when it comes to partisanship, with a roughly equal proportion identifying as Democrat and as Republican; as in the CivicPulse survey, a minority identified as Independent, and slightly more respondents identified as conservative rather than liberal.

Table 5.2. Descriptive Statistics of YouGov Sample

School board	22.7%
Other local board/commission	25.1%
City/town council	31.7%
Mayor	5.9%
City/district attorney	1.9%
Countywide office (e.g., supervisor)	10.7%
State legislator	12.7%
Other statewide office	2.3%
Federal office (US House/Senate)	2.7%
Judge	2.7%
Party office (e.g., precinct committee, delegate)	10.5%
Other	1.4%
Ever held office? Yes—local	58.8%
Ever held office? Yes—state	2.4%
Ever held office? Yes—federal	< 0.1%
Ever held office? Yes—other	1.7%
Ever held office? No	37.0%
Republican	43.8%
Democrat	44.2%
Independent	12.0%
"Very" or "somewhat" liberal	35.3%
"Very" or "somewhat" conservative	42.0%
Moderate	22.7%
White	85.8%
Black	2.8%
Hispanic	3.0%
Two or more races	2.9%
Male	47.6%
Female	52.4%

Note: Percentages for offices exceed 100 percent since some respondents have run for multiple offices.

CONJOINT EXPERIMENT: INDEPENDENT EFFECTS OF IN-PARTY AND OUT-PARTY AFFECT

One potential approach to isolate the effect of negative partisanship would be to use a simple vignette experiment to randomize the type of elite communication presented to respondents. A limitation of this design is that respondents may base their decisions on information not provided in the vignette. For example, respondents might infer that an elite who expresses negative partisanship is more ideologically extreme than an elite who expresses positive partisanship. A finding that the negative partisanship treatment reduced perceived electoral viability compared to the positive partisanship treatment would therefore be subject to internal validity concerns. That is, respondents' inferences about the ideology of the candidate may be correlated with the treatment, and may thus confound the experimental estimates. Researchers can "control" for this by keeping other information constant in the vignette, such as ideology of elite or type of election, so that any difference in perceptions can be attributed to the randomized attribute. The drawback here is that researchers can only test a one-dimensional hypothesis and are limited in the conclusions they can make. It would not be clear whether the results generalize to other situations outside of the one presented in the hypothetical vignette. Randomizing additional components of the vignette is one solution, but it is subject to stringent considerations of statistical power and diluting the treatment.

I therefore use an experimental approach called a paired-choice conjoint design, which enables me to estimate the causal effects of many dimensions simultaneously on elites' responses. In a conjoint experiment, respondents are asked to evaluate or choose between hypothetical profiles that contain multiple pieces of information. They complete this step several times, with each component of the profile randomized each time. This lends itself to intuitive causal estimations of the effects of various profile components on respondents' choices. For example, a common design in political science is to present respondents with side-by-side profiles of two political candidates. The profiles contain several attributes of the candidates, such as sex, race/ethnicity, age, and political experience. The levels for each attribute (such as "Male" or "Female" for sex) are randomized for each task. Respondents choose between two entirely different candidates several different times, allowing the researcher to estimate the causal effect of any given attribute level averaged over all other possible profile combinations. Because respondents register their evaluations more than once, the statistical power of the test (or the extent to which we can avoid false negatives) is increased and we can estimate the effect of each factor independently on respondents' answers.

100 CHAPTER FIVE

For this test, I modify the above candidate-choice example in a few ways. I am not necessarily interested in elites' vote preferences, but rather in their perceptions about *voters'* preferences. Respondents were presented with five pairs of political candidates side by side. They were first asked to imagine that the candidates were running against each other in a primary or general election in the respondent's congressional district. This was randomized so that about half of the sample was told that the candidates were facing each other in a general election and were always misaligned on partisanship. The other half was told the candidates were facing each other in a primary and were always aligned on partisanship. The type of election and who elites are looking to mobilize may play an important role in elites' strategies. On one hand, primary voters are more politically engaged, interested, and activated, suggesting that they are exactly the type of people that would place partisan interests above all else (e.g., Bakker, Lelkes, and Malka 2019; Huddy, Mason, and Aarøe 2015; Lavine, Johnston, and Steenbergen 2012). On the other hand, in primary elections candidates seek to defeat opponents in the same party; they may not focus on the out-party until they have an out-party challenger.

Respondents were asked to choose which of the candidates would do better among (general/primary) voters in their district. The question prompt emphasized that they should not select who they themselves would prefer as a representative, but rather who they think voters would like better. ("To be clear, we are not asking which candidate you personally would prefer, but rather which candidate you think would fare best among voters in a congressional [primary/general election].") The election type was randomized at the respondent level, meaning that respondents were asked who would win in a general or primary election for all five of the matchups. Below the main candidate choice outcome for each task, I included an open-text question to better understand the (reported) motivations for their selections: "If you want, let us know why you made the choice you did."

The candidate profiles appeared in a table with six attributes (gender, race/ethnicity, party, ideology, latest tweet, and political experience) for both candidates. An example of a conjoint task is shown in table 5.3 for a respondent assigned to the "general election" condition. The attributes were randomized for each candidate five different times so that for each respondent, five choice outcomes exist, representing which candidate won each matchup. The top row indicated the name of each candidate. Names were randomly assigned without replacement within each task so that two candidates could not have the same name in the same matchup. The names were drawn from a pool of forty-two names that have been validated to clearly cue race and gender (Butler and Homola 2017) (though the corresponding gender and race/ethnicity were also listed underneath the candidates'

Table 5.3. Example Conjoint Task

	CANDIDATE A	CANDIDATE B
Name	Abigail Smith	Carlos Torres
Gender	Woman	Man
Race/ethnicity	White	Hispanic
Party	Republican	Democrat
Ideology (based on candidate survey)	Moderate	Somewhat liberal
Latest tweet	"We should do everything it takes to make sure Republicans win the next election."	"Listening to Republicans makes me so angry and fearful for this country. What a disgrace."
Political experience	City councilor	State representative

names). The possible levels for the *Gender* attribute were Man or Woman. The possible levels for *Race/Ethnicity* were White, Black, or Hispanic.

The order of the next four rows was randomized and fixed at the respondent level. I am most interested in the *Latest Tweet* attribute, which held the positive and negative partisan treatments. As demonstrated in chapter 3, Twitter is a breeding ground for negative partisanship by members of Congress, so it is realistic to describe US House candidates sharing campaign messages or communicating with their constituents on this platform. However, the main purpose of listing the attribute as "Latest Tweet" was simply to deliver the treatment. Theoretically, this row could have read "Congressional Newsletter," "Campaign Speech," or any other mode of communication. Posing the statement as a recent post on Twitter is an ecologically valid implementation; the statements are short, cogent, and reflective of language used on political social media.

The statements for this attribute were randomly drawn from ten possible statements that varied along two dimensions (out-party/in-party and affective/electoral) for a total of four categories: out-party electoral, out-party affect, in-party electoral, in-party affect (see table 5.4). The first dimension varied the target of the partisan appeal: if the candidate was a Democrat, they either expressed a negative tweet about Republicans or a positive tweet about Democrats (and vice versa if the candidate was a Republican).

The second dimension varied whether the statements focused on electoral victory (if in-party) or loss (if out-party) or were positive (if in-party) or negative (if out-party) in affect. Consistent with my theoretical framework and findings earlier in the book that partisan statements are sometimes, but

102 CHAPTER FIVE

Table 5.4. Randomized Levels for "Latest Tweet" Attribute

Out-party electoral	"We should do everything it takes to make sure [Democrats/Republicans] lose the next election." "It's vital that [Democrats/Republicans] lose. They are bad for our country."
Out-party affect	"[Democrats/Republicans] are not good for this country. Shameful." "I am disgusted at today's [Democrats/Republicans]. They are dishonest, dangerous, and bad for America." "Listening to [Democrats/Republicans] makes me so angry and fearful for this country. What a disgrace."
In-party electoral	"We should do everything it takes to make sure [Democrats/Republicans] win the next election." "It's important that [Democrats/Republicans] win. We do great things for our country."
In-party affect	"We [Democrats/Republicans] are working hard to solve the nation's problems." "Show your support for [Democrats/Republicans] in Congress and follow us on Twitter!" "Proud of all the good work being done by my fellow Republicans."

not always, focused on elections, these are separate yet important forms of this representational style. Affective negative partisanship involves political incivility against the other party. The emphasis on *affect* is central: the statements should invoke negative feelings about the other party. Electoral negative partisanship is (arguably) more civil. By emphasizing victory in an election, the survey pits partisans against one another as if in a spectator sport. Scholars argue that with the increase of affective polarization, out-party loathing is more motivating for voters than in-party loyalty (Abramowitz and Webster 2016). This suggests that rhetoric about defeating the other party would be perceived as more effective than rhetoric about winning.

The *affect* statements draw on positive or negative sentiments about partisans and were designed to avoid explicit policy cues. An example of an out-party affect statement is: "I am disgusted at today's [Republicans/Democrats]. They are dishonest, dangerous, and bad for America." The *electoral* statements are focused on winning or losing elections, which naturally have more grounded implications in policy, even if they do not explicitly mention policy or an issue area. An example of an out-party electoral statement is: "We should do everything it takes to make sure [Republicans/Democrats] lose the next election."

Turning to the remaining attributes, *Ideology* was purported to come from a "candidate survey" and could take the values Moderate, Somewhat Liberal, or Very Liberal for Democratic candidates and Moderate, Somewhat Conservative, or Very Conservative for Republican candidates. Importantly, these values match an earlier question in the survey asking the elite respondents to estimate the ideology of "all people in [their] congressional district," "just Democratic primary voters in [their] congressional district," and "just Republican primary voters in [their] congressional district." I use these measures to create an *ideological distance* variable to estimate the relative importance of ideological congruence between the candidates and voters.

Party was listed as either Democrat or Republican, though whether the two candidates shared partisanship depended on whether the respondent was assigned to the general or the primary election condition. When respondents were evaluating a primary, the candidates were both Democrats or both Republicans. When respondents were evaluating a general election, one candidate was a Republican and the other was a Democrat, and which candidate was which was randomized.

Political experience served to provide more information in the table to distract respondents from the purpose of the conjoint. This field randomly populated from a list of ten possible values: None; Mayor; State Representative; City Councilor; School Board; District Attorney; City Treasurer; At-Large City Councilor; State Senator; Military Officer.

In the analysis that follows, I first focus on the partisan rhetoric and ideological distance attributes given theories about the relative importance of negative partisanship compared to policy representation (Iyengar, Sood, and Lelkes 2012; Costa 2021), but I do control for all of the other randomized attributes in the conjoint: race, gender, party ID, and political experience. I then turn to the effects of these other candidate attributes on elites' choices to examine how they compare.

NEGATIVE PARTISANSHIP IS STILL A LOSING STRATEGY

How does negative partisan rhetoric influence elites' perceptions of a candidate's electoral viability? I estimate average marginal component effects (AMCEs) by treating each profile presented as the unit of analysis. Across the 1,116 respondents, this results in 11,160 observations. The outcome of interest is whether the legislator profile was selected or not in a simple linear regression with indicators for each attribute level on the right-hand side of the equation. The AMCE can therefore be interpreted as the effect of a given attribute level relative to the excluded baseline level on the probability a legislator will be selected, averaged across all other possible combinations of the other attributes. Because multiple choice outcomes exist for each respondent in the survey, I use cluster-robust standard errors at the respondent level to correct for the possibility that individuals base their choices between latter pairs on profiles they saw earlier in the set of tasks.

For each type of election, I show the effect of partisan rhetoric and ideological distance between the candidate and voters in that election (controlling for the candidate's gender, race, partisanship, and political experience). The ideological distance variable takes the absolute value of the hypothetical candidate's ideology on the five-point scale subtracted from the respondent's placement of voters in their district. This variable can range from 0–4, with 0 meaning that voters and the candidate are perceived by the respondent to have the same placement on the ideological scale, 1 meaning they are one interval away on the five-point ideological scale, and so on as the values increase. Recall that the conjoint task asks about the respondent's district specifically ("Which candidate do you think would fare best in a [primary/general] election for Congress in your district?").

If the voter-driven hypothesis were true, then we would expect to find that respondents were more likely to select candidates who appealed to voters' negational partisan identities rather than those who appealed to their affirmational partisan identities. But this is not what I find. The left-hand plot in figure 5.6 shows that compared to in-party affect, in-party electoral statements and out-party affect statements decrease the probability that a candidate will be selected by 3.7 percentage points ($p < 0.05$). While this effect is small in magnitude, it underlies the importance of distinguishing between electoral and affective partisan rhetoric. Praising the merits of one's own party (in an affective sense) is more favored than focusing on "winning" the next election. If a candidate expressed out-party electoral rhetoric ("beating the other side"), they are less likely to be selected by about 6.6 percentage points ($p < 0.001$).

The right-hand plots in figures 5.6–5.8 show the effects for ideological distance. While the voter-driven theory does not necessarily *require* that elites place less importance on policy representation, the literature on affective polarization certainly suggests it. Therefore, an important part of the story is the relative attention elites give to ideological congruence compared to appealing to voters' partisan identities. Since respondents in this condition were asked which candidate would get the most support from voters in a general election in their district, I use the pre-treatment measure asking respondents to estimate the ideology of "all voters in [their] district." I find that as the ideological distance between a candidate and voters grows (and the perceived level of policy representation therefore shrinks), the candidate is less likely to be selected as winning the election. These effects are

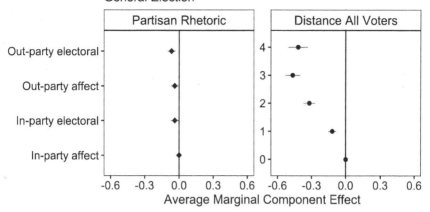

Figure 5.6. Effects of partisan statements and ideological distance on perceived electoral success in a general election

Note: Figure shows the difference in probability of selecting candidate using cluster-robust standard errors at the respondent level. "Distance All Voters" measured using perceived ideology of all voters in respondent's district. Horizontal lines represent 95 percent confidence intervals.

large in magnitude. Compared to a candidate who shares voters' ideology exactly, a candidate who is the farthest away on the ideological scale is almost 42 percentage points less likely to be selected as winning the general election.[6]

Figures 5.7 and 5.8 show the results for respondents randomized into the primary election condition. Recall that respondents completed all five conjoint tasks selecting the candidate most likely to win in either a general or a primary, and for primary elections, the candidates in each pair shared party affiliation, though party affiliation varied across pairs. As seen in figure 5.7, in-party statements had about the same effect. All else being equal, when a Democrat was running against a fellow Democrat, focusing on an in-party victory compared to hyping positive qualities of Democrats did not decrease that candidate's likelihood of being selected, as it did in a general election when Democrats and Republicans were pitted against one another. Out-party statements were also evaluated as being about the same, regardless of whether they were affective or electoral, but both undermined perceived electoral viability of the candidate (about 17 percentage points, $p < 0.001$). Note that this effect is much larger in magnitude than in the general election condition, because candidates are no longer favored to win based solely on their party ID. That is, in the general election matchups, respondents were most likely to select a candidate based on partisanship. In red districts, Republicans are most likely to win a general election; in blue

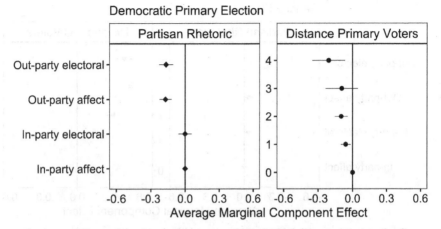

Figure 5.7. Effects of partisan statements and ideological distance on perceived electoral success in a Democratic primary election

Note: Figure shows the difference in probability of selecting candidate using cluster-robust standard errors at the respondent level. "Distance Primary Voters" measured using perceived ideology of only Democratic primary voters in respondent's district. Horizontal lines represent 95 percent confidence intervals.

districts, Democrats are most likely to win. In the primary election condition, we see what happens when this is taken out of the equation. When party ID does not override the other attributes, out-party rhetoric has a large negative effect.

On one hand, these findings seem intuitive. In a primary, candidates are focused on making the case to (literally) represent their own party, so focusing on the out-party is needless. On the other hand, this challenges prior understandings of the foundations of negative partisanship. As highly informed and engaged partisans, primary voters are exactly the type of people that are more motivated by out-group loathing than by in-group loyalty (Abramowitz and McCoy 2019; Bakker, Lelkes, and Malka 2019; Huddy, Mason, and Aarøe 2015; Lavine, Johnston, and Steenbergen 2012). One could reasonably expect that elites would invoke negative partisan rhetoric when they can get away with it in a primary election, and then shift to a less divisive communication style when appealing to the median voter in a general election.

To measure ideological distance between the candidate and the voters in this election, I used the perceived ideology of only Democratic voters. This means that elites were evaluating the ideology of a Democratic candidate compared to the ideology of only Democratic primary voters in the candidate's district. As before, I find that as candidates become less reflective of voters, their perceived likelihood of winning decreases. A Democratic candidate who is four intervals away from Democratic primary voters on the ideological scale was 21 percentage points less likely to be selected than a candidate who is the same ideology as primary voters, suggesting that substantive representation has a strong influence on perceived electoral success.[7]

The patterns for Republican primaries, shown in figure 5.8, are similar, with a few important caveats. First, the effects for out-party rhetoric (both affective and electoral) are still negative, though smaller in magnitude. When a Republican primary candidate dissed Democrats, rather than cheerleading Republicans, they were 6 to 7 percentage points less likely to be selected as winning the election ($p < 0.05$). Expressing in-party loyalty was more favorable than expressing out-party loathing, but the difference here is roughly half the size it is for Democratic primary candidates.

As for perceptions of substantive representation, Republican candidates are penalized when they are farther away from Republican primary voters on ideology, but only up to a certain point. The estimates for candidates that are three or four intervals away are non-significant and actually in the opposite direction. This imprecision is due to the fact that very few respondents reported that Republican primary voters in their district are "somewhat liberal" and "very liberal." While it is not surprising that Republican primary

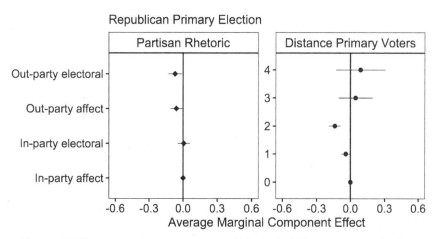

Figure 5.8. Effects of partisan statements and ideological distance on perceived electoral success in a Republican primary election

Note: Figure shows the difference in probability of selecting candidate using cluster-robust standard errors at the respondent level. "Distance Primary Voters" measured using perceived ideology of only Republican primary voters in respondent's district. Horizontal lines represent 95 percent confidence intervals.

voters are thought to be mostly conservative, this pattern has important implications for the book's argument about asymmetric negative representation. As discussed in chapter 2, affective polarization looks different for Republicans and Democrats. While both parties have increasingly sorted on ideology over the past several decades (Abramowitz 2010; Fiorina, Abrams, and Pope 2008; Fiorina 2017; Levendusky 2009a, 2009b), the Republican Party is generally more socially homogenous and ideologically extreme than the Democratic Party (Grossmann and Hopkins 2016; Hacker and Pierson 2005; Hare and Poole 2014; McCarty, Poole, and Rosenthal 2006; Theriault 2006). Some research thus suggests that the Republican Party drives affective polarization as well, with Republicans in Congress being more likely to include partisan language on social media (Russell 2018) or to further sow divisions between parties (Theriault 2013). Indeed, the findings presented here show that elites don't think partisan animosity is as big a problem for Republicans as it is for Democrats.

One distinctive finding from the above analysis that bears repeating is how perceptions of negative partisanship (out-party rhetoric) and partisan cheerleading (in-party rhetoric) diverge in consistent ways. Candidates who denigrate the other party were perceived to fare worse than candidates who praise their own party, and this effect was strongest in a Democratic primary election. There was also a negative and statistically significant effect for in-party electoral expressions for general election pairs, but this effect was null for primary elections. In other words, when a Democrat and a Republican are running against each other, fixating on winning the election is seen as ineffective compared to asserting the merits of the party. But in a primary election, where fellow partisans are running against each other, cheerleading for party victory is just as effective.

THE IMPORTANCE OF SUBSTANTIVE REPRESENTATION

The experimental results make clear that political elites think ideological congruence between voters and candidates is the most important factor when it comes to winning elections. For example, figure 5.9 shows the main effects again for ideological distance from voters in the district and partisan rhetoric, but also compared to the other attributes in the experiment: gender, race/ethnicity, political experience, and party affiliation. Ideological congruence is more important not only compared to partisan rhetoric, but also compared to all of these other factors. The magnitude of the coefficients for candidates who are out of step with their voters is substantively and significantly larger than the coefficients for the other randomized candidate characteristics.

Negative Partisanship as an Electoral Strategy 109

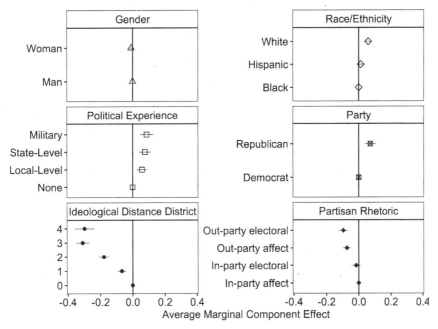

Figure 5.9. Ideological distance is strongest predictor of perceived electoral success
Note: Figure shows the difference in probability of selecting candidate using cluster-robust standard errors at the respondent level. Horizontal lines represent 95 percent confidence intervals.

The open-text answers for each candidate selection provide further qualitative evidence for how important the ideological label attribute was in the minds of respondents. Recall that after elites selected which of the two candidates is more likely to win an election, they were offered the opportunity to elaborate on why they made that choice. Most respondents (over 75 percent) did provide a reason for each of their selections. Above all other explanations for their choices, elites referenced ideology and the perceived ability of the candidates to substantively represent voters as driving their calculations of who would win in an election.

"In my district, voters are increasingly concerned about policy and a candidate's ideology."

"My district is more moderately conservative."

"In my district, candidates with some experience and with a more liberal leaning manner are more likely to be selected. Since Trump, my district has become less liberal. I believe Democrats in an attempt to swing the pendulum back would push for a liberal agenda and candidate."

"A 'somewhat conservative' person is better on the issues that matter."

"Liberal democrats will never win in this district."

"My district has been held by a Democrat for several years now and there is a strong conservative backlash that may elect a very conservative candidate."

"A moderate would do better than extreme conservative."

"I live in a very conservative district that votes upwards of 75% Republican."

"Liberals will only vote for liberals no matter how extreme."

"Somewhat liberal rather than very liberal."

"Somewhat conservative versus a moderate who may not consider policies that are fiscally prudent."

Most respondents all but ignored the partisan rhetoric in their explanations of why they selected certain candidates. Considering the nature of the design, this is surprising. The tweet quote is by far the longest and most obvious attribute in the conjoint table, and it draws on strong emotional language that often evokes strong emotional responses. Yet it was not a hugely discriminating factor in elites' perceptions compared to attributes like ideology and experience, and when it was, it was most often a mark against the candidate. Those who did remark on the quote expressed why such rhetoric would not garner support from voters, especially compared to a candidate who instead focuses on the issues.

"Candidate A is too critical of the opposite party thus is not apt to use good sound judgment on the issues."

"Neither candidate did themselves any favors by their unfortunate tweets: Jake's just shows a lack of imagination and Darrel's is disconnected from reality—as it applies to my community/state. In another district, it might be true, in which case perhaps he is the one who might do better—but not in my district."

> "Ms. Clark suggested a plan and included the voters to action. Mr. Banks is using emotions of anger & fear without a plan or call to action."

> "Her tweet would sink her."

> "Kristen stated what my party was doing with Javier attacking the other party."

> "Neither one due to their tweets attacking the other person, had to choose someone but neither are good choices."

> "Our district has a majority of conservative voters. While we have our fair share of divisive MAGA supporters, the majority of the majority are more moderate and appreciate a positive tone over negative attacks."

Overall, officials did not think negative *or* positive partisan statements would help a candidate win a congressional election. And it is clear from their answers that they were answering based not simply on their own personal tastes, but on how they thought voters would react. As an electoral strategy, elites cared about the ability of the candidates to represent voters based on their ideology and substantive focus on issues.

WHY DO POLITICAL ELITES EXPRESS NEGATIVE PARTISANSHIP?

Do elites think there is an electoral incentive to invoke negative partisanship? Based on the evidence presented in this chapter, the answer appears to be no. The first experiment showed that elites think elected officials will lose support from both undecided voters and core supporters if they insult the other party. This finding stands in contrast with the literature that suggests elites wield partisan attacks to appeal to their base. The second experiment demonstrated that, again contrary to many studies on affective polarization, elites think focusing on positive partisanship is more effective than negative partisanship, and that, overall, voters will prioritize ideological representation over partisan affect. These findings align with some conventional wisdom about how elites appeal to voters in a general election (e.g., Black 1958; Downs 1957; Gerber and Morton 1998), but challenge more contemporary research that suggests "us versus them" partisan politics overrides appealing to ideology (Iyengar and Krupenkin 2018; Mason 2018b). At the same time, considerations are asymmetric across parties, with elites predicting that Democratic voters will penalize out-party animosity more than Republican voters.

This leaves us with an important puzzle: if politicians don't think voters reward negative partisanship, then why do they engage in it? There are several possibilities. The first is that politicians *are* driven to engage in negative partisanship to satisfy voters, but I am unable to capture their true motivations in a survey. If elites are unlikely to share their true evaluations of partisan affective rhetoric, the findings reported here may be subject to social desirability bias. I argue that this is likely not the case for a few reasons. First, as discussed earlier, candidates and officials at lower levels of government do not have the same constraints as higher-ranking politicians and are thus less subject to considerations that would lead them to socially desirable responding. Second, in both surveys, respondents were explicitly reminded several times that their answers were completely anonymous and that it was important to give complete, honest answers. Third, the experiments were explicitly designed so that respondents were not asked about their *own* electoral strategies and motivations. In the first survey, elites were asked whether "an elected official" would lose or gain support if "they" insulted the other party. The candidates in the second experiment were also hypothetical, which is standard in conjoints. This approach allows respondents to separate their own potential motivation to respond desirably from their true evaluations of effective communication styles. Finally, conjoint experiments in particular have been found to reduce social desirability bias (Hainmueller, Hangartner, and Yamamoto 2015; Horiuchi, Markovich, and Yamamoto 2022). By providing respondents with many randomized attributes at once across several different tasks, my survey gives them many possible reasons (or "excuses") to support one candidate over another.

There are three other possibilities for why elites use negative representational styles that I test in the next several chapters. First, I investigate whether negative partisanship is expressive on the part of legislators themselves. After all, partisanship is a stronger social identity for those who run for office than for those who do not, and some scholars suggest that elites are more polarized than the mass public and that elite polarization is what drives mass polarization in the first place (Fiorina, Abrams, and Pope 2005). Research on affective polarization has documented how members of the mass public loathe the other side, but we have not systematically measured levels of affective polarization among elites in the same way. There is no reason to think this group of (politically motivated, interested, and ideological) individuals would be inoculated against the partisan divisions that face the rest of society. As such, the book's elite-driven hypothesis, tested in chapter 6, states that elites may be driven to engage in negative partisanship for their own psychic satisfaction.

Second, I test the book's exposure hypothesis. Politicians may be rewarded for negative partisanship in ways that have little to do with gar-

Negative Partisanship as an Electoral Strategy 113

nering more votes. Strong affective appeals attract media attention, boost politicians' national exposure and levels of out-of-state fundraising, and consequently provide them with leverage and power in office. The increasing number of safe districts means that many elected officials may care more about building their national influence than about securing votes for their next reelection campaign. Indeed, the reputations of some of the most notorious partisan warriors exceed their actual support in their district. Is negative representation motivated by a cycle of media exposure, financial rewards, and national-level influence? Are elites responding to a constituency group different from those I examine here? In this chapter, I showed that elites think primary voters and core supporters dislike out-party rhetoric just as much as everyone else, but there may be other subsets of the electorate that politicians are catering to. Political donors and activists tend to be more expressive about their partisanship; at the same time, these may be the groups legislators hear from the most. Money comes from all over; incumbent candidates for Congress regularly receive 40 to 60 percent of their donations from out of state.[8] It stands to reason that elites may engage in negative partisanship if it effectively solicits monetary contributions, if not votes.

What the findings from the last few chapters make clear is that politicians do engage in this behavior despite not thinking that it is electorally beneficial to do so. Having eliminated the most obvious motivation for this behavior, the following chapters test each of these alternative possibilities in turn.

6. THE HIDDEN LAYER OF POLARIZATION: ELITE ANIMOSITY

When they go low, we go high.

MICHELLE OBAMA, former First Lady

No. When they go low, we kick them.

ERIC HOLDER, former Attorney General to Barack Obama

Rep. Marjorie Taylor Greene is one of the institution's most controversial members. In the beginning of this book, I referred to how she was stripped of all her committee assignments for endorsing violent remarks against Democrats in 2021. In the couple of years since then, her attacks against the other party have only become more frequent, more personal, and more sensational. For example, she made headlines when she said, "Democrats are a party of pedophiles." For an interview with CBS's *60 Minutes*, the interviewer, Lesley Stahl, asked, "can't you fight for what you believe in without all that name-calling and without the personal attacks?" Greene replied, "Well, I would ask the same question to the other side, because all they've done is call me names and insult me non-stop since I've been here, Lesley." The day after the interview aired, Greene tweeted, "I'll say it again: Democrats are the party of pedophiles."

The increase in negative partisanship is well known, with many scholars tracking and documenting its ascendance in American politics. The coalitions of the Democratic and Republican parties have sorted along ideological lines, with most liberals and conservatives belonging to their respectively aligned parties (Levendusky 2009a), and also along other important social identities like race and religion (Mason 2018a). Ideological sorting leads to misperceptions about out-partisans' positions (Levendusky and Malhotra 2016a) and a lack of exposure to differing viewpoints (Roccas and Brewer 2002). Partisan media and campaigns also contribute to a climate of polarization and out-group hostility (Berry and Sobieraj 2013; Druckman, Levendusky, and McLain 2018; Levendusky and Malhotra 2016a; Michelitch and Utych 2018; Lelkes, Sood, and Iyengar 2017). By design, these explanations are voter-centric: they tell us why members of the mass public increasingly loathe the other side. While affective divisions among ordinary citizens are more easily measured, the animosity harbored and expressed by political elites—those who are in power and set the agenda—can shape legislative outcomes, influence the quality of public debate, and have long-term implications for the stability of democratic institutions.

Scholarship on affective polarization implicitly assumes that expressions of negative partisanship at the elite level must be strategic posturing in response to mass-level trends. If voters loathe the out-party, then candidates and officials invoke out-party loathing to give voters what they want. And the cycle is reciprocal: people in the mass public feel more negatively about out-partisans the more they observe elite-level negativity and polarization (e.g., Banda and Cluverius 2018; Huddy and Yair 2021; Stapleton and Dawkins 2022). While we typically think of politicians as highly strategic actors, I argue that the mechanism in the causal chain between affective polarization at the mass level and negative partisanship at the elite level is *not* that elites strategically do what their voters want. Rather, an environment of polarization provides incentives for elites to use negative styles of representation, even if they do not think this will win them votes. For starters, elites may have strong feelings of partisan animosity themselves.

Yet affective polarization and negative partisan identity among American political *elites* have so far not been systematically studied. Enders (2021) examines these phenomena among US party delegates, revealing higher levels of polarization among delegates compared to the general populace. However, the data only extend to 2004 and the political landscape in the US has dramatically shifted in the years since then, with increasing polarization and other changes. Another recent study by Lucas and Sheffer (2023) explores the phenomenon of elite affective polarization in the Canadian context. Their research demonstrates that Canadian local politicians are, on average, less affectively polarized than the citizens they represent. Their findings also indicate considerable variation, especially among politicians who are ideologues or partisans, or who harbor strong political ambitions. Despite these important insights, the current US political landscape remains an uncharted territory in this line of research, emphasizing the need for studies that focus on American political elites.

Just as the conversation about mass-level affective polarization has moved well beyond the academic realm, studying elite-level partisan animosity is not merely an academic exercise; it holds profound implications for the functioning of democratic institutions and the efficacy of governance. If political elites are themselves deeply entrenched in partisan animosity, this could alter our understanding of legislative gridlock, the quality of public discourse, and the overall stability of democratic systems. Furthermore, it would challenge the assumption that elite expressions of negative partisanship are merely strategic responses to voter sentiment. Political elites may be not just reflective, but constitutive agents in the polarization process, shaping and being shaped by a political environment that encourages negative styles of representation.

* * *

Politicians think talking about issues is a better electoral strategy than talking about partisanship, and specifically better than attacking the other party. In chapter 5, across two studies, candidates and politicians reported that elected officials who insult the other party are likely to lose support among undecided voters, core supporters, and even primary voters. I also showed that legislators who invoke negative partisan appeals in constituent newsletters and tweets do not perform better in the next election. If politicians understand that they do not benefit from negative partisan appeals in terms of votes, then why do they do it? In this chapter, I argue that there are other internal motivations that drive this behavior. As opposed to the voter-driven hypothesis, this chapter follows a top-down framework. The *elite-driven hypothesis* posits that negative partisanship is expressive of candidates' and politicians' own views and identities. This forms a "hidden layer" of polarization, one driven by the intrinsic motivations of elites rather than merely reflective of voter sentiments. Even though they think it is not necessarily a winning strategy, elites engage in this behavior because they themselves are motivated by their negational, affective identities. Simply, they like expressing how they actually feel about the other side. Some part of this behavior may not be a means unto an end, but an end in itself. Expressing negative partisanship may also help satisfy strategic goals, even if it doesn't directly attract votes. Accordingly, the *exposure hypothesis*, examined in chapter 7, states that negative affective appeals attract attention on both social media and more traditional news outlets, boost politicians' national exposure, increase out-of-state fundraising, and consequently provide the politicians who use them with leverage and power in office. The extrinsic incentive to attack the other party, therefore, is that it wins not votes, but attention.

Findings from elite surveys and experiments provide evidence that negative representation is perpetuated by feelings of partisan animosity held by politicians themselves. Politicians loathe the out-party just as much as, if not more than, members of the mass public. These same politicians perceive that campaigns have become more negative over time, which creates a domino effect where politicians think it is "okay" to attack the out-party because the other side is going to do it anyway.

THEY'RE JUST LIKE US: PARTISAN ANTIPATHY AMONG POLITICIANS

How do politicians feel about members of the other party? Compared to the average citizen, elites engage in more substantive interpersonal interactions with members of opposing parties. They share legislative spaces with their adversaries and must collaborate with them to realize policy objectives (Kirkland 2011; Reingold 1996; Sheffer et al. 2023). Such interactions and institutional settings encourage civil norms and experiences of cooperation that are more prevalent than the public commonly perceives (Best and Vogel 2014; Caldeira and Patterson 1987; Hibbing and Theiss-Morse 2002). These aspects of political life may mitigate the likelihood of politicians harboring intense negative feelings toward their political opponents. Increased interactions with out-partisans tends to reduce affective polarization and antagonism against the other side (Kalla and Broockman 2022).

On the other hand, there are a few reasons to think elites, like voters in the mass public, do experience animosity toward the other side. Partisanship is a stronger social identity for those who run for office than for those who do not, and people who run for office are more ideologically extreme than ordinary citizens (Hall 2019). Ideological extremity is associated with stronger partisan affect (see chapter 9; also see Bougher 2017; Webster and Abramowitz 2017), so it would follow that political elites, as extreme ideologues, have high levels of partisan antipathy themselves. Notwithstanding classic characterizations of elites as purely rational actors seeking reelection (Downs 1957; Mayhew 1974), there is also evidence to support the idea that politicians are influenced by their own values and personal characteristics, not just those of their constituents (Peterson and Grose 2021; Joly, Hofmans, and Loewen 2018). It is unlikely that this group of politically motivated, interested, and ideological individuals would be totally inoculated against the partisan divisions that pervade the rest of society.

In the February 2021 survey of political candidates and officeholders described in chapter 5, I included the standard "feeling thermometer" question to measure partisan affect. Feeling thermometer questions have long been used by political scientists as a way of gauging not just whether respondents like or dislike a particular politician or group, but also how intense those feelings are. The thermometer ranges from 0 (the coldest or most unfavorable they could feel toward the target group) to 100 (the warmest or most favorable they could feel).[1] Here I show how elites rate the out-party on this scale. Candidates and politicians who strongly dislike members of the other party might use a communication style rooted in negative partisanship, regardless of how they feel about their own party.

To compare elites to citizens, I use the same feeling thermometer question asked in the 2020 wave of the American National Election Studies (ANES), a representative sample of American adults. Figure 6.1 shows the probability density distribution for elites compared to the ANES sample of adults across feeling thermometer ratings for the other party (Democrats' ratings for Republicans and Republicans' ratings for Democrats) on the 0–100 point scale. Higher values on the x-axis mean that respondents rate out-partisans favorably and thus have low partisan animus. Lower values on the x-axis mean that respondents rate out-partisans unfavorably and thus have high partisan animus. Both distributions are skewed to the right, but it is clear the mass sample has greater variance, with peaks around the 0, 15, and 30 points on the 100-point scale. The mean out-party rating for the elite sample is 15.9, with a standard deviation of 20.7.[2] Over 11 percent of politicians gave opposite partisans the lowest possible rating of 0, and 60 percent gave opposite partisans a rating of 10 or lower. By contrast, the mean in the mass sample is 19.3 (the standard deviation is 35, reflecting the greater variance)—still negative, but not as negative as the sample of politicians.[3]

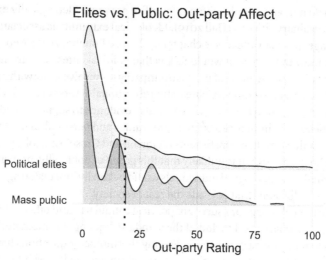

Figure 6.1. Politicians report more partisan animosity than do members of mass public

Note: Plot shows the density probability distribution of feeling thermometer ratings for opposite partisans (0–100). Vertical dotted line shows the mean for the samples combined. Solid vertical lines show the mean for political elites (YouGov sample) and the mass public (ANES sample).

The difference in out-party affect between these two groups is statistically significant ($p < 0.001$), indicating that elites do in fact dislike out-partisans more than do members of the mass public.

Table 6.1 shows results from an ordinary least squares regression model that estimates the association between ratings of the parties and several key characteristics of elites. Candidates who have actually won an election and held office give a slightly higher rating (+3.61) of the out-party than do elites who have only run for office but never won ($p < 0.01$), suggesting there might be a positive effect of exposure to the other side once candidates gain office and regularly interact with people with whom they disagree with. Conservatives have lower ratings of the other party than liberals do, but they also rate their own party lower, indicating a general distaste for partisan politics. In general, the same characteristics are associated with partisan affect in the mass public (discussed in chapter 9). Factors like how old a person is, their race and gender, their interest in current affairs, and their partisan affiliation all influence how they feel about the parties, with one important difference between politicians and the mass public: the effect of being a Trump supporter. Among elites, voting for Donald Trump in 2016 is not associated with a statistically significant change in feelings about the parties. Among citizens, Trump voters have particularly high negative partisan affect; the difference between their in-party and out-party ratings is over 32 points—almost a full third of the scale. I analyze negative partisan affect among voters in greater detail later in the book, but for now it is important to note that elites are not impervious to the personal and demographic driving forces of affective polarization, nor is animosity toward out-partisans merely concentrated among Trump's circle of supporters.

Of course, a feeling thermometer is a somewhat blunt instrument for capturing negative party affect. To provide more detail on how elites feel about out-partisans, I also asked them an open-ended text question on what words they would use to describe Republicans and Democrats. The question asked: "What words come to mind when you think of the following groups? You can write as much or as little as you want. Recall that whatever you write is confidential and will not be linked to your name."[4] The first two plots in figure 6.2 show the twenty most common words politicians use to describe the other party (top left-hand plot) and their own party (bottom left-hand plot). The following two plots on the right show results by party (the words Republicans use to describe Democrats and vice versa).

It is clear that elites use primarily negative—and often quite harsh—words to describe the other party compared to their own party. Applying a sentiment coding of terms to the responses shows that elites were about 2.8 times more likely to use negative words to describe out-partisans than they were to use positive words. Some of the words are ideological in nature (i.e.,

Table 6.1. Estimating Partisan Affect among Elites

Predictors	OUT-PARTY RATING Coef. (s.e.)	IN-PARTY RATING Coef. (s.e.)	IN-PARTY–OUT-PARTY Coef. (s.e.)
Intercept	25.77 *** (3.99)	66.57 *** (4.50)	40.79 *** (6.39)
Has held office	3.61 ** (1.28)	0.42 (1.43)	−3.19 (2.05)
Republican	−2.78 (2.64)	−7.10 * (2.98)	−4.32 (4.22)
Conservative	−5.97 * (2.64)	−6.21 * (2.98)	−0.36 (4.23)
Moderate	6.18 ** (1.90)	−9.06 *** (2.14)	−15.23 *** (3.04)
White	−3.03 (1.95)	−1.32 (2.19)	1.61 (3.13)
Age	−0.13 ** (0.05)	0.11 * (0.06)	0.25 ** (0.08)
Male	−0.85 (1.26)	3.86 ** (1.41)	4.66 * (2.01)
Voted 3rd party Pres2016	6.10 * (2.82)	−15.25 *** (3.18)	−21.27 *** (4.51)
Voted Trump Pres2016	5.03 (2.75)	−0.16 (3.10)	−5.24 (4.40)
Did not vote Pres2016	14.09 *** (3.16)	1.33 (3.57)	−12.77 * (5.06)
Church attendance	−2.04 *** (0.37)	0.39 (0.41)	−1.61 ** (0.59)
High news interest	−8.78 *** (2.00)	2.84 (2.26)	11.51 *** (3.21)
Observations	966	980	964
R^2 / R^2 adjusted	0.177 / 0.167	0.130 / 0.119	0.161 / 0.150

Note: $^*\,p < 0.05$; $^{**}\,p < 0.01$; $^{***}\,p < 0.001$; coefficients estimated from ordinary least squares regression analysis.

the top word Republican elites use to describe Democrats is "liberal"; the fourth most common word Democratic elites use to describe Republicans is "conservative"), illustrating the connection between ideology and partisan affect. However, most of the words used are affective, personal, or more trait-based: "evil," "dishonest," "liars," "greedy," and "hate" are among the top words elites used to describe people who affiliate with the other party. These words are not merely negative—they are extreme.

Clearly, the candidates and politicians I surveyed have strong negative feelings toward out-partisans. Recall that the sample is relatively diverse when it comes to the type of elite: it contains people across the ideological spectrum; Democrats, Republicans, and independents; and people who have run for and held political office at the local, state, and even federal levels. The patterns provide suggestive evidence that negative representation is at least partially elite-driven; it is possible that elites are motivated by their own affective proclivities. The lack of scholarship at the elite level underlies an assumption that politicians are inoculated against trends of affective polarization. Indeed, it might be easy to think of politicians as merely *performing* negative partisanship but not really *feeling* it the same way many Americans do. But it turns out elites are just like us, or even worse. Rather than just strategically pandering to constituents' partisan identities, they seem to be invoking their own.

A FALSE CONSENSUS EFFECT? POLITICIANS WHO DISLIKE THE OTHER SIDE

That politicians feel negative partisanship in much the same way that voters do is still likely just part of the story. After all, if they thought voters would not want to hear expressions of negativity toward the other party, then why wouldn't they do a better job of hiding how they really feel? It is possible that politicians *on average* do not think negative partisanship wins votes, but politicians who are particularly high in negative partisan affect do. The "false consensus effect" is when people assume that their beliefs and values are shared by the public at large (Furnas and LaPira 2024; Marks and Miller 1987; Ross, Green, and House 1977). Stemming from an "egocentric bias," the false consensus effect in this context would mean that out-party-loathing elites think negative representation wins elections precisely because voters, like them, loathe the out-party and prioritize this out-group identity.

To explore whether negative affect shapes elites' perceptions of negative partisanship as an electoral strategy, I reanalyze the conjoint results from chapter 5 *conditional on politicians' levels of partisan animosity*. Recall that in this experiment, elite respondents selected among two hypothetical

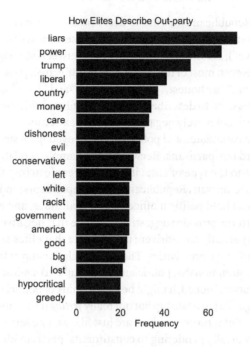
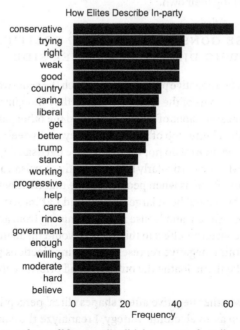

Figure 6.2. Top words candidates and politicians use to describe partisans

Note: Plots show frequencies of top twenty words used by political candidates and elected officials to describe partisans.

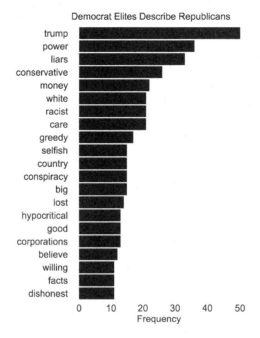

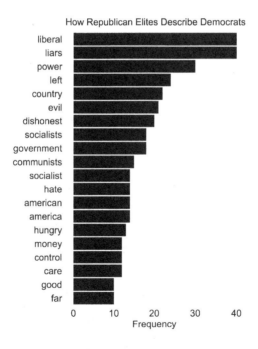

political candidates for Congress based on who they thought would be more likely to win an election in their district. I randomized the race, gender, political experience, ideology, and partisan rhetoric of the candidates, with my focus being on the rhetoric (positive in-party or negative out-party) and the perceived ideological distance on a scale from 0 to 4 between the candidates and the voters in the district. Respondents who gave a feeling thermometer rating of 0 to the other party are coded as being high in negative partisan affect. Using such a strict cutoff enables me to be sure that these are respondents with extreme levels of partisan animosity; recall that over 11 percent of respondents gave opposite partisans a rating of 0.

Figure 6.3 shows how often candidates with certain attributes were selected separately for respondents who gave the out-party a 0 and for everyone else.[5] If elites with high partisan animosity think voters will reward negative partisan rhetoric, then the mean selection rate for that candidate attribute level should be above 0.50. We might also expect differences in the effects of ideological distance: elites high in partisan animosity may think voters care less about ideology and more about partisan rhetoric.

This is not (quite) what I find. Candidates who used negative out-partisan rhetoric were selected less than half (45.6 percent) of the time, while

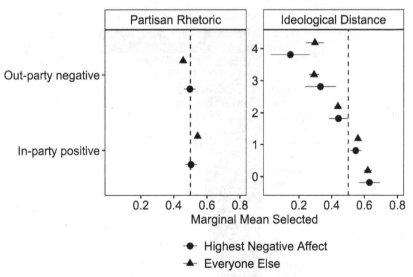

Figure 6.3. How partisan rhetoric and ideological distance influence elite perceptions of electoral success

Note: Plot shows estimated marginal mean probability of winning election for partisan rhetoric and perceived ideological distance attributes across level of partisan animus. Model includes terms for other attributes not shown here: race, gender, and political experience. Horizontal lines represent 95 percent confidence intervals. Cluster-robust standard errors by subject.

candidates who used positive in-partisan rhetoric were selected more than half (54.4 percent) of the time. These results mirror those from the pooled analysis in chapter 5, but importantly, they only apply to respondents who did not report the highest level of negative partisan affect. Among respondents who are extremely high in negative partisan affect, the type of partisan rhetoric used by a candidate made essentially no difference in how often that candidate was perceived as being more electable. These elites did not think expressions of negative partisanship were harmful to a candidate's electoral viability in the way that other elites did. While the differences in selection probability for these two groups is relatively small (with negative affect elites selecting an out-party rhetoric candidate 49.6 percent of the time and everyone else selecting an out-party rhetoric candidate 45.6 percent of the time), they are statistically significant at the 0.05 level.

While there are (small) differences between elites high in negative affect and everyone else, the false consensus theory suggests that these elites use negative partisanship because they think it is what voters actively want. Here, affective partisan statements are not perceived as a particularly successful electoral strategy, even by elites who are highly affectively polarized themselves. For these respondents, partisan rhetoric had no meaningful effect at all on perceptions of electoral success. Moreover, perceived ideological distance between voters and candidates is still the most important predictor of electoral viability: even elites who report extremely high levels of negative partisan affect think that voters will prioritize ideological representation rather than rhetoric based on affective, partisan interests. Overall, the false consensus explanation does not appear to go very far in explaining why politicians engage in this behavior, but the results do suggest that there are opportunities to do so without incurring serious penalties. Elites themselves strongly dislike the other party, and disliking the other party reduces perceived electoral penalties for attacking the other party.

DO TWO WRONGS MAKE A RIGHT? NEGATIVE PARTISANSHIP IN A HOSTILE ENVIRONMENT

Crucially, the previous set of results examines each candidate profile independently of the other candidate profile in its matchup. Even though politicians were shown two candidate profiles side by side and asked which candidate would fare better among voters, I estimate the mean selection rate for a profile with a given characteristic averaged over all other possible combinations of the characteristics, as is standard in conjoint analysis, but not the mean selection rate for a profile with a given characteristic when *going up against a different characteristic* in the opposite candidate profile. This distinction is important: negative partisanship by elites is not communicated in a vacuum. Earlier we saw that many instances of elite out-partisan rhetoric are reactive: representatives take down the other party when someone in the other party does it first. It is possible that out-party rhetoric has a negative (or null) effect compared to in-party rhetoric on its own, but not when we consider what the other candidate in the race is doing. When "they go low," do politicians think it's best to "go high," as Michelle Obama famously stated at the 2016 Democratic National Convention, or to "kick them," as President Obama's Attorney General Eric Holder famously retorted soon afterward?

Figure 6.4 shows the effect of a candidate's rhetoric *and* the other candidate's rhetoric.[6] When the opponent in a conjoint task made a negative out-partisan appeal, making a positive in-party appeal boosted perceived electoral chances by almost 7 percentage points. Before, the main analysis of any given candidate's rhetoric showed that positive in-partisan appeals had a primarily null effect on perceptions of electoral success. Here, we see that is only the case when *both* candidates in an election use positive partisan appeals. If the other candidate is denigrating the out-party, elites think voters will reward candidates who stay positive. In sum, elites think that "going high" when the opponent "goes low" is a worthwhile strategy.

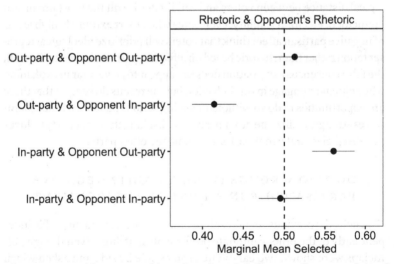

Figure 6.4. How (the opponent's) partisan rhetoric influences elite perceptions of electoral success

Note: Plot shows estimated marginal mean probability of winning election for candidates who use out-party or in-party rhetoric when their opponent also uses out-party and in-party rhetoric. Model includes terms for other attributes not shown here: race, gender, and political experience. Horizontal lines represent 95 percent confidence intervals. Cluster-robust standard errors by subject.

We know that most elites (except for those who are extremely high in negative partisanship) think voters will penalize candidates for denigrating the out-party. But does expressing partisan antipathy have the same effect if the other candidate does it too? The estimates for "out-party–in-party" and "out-party–out-party"—which show the effect of out-partisan rhetoric when the other candidate uses in-partisan rhetoric and out-partisan rhetoric, respectively—in figure 6.4 suggest a more nuanced picture. Indeed, candidates who make an out-partisan appeal were still perceived as more likely to win an election, but only when the opponent made a positive in-party appeal; in this scenario, candidates were selected as more likely to win an election only 41 percent of the time. Importantly, making a negative out-partisan appeal had virtually no effect on perceived electoral viability if the other side *also* made such an appeal. This is the case even for elites who are *not* high in negative partisan affect, such that the negative effects of partisan attacks seen in figure 6.3 and in chapter 5 all but disappear. In fact, while in-party rhetoric ("going high") results in a positive boost to one's perceived electoral success, the difference between "going high" and "going low" when the opponent uses out-party rhetoric is not actually statistically significant.

These findings shed light on when and how politicians may elect to attack the out-party. Any given election may present a domino effect where once a candidate attacks the other side, using similar rhetoric is no longer considered detrimental to one's electoral chances. Indeed, political environments and campaigns are, in general, already perceived to be characterized by negativity. In the 2020 survey fielded on local politicians, I asked "over time, do you think political campaigns have become more positive or negative, or have they mostly stayed the same?" I asked politicians to answer this question for campaigns at each level of government: in national elections, in state elections, and in local elections. About 90 percent of public officials answered that national election campaigns have become "much more" or "somewhat more" negative over time (see figure 6.5). About 70 percent said the same about state election campaigns. Local election campaigns are not as bad: 45 percent of officials answered that local campaigns have stayed the same, 37 percent said they have become more negative, and 15 percent said they have become more positive.

I also asked an open-ended question in the survey inviting respondents to describe in their own words how campaigns (at any level) have changed over time. The vast majority of responses spoke to how the political environment, even at the local level, has become more negative and characterized by teamsmanship. The following responses show the range of officials' statements about this, but illustrate a common theme:

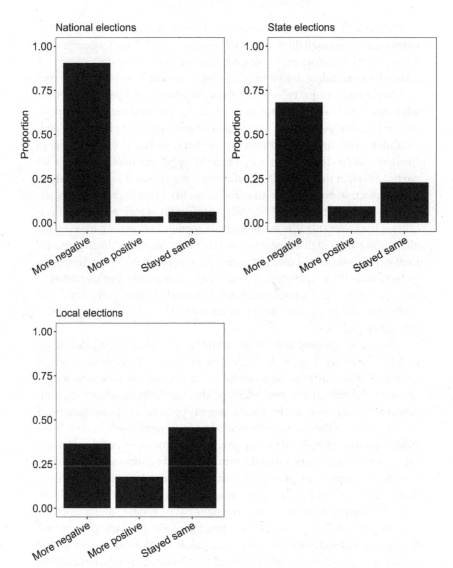

Figure 6.5. How local politicians perceive campaigns have changed over time
Note: Plots show the proportion of elite respondents who answered that national, state, and local election campaigns have become much more or somewhat more negative, much more or somewhat more positive, or stayed the same.

The Hidden Layer of Polarization   129

"Partisanship has infiltrated into races even for positions that are really nonpartisan in nature."

"Yes, the widespread acceptance of lies and falsehoods if they support one's political allegiances. The allegiance comes before truth much like allegiance to a sports team. The Lions suck, but we still cheer for them. We get mad, make excuses, blame the refs and cheer for them again next week. That is fine for sports but terrible in politics. Campaigns exploit fear, make ruthless villains of their opponents, blame the media for questioning their failures and divide people rather than working toward the best solutions."

"Much more partisan and mean spirited."

"They have devolved into a slugfest."

"They have degenerated into name calling and negativity."

"OMG. . . . Really? Partisanship and identity politics are changing the elected official campaign landscape forever. Social media has become a tool of disinformation that is purposefully exploited by those with a hidden agenda. It's embarrassing. Makes me care less if I campaign again frankly."

"I think they have gotten more divisive and destructive. The rhetoric during a campaign has lost any civility in recent years. While campaigns have always taken on opponents they weren't always so destructive. [Former Sen. Lloyd] Bentsen's interchange with [Former Sen.] Dan Quayle was explosive—so to speak—but it was still civil. In recent years campaigns have gotten super destructive, less civil, which says a lot about where we are as a country."

Many responses additionally highlighted how the increased negativity comes at the expense of focusing on important issues:

"Trend is to besmirch the opposition, rather than to put forth and expound on positions and policy structure."

"They are very divisive. . . . It is difficult to understand where candidates really stand on particular issues. Because they seem to spend more time speaking negatively of their opponent rather than spending that time to educate the voters on particular stances."

"They are way too personalized. Campaigns do not focus on broad ideas but specific triggers for individual voters."

"Less emphasis on policy positions and more on personal attacks, fear-mongering and outright lies."

"Yes, focus too much on negativity, need to shift back to proactive policy."

"Aggressive and less about the issues."

Clearly, there is a perception among elites that candidates all too often focus on partisan or personal attacks. Given this perception, it is natural to think that most candidates begin their campaigns with the assumption that it will ultimately turn negative, perhaps even uncivil. At the same time, the conjoint analysis demonstrates that they think voters reward candidates who focus on positive statements about their own side if the other side makes out-partisan appeals. In a context of negativity, then, why don't elites always "go high"? If elites do not think voters penalize candidates who attack the other side, are there other external incentives or benefits to doing so?

CONCLUSION

Politicians may be driven to engage in negative partisanship for their own psychic satisfaction, to reflect contemporary trends of negativity and hostile discourse, and because it draws more media attention and thus increases exposure and power. Findings from elite surveys and experiments provide evidence that negative representation is partly perpetuated by feelings of partisan animosity among politicians themselves. Moreover, the mixed and weak results regarding partisan affect on perceptions of the electoral incentive only underscore the importance of the results regarding ideological congruence. Both experimental and survey data show that elites perceive substantive representation to be the most important to voters and believe that voters will not reward expressions of negative partisanship. Elites do not always think expressions of negative partisanship come with a penalty; under certain conditions, the benefits outweigh the costs.

Importantly, I find that politicians have at least as much animosity toward the other party as ordinary partisans do. There are important positional differences between public officials and members of the mass public. Politicians interact with opposing partisans all the time, unlike ordinary people (making conflict salient, but also increasing opportunities for humanization). For this reason, we might expect these individuals to feel less distaste for the opposing party. Yet, my survey of politicians shows that this is not the case. These politicians also have the power to hurt opposing partisans through their actions in ways that ordinary people do not. Ordinary partisans are mostly on the sidelines cheering for the other side to lose the fight, but politicians are in a position to throw (and land) actual punches.

This hidden layer of polarization—elite antipathy—not only adds complexity to our understandings of why politicians resort to negative partisanship and to scholarship on affective polarization in general, but also suggests a positive feedback loop of affective polarization and the use of negative representational styles. The more the parties converge around other social identities, the more hostile the discourse becomes surrounding the parties. Politicians perceive increased negativity at both elite and mass levels: they report that campaigns have become more negative over time, and they are also themselves more affectively polarized than the mass public. At the same time, elites think negative partisan rhetoric does not necessarily lose elections when both candidates use it—and candidates inevitably do use it. In campaigns that are characterized by negativity, attacking the out-party is viewed as fair game.

7. REAPING THE REWARDS: MEDIA, MONEY, AND INFLUENCE

I think she likes the attention. I think she likes being a well-known name, and being a Democratic sweetheart.

SASHA GEORGIADES, former aide to Rep. Katie Porter

When long-serving California Sen. Dianne Feinstein announced that she would be retiring at the end of her term in 2024, three Democratic members of the US House quickly announced their intention to run for the seat: Adam Schiff, Barbara Lee, and Katie Porter. While Schiff and Lee had represented California in the US House for decades, Porter was in just her third term. Yet, her candidacy was taken just as seriously as Schiff's and Lee's thanks to the fact that she had quickly established a prominent national reputation in just a few short years in Congress. That reputation was built at least partly on incisive critiques of Republicans during committee hearings, the clips of which were shared so much on social media by Democratic partisans from all over the country that some news outlets referred to her as a "YouTube celebrity."[1] This attention helped her raise more money than any other House Democrat during the 2022 election cycle, a feat that was especially astounding given that she refused to accept contributions from PACs. A major part of the reason she was able to raise so much during the cycle was her national reputation, which allowed her to attract donations from all over the country. No House candidate raised more money from outside their own state than Porter did during the same election cycle.

What Porter's brief time in Congress shows us is that while members of Congress are often viewed as single-mindedly focused on reelection, it has long been understood that their goals are far more diverse. Legislators are certainly seeking reelection, but many are also seeking much more, including a prominent national profile like the one Porter quickly achieved. Being well known is one quick path to achieving power and influence within (and beyond) the chamber, the kind of influence that makes it possible for a third-term congresswoman to challenge her much more senior colleagues for a highly coveted Senate seat. The desire to achieve such power and influence leads politicians to carefully craft media strategies to gain attention (Ansolabehere, Behr, and Iyengar 1993; Cook 1989, 1998; Hess 1986). Considering that most members of Congress represent constituencies that lean heavily toward their own party, few members run a high risk of electoral defeat anyway.[2] The increasing number of safe districts means that many elected officials may care more about building their national influence than they do about securing more votes for their next reelection campaign. Indeed, for some of the most notorious partisan warriors, their national reputation exceeds their actual support in their own district. In such a context, politicians may be rewarded for negative partisanship in ways that have little to do with garnering more votes.

In this chapter, I document the external motivations and rewards that drive negative representation. While negative representation does not appear to aid legislators in achieving their goal of being reelected, the use of partisan rhetoric by political elites is instead a consequence of the cycle of affective polarization in which negativity is rewarded with national exposure, attention, and ultimately influence. Expressing negative partisanship helps satisfy other strategic goals, even if it does not directly attract votes. Accordingly, the *exposure hypothesis* states that negative affective appeals attract attention both on social media and in more traditional news outlets, boost politicians' national exposure, increase out-of-state fundraising, and consequently provide them with leverage and power in office. The extrinsic incentive to attack the other party, therefore, is not necessarily that it wins votes directly, but that it attracts attention and resources. I use a multimethod approach to test these hypotheses. Findings from several analyses of social media posts, open-ended responses from elites, television news coverage, and fundraising data provide evidence that negative representation is associated with rewards: it increases attention on social media and fundraising dollars for a politicians' campaign, especially donations from out of state.

NEGATIVE REPRESENTATION MAY NOT GET VOTES, BUT IT GETS "LIKES"

A large body of research emphasizes the greater attention-capturing ability of negative content over positive content on social media platforms (Brady, Gantman, and Van Bavel 2020; Meffert et al. 2006; Rozin and Royzman 2001). For example, during pivotal events such as the 2016 elections and the Ferguson protests, negativity on Twitter spread farther than positive content (Schöne, Parkinson, and Goldenberg 2021). Fine and Hunt (2023) analyzed tweets by US senators and found that messages laced with negativity or attacks had a higher likelihood of being retweeted, overshadowing the policy substance contained within these tweets. Overall, legislators who employ polarizing language online garner more public attention (Ballard et al. 2022; Rathje, Van Bavel, and Van Der Linden 2021). The consistent finding that negative language and divisive content are more likely to be disseminated on social media platforms carries significant implications for politics.

The emphasis on negativity may distort public perceptions and prioritize contentious issues over substantive policy discussion. This tendency for negativity to dominate online interactions has a cascading effect on political engagement and campaigning. Politicians who utilize polarizing language not only capture more public attention but also secure greater campaign funding (Kowal 2023). Consequently, this dynamic could incentivize politicians to employ a strategy of divisiveness and confrontation rather than cooperation and substantive policymaking.

Chapter 3 demonstrated that social media is a breeding ground for negative styles of representation. Across more than 1.3 million tweets written by members of Congress from 2009 to 2020, mentions of the out-party surpassed mentions of the in-party once Donald Trump took office. Moreover, tweets that invoke the out-party have become uniquely more negative in sentiment over the past decade. This is not just an artifact of overall levels of negativity increasing on social media: tweets by members of Congress that do not mention the other party have not become more negative over time. Elites tweet about the out-party more frequently and in a more negative way than they did just a decade ago. In this section, I explore whether invoking the out-party predicts online engagement and attention.

Figure 7.1 shows the average number of likes and retweets for congressional tweets that mention their own party, the other party, both parties, or neither party.[3] The pattern is dramatic and clear: legislators get more reactions when they talk about the out-party. Tweets that use no partisan language receive an average of 711 likes and retweets. When legislators tweet about their own party, they receive an average of 1,297 likes and retweets, and if they tweet about both parties, they receive an average of 1,977 likes and retweets. When they *only* tweet about the other party, they receive 2,700 likes and retweets on average.

One challenge with examining the relationship between the attention a tweet receives and whether it uses partisan language is that legislators who attack the other party may also be more popular on Twitter and have more followers to like and retweet their posts. Does tweeting about the other party attract attention, or do those who already receive attention attack the other party more? Table 7.1 shows the results from ordinary least squares

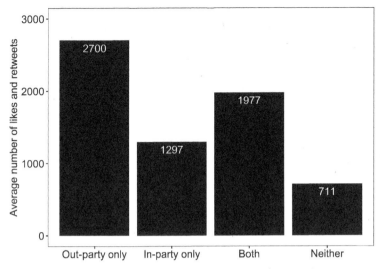

Figure 7.1. Popularity of congressional tweets containing partisan language

Note: Congressional tweets from 2009 to 2020 by members in the 116th Congress (n = 1,358,680). Plot shows average number of likes and retweets for tweets that contain mentions of the out-party only, the in-party only, both in-party and out-party, and neither in-party nor out-party.

regression models including fixed effects for the legislator who wrote the tweet and the congressional session in which it was posted. The models also control for how many negative words and positive words are contained in each tweet using a sentiment coding (Hu and Liu 2004). This approach allows me to isolate the target of the tweet from other reasons that might increase its engagement.

The analysis provides further evidence that when legislators invoke the other party on Twitter, they receive more attention. As seen in the first model, compared to tweets that do not mention the parties at all, tweets that mention the out-party receive over 1,000 likes and retweets more on average, while mentioning both in-party and out-party in a tweet increases likes and retweets by only half that amount ($p < 0.001$). In-party mentions do not have a statistically significant effect on engagement. Importantly, as the number of negative words increases in a tweet, so does the engagement; with each additional word coded as negative in sentiment, the number of likes and retweets of the tweet increases by 200 on average ($p < 0.001$). As the number of positive words in a tweet increases, engagement decreases slightly ($p < 0.05$). This finding is consistent with research showing that negativity spreads farther on social media (Crockett 2017; Rathje, Van Bavel, and Van Der Linden 2021). But it is important to emphasize that tweeting about the other party generates more likes and retweets even controlling

Table 7.1. Estimated Effects of Partisan Tweets on Engagement

Predictors	LIKES AND RETWEETS Coef. (s.e.)	LIKES Coef. (s.e.)
Intercept	−899.96 *** (166.67)	−490.24 *** (78.62)
In-party mention	88.08 (51.07)	22.27 (24.09)
Out-party mention	1009.89 *** (36.41)	532.22 *** (17.18)
Mention both	574.52 *** (90.37)	210.54 *** (42.63)
Negative words	200.60 *** (5.73)	103.82 *** (2.70)
Positive words	−11.36 * (5.47)	0.08 (2.58)
Legislator fixed effects		
Congress fixed effects		
Observations	1,358,680	1,358,680
R^2 / R^2 adjusted	0.087 / 0.087	0.181 / 0.181

Note: $^*p < 0.05$; $^{**}p < 0.01$; $^{***}p < 0.001$; coefficients estimated from ordinary least squares regression analysis. Fixed effects by legislator and congressional session.

for the fact that those tweets tend to be more negative. Negativity attracts attention on Twitter, but so too does targeting the other party. While I am primarily interested in whether negative representation receives more attention regardless of whether that attention is positive or negative in nature, it is possible that some of the retweets were not meant as an endorsement of the message. That is, if people were reposting the tweets to criticize the negative language that was used, this would have different implications about the type of engagement negative representation stimulates. The second model shows the results just for likes (excluding retweets), which are a more direct measure of *positive* engagement (think of the common Twitter bio refrain: "RTs do not equal endorsement"); the results mirror those in the first model.

It is clear, then, that elected officials can gain much more notoriety for themselves by using their social media accounts to bash the other side rather than to focus on other matters. This finding extends the existing body of research on negativity in social media by showing that tweets targeting the other party are more engaging, even when controlling for negative sentiment. Prior research has primarily focused on the emotional tone of social media posts, finding that negative content tends to attract more attention. But this analysis shows that even when accounting for the tone, mentioning the out-party leads to markedly higher levels of engagement. This suggests that public attention on social media is not solely driven by the emotional valence of a message, but is also significantly influenced by the target being discussed. It is important to study negative representation as a concept, rather than simply focusing on political incivility.

The role of social media in this dynamic is hardly lost on politicians themselves. Responding to the same open-text question about how campaigns have changed over time, 17 percent of politicians mentioned social media or the internet, and many explicitly drew a connection between social media and heightened negativity. For example:

> "More aggressive and negative. They focus more on how the opponent can't do something instead of staying focused on the candidate. Local elections don't seem to be as bad as state and federal but because of the internet and social media, things can be distorted quickly and it is hard to defend against it while trying to focus on your own campaign and positive message."

> "People seem to be talking in sound bites on social media more than in-depth verified info."

> "They have gotten more personal and as such a little meaner. Social media has changed the whole landscape of the process."

Others focused more generally on the importance of developing and maintaining an online presence:

> "Campaigns have become the new reality television pastime. Candidates need to connect with the voters and unfortunately network television is the way to accomplish the goal."

> "Campaigns require a social media presence. The day of door-to-door connections are less important."

> "Social Media gives a great chance to be heard at the voters convenience."

"Social Media! Campaigns used to be in person and TV only. Now with social media you connect with a lot more people."

"Different methods of reaching voters. Internet, social media."

Overall, the internet and mobile technology have revolutionized communication, especially in politics. Politicians use social media to interact with their base and spread their message to target demographics. The primary advantage of social media is that it allows political candidates to communicate with a broad audience without geographic restrictions, such as how Porter's YouTube clips made her nationally famous. The elites in my survey expressed cynicism about this form of communication, likening it to reality television and lamenting the end of traditional campaigning.

TELEVISION NEWS MEDIA HEIGHTENS NEGATIVITY

That negative, out-party appeals strongly predict engagement on Twitter is important not just in and of itself, but also because it is a proxy for how elites reach an audience through more traditional channels. By prioritizing virility on Twitter, politicians can bypass traditional media outlets and "hack" the coverage formula. In the post-broadcast news environment (Prior 2007), partisan and ideological media offer an external incentive for politicians to inflame partisan identities and engage in high-profile rhetorical warfare. Indeed, the downstream effects of popularity on social media are profound. The more attention a representative receives on Twitter, the more likely they are to gain national attention through the news media.

To examine the relationship between news media, social media, and the negative-attention cycle, I use the Internet Archive's Television News Archive Explorer to examine coverage from 2009 to August 2023, month by month.[4] Each broadcast is divided into a series of fifteen-second news segments which are transcribed into a searchable database.[5] The first question I address with this database is: how does television news contribute to the vicious cycle of negative representation and affective polarization generally? Figure 7.2 shows the percentage of segments on Fox News (top) and MSNBC (bottom) that mention the parties as a whole (e.g., "Democrats," rather than a specific Democrat like "Nancy Pelosi"). Fox News, which is aligned with the Right, had more segments about Republicans than Democrats until 2017. Once Trump was inaugurated as president, however, Fox covered the Democratic Party much more than the Republican Party. MSNBC, which is aligned with the Left, showed the opposite pattern. Starting in 2010, more segments covered the Republican Party than the Democratic Party until the end of 2018, when Democrats took back power in

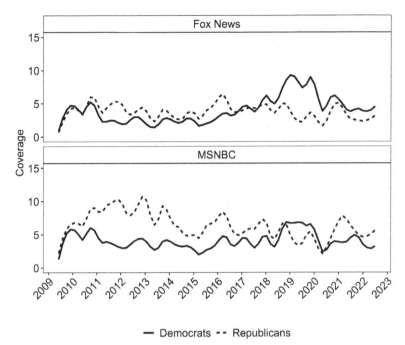

Figure 7.2. Television news coverage of the parties by Fox and MSNBC
Note: Percentage of fifteen-second news segments per month on Fox News and MSNBC that reference the Democratic Party (solid line) and the Republican Party (dotted line).

Congress. For a brief stint, from 2019 until midway through 2020, MSNBC mentioned the Democratic Party more often, but then it reversed the trend again and covered Republicans more frequently in 2021 and 2022. These patterns are telling: it appears that each outlet prefers to cover their preferred party *less* once that party is in a position of power, choosing instead to focus more attention on the out-of-power opposition. From a normative perspective, if the news media is meant to help Americans hold their elected officials accountable for what they do in office, then this trend is precisely the opposite of what we would hope to see.

A second question these data can help answer is: What is the role of television news in amplifying the social media behavior of politicians? Specifically, are news outlets more likely to cover congressional tweets when they are negative and contain attacks than when they are positive and talk about compromise? Figure 7.3 shows the percentage of news coverage by Fox News, MSNBC, and CNN specifically about Congress and Twitter. In order for a news segment to match my search, the clip must have contained the word "Congress" along with "Twitter," "tweet," or "tweeted" somewhere

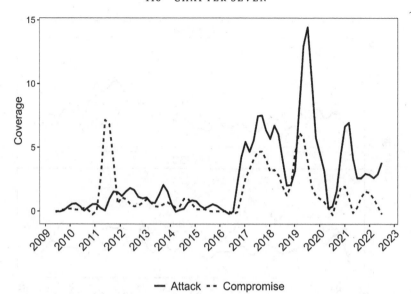

Figure 7.3. Television news coverage of congressional tweets characterized as "attack" or "compromise"

Note: Percentage of fifteen-second news segments per month on Fox News and MSNBC that reference tweets by members of Congress in the context of "compromise" (dotted line) and "attack" (solid line).

in the fifteen-second clip. Among this subset of segments, I then search for other words that appeared in the same clip or in the fifteen-second clip immediately before or after it. Specifically, I plot the volume of segments about Congress members' tweets that included language suggesting that they were about an "attack" and compare that to those that contained language indicating that the segment was about "bipartisanship" or "compromise."[6]

In general, up until 2017 the news media very rarely covered a tweet by a member of Congress in either context, "attack" or "compromise" (with the exception of mid-2011, when there was a spike in "compromise" coverage). Then, once Trump became president, coverage about tweets in Congress increased, for both "attacks" and instances of "compromise." That said, significantly more segments were focused on tweets in Congress as attacks. This is especially true for mid-2019, when almost 15 percent of all news segments on these television news outlets referred to Congress members' use of Twitter in the context of an attack, compared to 6 percent in the context of compromise.

These findings generally follow what we would expect given research on negativity bias in the news media (Fridkin and Kenney 2004; Soroka 2012;

Soroka and McAdams 2015). The agenda-setting power of the news media means that they decide what is newsworthy, what we pay attention to. And there is a large body of evidence that suggests people are more likely to pay attention to negative news stories than to positive news stories. For example, attack ads are more likely than positive ads to focus on salient issues and thus are more informative (Geer 2008). Negativity in the news also has the power to generate emotions, like anger or anxiety, that tend to increase attention (Gervais 2017; Marcus, Neuman, and MacKuen 2000; Valentino et al. 2011). When members of Congress tweet about their more traditional duties having to do with actual representation, like legislative compromise, this is not necessarily newsworthy. This does not mean that members of Congress never actually tweet about compromise or bipartisanship; we know from the patterns analyzed earlier in the book that they do, especially when they use specific policy or issue-area words. Over a third of all legislator tweets analyzed contained policy language, and legislators on average mentioned policy 570 times on Twitter. The findings here show that when they condemn the other side it is more likely to be picked up and amplified in the news than when they mention compromise. This suggests there is an incentive for members of Congress to attack the other side on Twitter. If such tweets are more likely to get liked and retweeted and are then more likely to be picked up by major television news stations, legislators receive free media coverage and increased potential to boost their national exposure and influence.

A further implication is that news negativity may reduce penalties for out-group rhetoric by politicians. Viewers become desensitized to negativity with repeated exposure over time (Bushman and Anderson 2009; Scharrer 2008), thus heightening the role of partisan attacks in the political landscape. The news media itself is a contributor to the cycle of communication about out-groups. The more out-group discourse is covered in the media or, more importantly, perpetuated by television news itself, the greater the potential that people will be desensitized to this type of communication and come to expect it as part of the political ecosystem. Partisan media portray the opposition as having radical beliefs, which increases perceived polarization among the mass public (Levendusky and Malhotra 2016a). Members of Congress tweet about policy issues a lot, but since that is not what gets retweeted or picked up by cable newscasts, that is not what Americans see.

MONEY, MONEY, MONEY: NEGATIVE REPRESENTATION RAISES DONATIONS

American political campaigns, especially at the federal level, have become increasingly expensive, requiring politicians to fundraise more and more intensively. Not only can the money legislators raise be used to support their own future campaigns; the most prominent fundraisers can also spread the wealth to their colleagues, an ability that gives them an additional source of power and influence. As social media continues to emerge as a dominant form of political communication, legislators and candidates leverage these platforms for mobilization. While direct fundraising appeals on platforms like Twitter or Facebook might not always resonate widely, creating captivating content is vital as candidates vie for attention online. Research shows that viral posts amplify a candidate's profile, attracting more funds to their campaign accounts (Kowal 2023). Some of this engagement stems from "polarizing" rhetoric that denigrates out-groups in favor of in-groups, which leads to increases in both the amount of money raised by a candidate and the number of donors giving to a candidate (Ballard et al. 2022).

According to a recent OpenSecrets report, successful Senate candidates raised an average of $7.3 million in 2000. By 2022, this skyrocketed to $26.5 million. Successful House candidates in 2000 raised an average of $840,300; by 2022 this increased to around $2.8 million. In that same election cycle, Rep. Katie Porter used her national reputation to raise more than $25 million. The escalation in fundraising is partly attributed to the US Supreme Court's 2010 decision in *Citizens United v. Federal Election Commission*. The verdict enabled non-candidate-affiliated political groups to receive unlimited funds from individual and corporate donors. The 2022 electoral cycle saw these outside groups inject over $2 billion into political campaigns. Federal political campaigns are still bound by contribution limits. To counteract the massive spending by outside groups, candidates have extended their fundraising strategies to include donors beyond their state borders.

Indeed, there has been a noticeable shift away from in-state contributions, with Senate candidates receiving less than half of their donations from in-state sources since 2014. Most contributions to House candidates were from in-state donors between 1998 and 2016, yet by 2022 the percentage of contributions from in-state donors had dropped by more than 10 percentage points (OpenSecrets). Research suggests that out-of-state contributions are more valuable to non-incumbents, as they indicate support from groups in the extended party network (Baker 2022). While out-of-state donations do not often correlate with success in elections, it is a good signal of national notoriety. The candidates who receive the most out-of-state funds include those running against high-profile, polarizing candidates (for instance, Amy McGrath, who raised over 97 percent out-of-state funds to run against Mitch McConnell) and individuals with national reputations (e.g., Reps. Liz Cheney, with over 96 percent of 2021–2022 funds from out of state, and Steve Scalise, with 94 percent from out of state).

The increase in out-of-state donations is just one example of the nationalization of congressional politics. But these patterns can provide important insight into how legislative communication offers opportunities for members of Congress to increase their national profile. While members of Congress have always had some national-level duties, modern communication channels allow them to engage a national audience more rapidly and cost-effectively. This nationwide reach translates to an influx of fundraising, particularly donations from beyond their state borders. The escalating costs of American elections compel candidates to perpetually solicit donations. And to be sure, the politicians who are best known for negative representation on social media are also some of the institution's most prolific fundraisers.

Is negative partisan rhetoric associated with an increase in fundraising, particularly from out-of-state donors? So far, we've seen that negative representation increases social media attention and coverage on partisan television news. The implication is that members engaging in negative partisan representation benefit in terms of attracting activists, raising money, and raising their national prominence, even if this behavior does not directly attract votes. I further test this implication using campaign finance data. I explore whether legislators who use negative representation styles receive more out-of-state donations than other legislators. Using out-of-state donations enables me to examine whether partisan attacks draw donations from people beyond a representative's constituency. As a preview, I find that negative partisan rhetoric in tweets, but not necessarily in newsletters, is associated with an increase in total fundraising dollars as well as out-of-state donations. This is consistent with expectations: newsletters are narrowcast communications sent to constituents within a member's district or state, whereas tweets are broadcast to a much larger audience. Social media posts reach potential donors in other districts and states, and as documented in the media analyses above, tweets that focus on the opposing party are much more likely to be liked and retweeted. Negative representation is a reputation-building activity, increasing legislators' notoriety on the national stage.

Analyzing the Relationship between Fundraising and Communication

For the analyses below, I use fundraising data provided by OpenSecrets that was collected from Federal Election Commission filings. First, I examine how language in tweets is associated with total fundraising dollars and out-of-state donations; next I examine language in newsletters. Recall that the Twitter data focus on members in the 116th Congress, so I limit my analyses to incumbents and analyze how much money they raised during that session's election cycle. For a clear comparison between social media and newsletters, I focus on the 116th Congress for newsletter as well. These are the same members of the House during the same time period, just on different communication mediums. Analyzing the results for the full set of newsletters over time, from the 111th to the 116th Congress, shows similar results. The figures below are based on predicted values from ordinary least squares regression models that include several relevant control variables, such as gender, race, party affiliation, seniority, party leadership status, ideological extremity, vote share, and legislative effectiveness score. The models also include all rhetoric variables (out-party, in-party, policy, and bipartisanship), which means that the figures show the relationship between fundraising and out-party language (for example) while holding constant the number of tweets/newsletters that mentioned the in-party, policy, and bipartisanship.

NEGATIVE REPRESENTATION ON SOCIAL MEDIA YIELDS MORE MONEY

First, I start with estimating the relationship between negative partisan rhetoric and total dollars raised by a member of Congress during the election cycle. As seen in the bottom portion of figure 7.4, the frequency with which legislators tweet about the out-party is positively associated with fundraising totals. Specifically, for every additional mention of the out-party, a legislator is predicted to raise an extra $6,160, which is statistically significant ($p < 0.001$). It bears repeating that this estimate is associated with just a one-unit increase in rhetoric: if a legislator tweeted about the other party just *one additional time* during 2019–2020, their campaign raked in an additional $6,100. When modeling fundraising as a function of how many more times the opposite party is mentioned than the in-party, this increases to over $8,000.

The models in the appendix to this chapter show that this is not always the case for other types of rhetoric. The number of times a legislator discusses their own party on Twitter, or discusses bipartisanship or compromise, has no statistically significant effect on how much money they receive. The number of times they talk about policy, however, actually has a small but statistically significant *negative* effect on total dollars fundraised.

A striking comparison can be made to congressional newsletters. Each additional mention of the out-party in newsletters is associated with a *decrease* in total dollars fundraised of $15,820 ($p < 0.001$). With each additional mention of the opposite party over the in-party, fundraising decreases by over $19,500. There are also different patterns when it comes to other types of rhetoric as well. Each additional mention of the *in-party* in

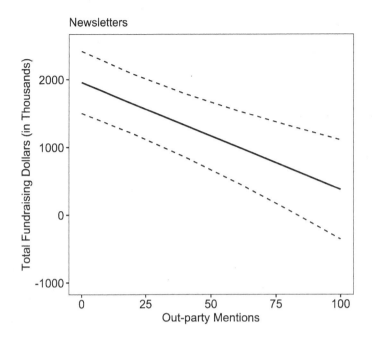

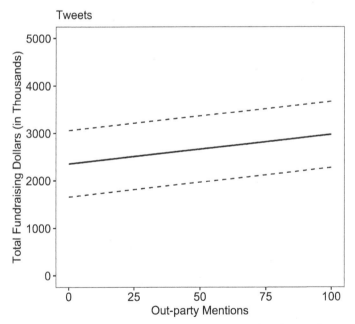

Figure 7.4. Total fundraising dollars and out-party mentions in newsletters and tweets

Note: Figure shows predicted values from ordinary least squares regression model including controls on effect of out-party mentions in newsletters (*top*) and tweets (*bottom*) on total fundraising dollars in thousands. Area between dotted lines represents 95 percent confidence interval.

newsletters *increases* total dollars raised by $38,180. When legislators talk about bipartisanship in newsletters, they receive almost $8,500 more in donations. These substantively large, statistically significant relationships suggest that rhetoric is not only used very differently in newsletters and in social media, but also has different downstream effects, and therefore offers different types of incentives to politicians navigating their strategic communication.

ATTENTION FROM OUT OF STATE

Of course, given arguments about negative partisanship and national prominence, I am most interested to see if these relationships hold when examining donations coming from beyond state borders. Out-of-state donations are indicative of national attention and the possibility of broader influence. Figure 7.5 shows that for each additional out-party mention on Twitter, a legislator is predicted to raise an additional $1,230 from out-of-state sources ($p < 0.01$). This increase rises slightly ($1,480) when we consider the number of times a legislator tweets about the other party in comparison to their own party. As legislators increasingly emphasize the opposite party over their own party on social media, they receive more out-of-state money. Emphasizing the opposition appears to resonate with a broader national audience, providing legislators with a significant fundraising advantage.

Importantly, the top plot in figure 7.5 shows that there is not much of an association between negative partisan rhetoric in newsletters and out-of-state fundraising—the line is relatively flat. If anything, there is a slight downward slope as out-party rhetoric increases, but the trend is not statistically significant. Recall that newsletters are primarily used to explain roll call votes, discuss policy, and highlight specific projects the member has undertaken for their district (also see Clarke, Jenkins, and Micatka 2020; Cormack 2016a, 2016b; Lipinski 2001; Yiannakis 1982). Contrastingly, Twitter, being a modern social media platform, functions within a reward-based system that often favors sharp, polarized soundbites. Indeed, chapter 3 showed that legislators on social media resort to more partisan and polarizing language, especially when their party isn't in power. Partisan language is used more frequently on social media, and policy discussions, although prevalent in both mediums, appear in almost every newsletter, but in only one in every three Twitter posts. Newsletters almost always incorporate policy discussions, even when referencing the opposing party. However, a significant portion of tweets mentioning the opposing party do not delve into policy at all. Compared to newsletters, Twitter shows less overlap between negative party mentions and other forms of rhetoric. While newsletters can contain mentions of party affiliations and dynamics, their extended format

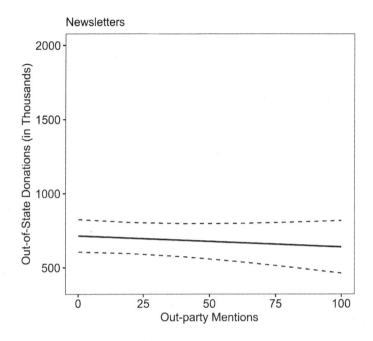

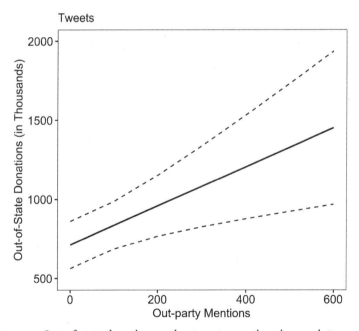

Figure 7.5. Out-of-state donations and out-party mentions in newsletters and tweets

Note: Figure shows predicted values from ordinary least squares regression model including controls on effect of out-party mentions in newsletters (*top*) and tweets (*bottom*) on fundraising dollars from out of state in thousands. Area between dotted lines represents 95 percent confidence interval.

also often allows for a more balanced tone. Even if a legislator criticizes the opposing party, they frequently balance this with positive content elsewhere in the document. Over the years, newsletters have displayed an evolution toward a more optimistic and constructive tone, showcasing the desire to build rapport and trust with constituents. Unlike the sentiment in newsletters, the sentiment in tweets, especially those mentioning the opposing party, has become increasingly negative over the years.

The fundamental difference between newsletters and social media lies in their intended audience and their format. Designed for a more localized, constituent-based audience, newsletters focus more on policy and bipartisanship. Their primary goal is to maintain communication with those the legislators represent directly. Twitter, on the other hand, with its global reach, caters to a wider audience. This broad spectrum of users, combined with the platform's brief and instantaneous nature, positions Twitter as a tool for instant engagement, attention-grabbing, and heightened partisanship. Content aimed at constituents (newsletters) is less devoted to negative partisanship. But content aimed at broader audiences (social media) looks to gain competitive advantage by offering more exciting soundbites that get picked up on the global stage.

When amplified on platforms like social media and traditional news outlets, negative representation can substantially enhance a politician's national visibility. This heightened exposure not only bolsters out-of-state fundraising, but also endows politicians with increased leverage and authority in their official capacities. In the context of examining the exposure hypothesis, the distinction between social media and newsletters in reach and immediacy is pivotal. Tweets, with their real-time dissemination and vast potential for virality, are inherently more suited to capturing wide attention. Their brief, often incisive nature can capture attention to spark media coverage and national notoriety. On the other hand, given the findings in chapter 5 that political elites think insulting the other party turns voters off, it makes sense that legislators do not use newsletters to engage heavily in negative representation.

Once again, this effect is unique to negative representation. On Twitter, no other type of language has a statistically significant association with out-of-state donations. It is only when they focus on the other party that legislators reap the financial rewards, both overall and specifically from beyond their state's borders. In newsletters, policy language and bipartisan/compromising language do not have a statistically significant association with out-of-state donations, but when legislators talk about their *own* party, donations increase slightly (but significantly). This again underscores the ways legislators use the different forms of communication and their implications for representation.

CONCLUSION

In the beginning of this book, I described the economic theory of markets with asymmetric information and how they lead to a "race to the bottom." In such markets, buyers are unable to accurately assess the quality of goods or services being offered. Sellers of high-quality goods may exit the market, leaving only low-quality goods (or "lemons") available. This can lead to a downward spiral in which the average quality of goods on the market decreases, leading to lower demand and eventually market collapse. In the context of political representation, asymmetric information could result from deceptive campaign promises, biased media coverage, or gaps between perceptions and reality. The vicious cycle of negativity and attention contributes to a race to the bottom by promoting negative, partisan rhetoric over positive, compromising rhetoric. The more negative representation is used and the more it is perceived as the norm, the more self-reinforcing it becomes. An information environment that rewards provocation in turn rewards elite partisan attacks with more fame and exposure, further contributing to the cycle.

Elite communication on social media that contains out-party appeals receives significantly more attention than communication that contains in-party appeals or does not mention partisanship at all. And partisan television news outlets like Fox News and MSNBC are more likely to cover partisan attacks by Congress members on Twitter than to cover efforts toward compromise and bipartisanship by Congress members on Twitter. In recent years, these outlets also tend to cover the opposing party more, adding to the polarization ecosystem. This level of national attention translates to financial rewards as well; legislators who engage in negative representation on social media receive more money for their campaigns, both overall and specifically from beyond their own state, suggesting that the behavior helps build national-level influence.

Ultimately, even though elites do not think Americans favor elite expressions of partisan animosity, the broader environment of affective polarization makes the use of negational representational styles all too common. While the approach of attacking opponents may seem counterproductive or damaging to civil discourse, there are tangible advantages for politicians who employ such strategies. By capitalizing on the media's penchant for covering controversial and conflict-driven stories, these politicians can effectively amplify their own voices and increase their influence. Members who frequently employ negative rhetoric often emerge as some of the institution's most prominent fundraisers outside of party leadership. By engaging in this behavior, these members raise their profile, becoming influential figures in national discourse and, frequently, within their own party.

Given the partisan leanings of many congressional districts, the electoral risks associated with consistent oppositional rhetoric are minimal. In fact, for many members, the benefits—increased visibility, enhanced fundraising, and greater influence—likely outweigh any potential electoral drawbacks. Even if some constituents find this behavior distasteful, the net gains for the legislator are often positive. For the minority party in Congress, the need for a unified, oppositional stance to shape media narratives and build a compelling case for reclaiming power provides an incentive for individual legislators to amplify their out-party rhetoric, especially on platforms like Twitter that offer a broader reach. In the rest of the book I examine negative representation from the bottom up through the lens of constituents and show the destructive effects such a feedback loop generates for democratic representation.

8. AMERICANS DON'T LIKE NEGATIVE REPRESENTATION

It is clear that the affective distance between Democrats and Republicans has increased. Opposite partisans not only differ in their ideological policy positions, but also increasingly dislike one another. Animus against the other party, rather than affinity for one's own party, is the main driver of the affective gap in feelings between partisans. In some cases, this hostility is more important for voters' political attitudes than loyalty to their own party (Abramowitz and Webster 2016; Amira, Wright, and Goya-Tocchetto 2021—though see Lelkes 2018).

If negative partisanship dominates how Americans view one another in the mass public, then surely it also affects how Americans view politicians (Abramowitz and Webster 2016; Druckman and Levendusky 2019; Iyengar and Krupenkin 2018). While evidence clearly demonstrates that partisans loathe members of the opposing party, less research has examined how people feel about political elites engaging in negative partisanship compared to focusing on policy issues. What is the relative value of policy congruence, constituency service, and partisan affect by legislators? Are expressions of negative partisanship actually favored? For the hyperpolarized context, many claim that Americans will reward elected officials who cater to their affective partisan identities. As discussed throughout this book, one's negational identity—or "who one is not"—rather than affirmational identity—or "who one is"—is a meaningful source of political behavior and voter decision-making (Zhong, Galinsky, and Unzueta 2008). Moreover, some scholars have argued that when asked to evaluate the other party, people actually think of *elite* members of that party, such as the president or members of Congress (Druckman and Levendusky 2019). The natural extension of this body of work has been to suggest that citizens hold representatives accountable based on the extent to which those representatives meet their affective, partisan interests rather than their ideological interests (e.g., Iyengar and Krupenkin 2018). While there are seemingly endless examples of voters cheering on politicians when they attack the other side, anecdotal data alone cannot conclusively determine whether people respond favorably to negative representation. We lack generalizable empirical evidence, despite the fact that many scholars and analysts have interpreted politicians' persistent use of negative partisanship as proof that citizens support such appeals.

In this section of the book, I turn the focus to members of the mass public. So far, I have examined negative partisan representation from the top down, from the side of representatives. Understanding representation in an age of negative partisanship also requires an examination from the bottom up. How do the *represented* feel about communication styles based on out-partisan identities? In this chapter, I report results of three experiments on mass public samples to understand how voters perceive different representational styles from politicians.[1]

I argue that counter to many contemporary narratives, people still want representation based on issues, not partisan affect. While social-psychological theories about partisan identities may explain how people view other-partisans (elites or otherwise), it need not mean that they want representatives who invoke their partisan identities if it comes at the expense of their policy positions or quality service responsiveness. Across three survey experiments, I find that affective partisan rhetoric is not rewarded, and in most cases significantly harms citizens' evaluations of legislators. This remains true even when people evaluate a legislator of their own party. Additionally, positive, in-party sentiments are evaluated more favorably than negative, out-party ones. Overall, people rate representatives the highest when they share their issue positions and priorities.

The implication of these findings is that people react in ways that we would expect them to in a healthy, functioning representative democracy rather than a democracy characterized by party tribalism. Partisanship may very well be a social identity (Campbell et al. 1960; Green, Palmquist, and Schickler 2004), even one that trumps ideological principles (Barber and Pope 2019) and leads to bias against members of the out-party (Cassese 2021; Martherus et al. 2021; Mason 2018a). But at the same time, people prioritize policy and constituency service rather than affective group-orientations. Citizens are focused on the policies and actions of their elected representatives and hold them accountable for their performance and service to their constituents. Politicians who often take part in expressive partisanship may thus be out of line with what their constituents want. And concerns about affective polarization in terms of what it means for *perceptions of representation* may be overblown.

PERCEPTIONS OF REPRESENTATION

Representative democracy rests on the idea that legislators serve on behalf of their constituents. Conventional wisdom therefore posits that citizens desire representatives who share their policy positions (e.g., Ansolabehere and Jones 2010; Downs 1957). Typically, policy congruence is applied to models of elections and vote choice, but it impacts more general legislator evaluations as well. Evaluations of representational styles, congressional approval, and trust in government are all influenced by the extent to which citizens perceive that they are getting quality substantive representation (Griffin and Flavin 2011; Lapinski et al. 2016; Mansbridge 1999; Parker and Goodman 2009).

But representation is multidimensional. Elected officials can represent their constituents in a variety of ways, such as allocating resources to their district or providing service responsiveness through casework. There are additional forms of representation that require no action at all; for example, descriptive or symbolic representatives "stand for" their constituents rather than "act for" them (Pitkin 1967). Representational styles are often symbolic or rhetorical in nature (Eulau and Karps 1977; Fenno 1978; Grimmer 2013), and thus citizens' perceptions of representation rely in part on how the representative makes them feel. Evaluations of constituency service have been found to rely heavily on the legislators' tone in response to service requests, rather than on whether the legislator substantively answered the request (Costa 2021). People respond to whether representatives make them feel heard. In turn, legislators spend a great deal of energy strategizing how to explain their representational choices to constituents (Fenno 1978; Grose, Malhotra, and Parks Van Houweling 2015; Kingdon 1989).

Citizens mostly evaluate representation based on what representatives *do* for them. People generally prefer different representational styles depending on the outcome each style produces. For example, where district allocation is more important to a community or constituency group, that is what those constituents prioritize (Griffin and Flavin 2011; Harden 2015). A citizen's support of certain procedural behaviors is conditional on whether those procedures lead to outcomes with which they personally agree (Doherty 2015). Even when people make communal considerations in evaluating representation—that is, whether a legislator provides quality representation for the whole district, not just them personally—they are likely drawing on shared substantive interests (Christenson and Makse 2015; Costa, Johnson, and Schaffner 2018).

DO AMERICANS STILL WANT SUBSTANTIVE REPRESENTATION IN AN AGE OF NEGATIVE PARTISANSHIP?

A growing body of research challenges the importance of policy congruence and substantive representation for mass political behavior in the current hyperpolarized context. Instead, negative partisanship has come to characterize American politics. Most research on negative partisanship focuses on partisans' attitudes toward other members of the mass public, and not toward political elites. Nevertheless, that many studies have upheld the presence of negative partisanship in the mass public, as well as the observation that elected officials often take to public platforms to express negative affect toward the out-party, has led many to suggest that citizens *favor* this type of politics over policy congruence and substantive representation.

Social identity theories have long posited that how individuals define themselves as members of groups helps to explain their attitudes and behavior (Tajfel 1982). In political science, these theories have been used to better understand party affiliation (Campbell et al. 1960; Green, Palmquist, and Schickler 2004), group conflict (Elkins and de Figueiredo 2003), and policy preferences (Burns and Gimpel 2000). Group theories have been used less to investigate forms of representation based on who a representative's constituents are *not*, even though politicians often publicly express disdain for the other side. While there is some research on citizen evaluations of legislative bipartisanship and willingness to compromise (e.g., Harbridge and Malhotra 2011), there are few, if any, close examinations of whether people reward an affective style of representation centered around negative partisanship.

The two types of negative representation defined in this book (affective and electoral) can spur reactions from the public. Affective polarization in the mass public is partly thought to be driven caused by hostile campaign environments (Iyengar, Sood, and Lelkes 2012; Iyengar et al. 2019). If this is the case, then negative partisan affect expressed by politicians would increase partisans' negative affect toward the other party. Disagreeable incivility by elites—incivility that targets one's in-group—induces anger and increases use of incivility from members of the targeted group. Like-minded incivility by elites—incivility toward the out-group—increases one's own hostility toward the out-group (Gervais 2017; Mutz and Reeves 2005; Mutz 2015) and effectively increases mobilization (Jerit 2004). Inferred from this is the notion that while elite incivility toward the out-group may evoke anger, it may also rile up *support* for the elite in question.

Second, representatives can focus on out-group electoral loss (or in-group victory) without particular use of incivility. Affective polarization is largely driven by out-party loathing that subsumes in-party loyalty. While uncivil affective representation may turn some constituents off (Klar and Krupnikov 2016; Lelkes and Westwood 2017), those constituents still may favor elite rhetoric that invokes partisan motivations in other ways. For instance, Barber and Pope (2019) find that party loyalists are quick to abandon ideological principles if given a cue by a powerful in-party elite (such as President Trump). Party loyalists may therefore also prioritize electoral gains for their "tribe" regardless of what that would mean for policy outcomes.

A clear narrative has developed among scholars of American politics that political behavior revolves around heightened levels of partisanship. The general sentiment consistent across narratives is that partisanship is more important than anything else for many aspects of political behavior, including evaluations of legislative behavior and representational styles. But whether partisan negative representation is favored has not actually been empirically demonstrated. How do citizens weigh the relative value of ideology and policy congruence, constituency service, and partisan rhetoric? In answering this question, I take into account both incivility and electoral-based forms of affective representation, as well as how out-party versus in-party rhetoric affects evaluations of representatives.

THE EXPERIMENTS

As described above, perceptions of representation are multidimensional. Constituents generally prefer representatives who share their party and ideology, and in some cases their race and gender. We also know that campaign rhetoric, particularly incivility or rhetoric meant to evoke negative emotions, influences evaluations of legislators. However, observational research and even much experimental work cannot disentangle the impact of various coexisting legislative behaviors on individuals' evaluations.

The three studies presented in this chapter are variations on the conjoint experimental design described in chapter 5 in which elites selected among a pair of candidates whose characteristics varied. To implement the experiments, I independently randomize attributes of legislators to examine the relative impact of issue representation, constituency service, and expressions of partisan affect on individuals' evaluations. I describe the design of each experiment in the sections that follow, but table 8.1 summarizes the main components of each study.

Before getting into the specifics of each study, I take note of two features of the experiments. First, as in the conjoint experiment used to study *elite* perceptions of electoral viability, the legislators who appear in the vignettes are hypothetical, which is standard in conjoints. This has the benefit of reducing confounding as it limits respondents' reactions to the information provided as much as possible. As in other survey experiments, this can come with the potential drawback of compromising ecological validity. Hainmueller, Hangartner, and Yamamoto (2015) show how conjoint experiments can recover behavioral benchmarks, but the case of affective representation may be particular if social desirability bias leads respondents to express disapproval of incivility in surveys but not in the real world. While I model

156 CHAPTER EIGHT

Table 8.1. Summary of Three Experiments

	STUDY 1	STUDY 2	STUDY 3
Sample	Lucid (n respondents = 1,506)	CCES (YouGov) (n respondents = 1,000)	Lucid (n respondents = 3,030)
Number of tasks	6	3	1
Issues	Immigration, healthcare	Gun control, income tax	Varies
Issue importance?	No	No	Yes
Type of partisan rhetoric	Out-party (incivility)	Out-party, in-party (incivility, cheerleading)	Out-party, in-party (electoral)

Note: "Issue importance?" is an indicator of whether the study took into account how important the issues (used to measure policy representation) are to the experimental subjects.

the information provided in the experiments on real examples, I am careful to note that the results may not always generalize to *elections*. That is, the experimental designs enable me to estimate the relative independent impact of substantive and affective representation on how people evaluate elite behavior, but it is harder to say for sure how these evaluations translate to vote choice.[2] We saw in chapter 5 how negative partisan rhetoric by a representative correlates with that representative's vote share. This chapter focuses more on the public attitudinal outcomes of such expressions by elites. The experiments may not directly translate to whether people would *vote* for a candidate who uses negative partisan rhetoric, and this is not the aim. Rather, I am now interested in whether people report that they *favor* this behavior of representatives in office compared to other behaviors and characteristics.

Second, I use individual issue treatments to measure what can essentially be considered ideological representation. This reflects how the literature has characterized both policy congruence between representatives and constituents (e.g., Rogers 2017; Stimson, MacKuen, and Erikson 1995) and policy-based polarization (e.g., Hill and Tausanovitch 2015; Poole and Rosenthal 1984). Iyengar, Sood, and Lelkes (2012) use measures of individual policy preferences to demonstrate that partisan polarization is largely based on "affect, *not ideology*" (emphasis mine). While ideology itself is conceived to be an abstract organization of values, issue positions are how those values manifest. Even while people struggle to articulate a cohesive ideology (Converse 1964; Kinder and Kalmoe 2017), they are able to take clear and consistent stands on individual issues (Achen 1975; Ansolabehere, Rodden, and Snyder 2008). Using individual policy issues in the following experiments therefore gives a clearer sense of substantive representation rather than ideological labels of elected officials. If I find that individuals prefer policy congruence across this set of issues over partisan affect, this would be evidence in favor of representation on ideology, regardless of whether those individuals would accurately describe their policy preferences in ideological terms.

Finally, it is worth noting that the survey evidence about the public's (and elites' in chapter 5) attitudes cannot by itself give us a concrete explanation of why negative representation happens—and, to be sure, it is not intended to. These surveys are designed to offer a valuable snapshot of how negative representation influences attitudes about legislators. The experiments capture what people think they prefer in terms of legislative behavior. It's essential to differentiate between these reported preferences and the actual utility or benefits negative representation may offer to politicians. While the public claims to penalize or look unfavorably upon negative representation, this does not negate the potential advantages such practices may confer, such as garnering increased media attention or enhancing fundraising capabilities (as shown in chapter 7). The validity of self-reports as a reliable measure of actual beliefs or behaviors is an entirely separate question on the methodological constraints of survey research. Despite these constraints, survey data, and especially experimental data, remain critically important. Experiments allow for controlled comparisons, which go beyond capturing top-of-the-head opinions to reveal more authentic perceptions of negative representation. What people report is meaningful in its own right because it provides insights into what they expressively believe about the virtues of partisanship versus policy. In this way, this chapter offers a different angle from which to study the complicated dynamics surrounding negative representation.

STUDY 1: DO CITIZENS FAVOR NEGATIVE PARTISANSHIP OVER POLICY CONGRUENCE?

The first conjoint was fielded using Lucid in December 2018 on a sample of 1,506 individuals. Lucid is a respondent aggregator that directs a demographically balanced online panel to a survey hosted on the Qualtrics platform.[3] Within the survey, respondents were first asked whether they support or oppose a variety of policy proposals regarding immigration, healthcare, gun reform, and the corporate tax rate. For the purposes of this study, I was only interested in their positions on two issues: increasing spending on security along the US-Mexico border and Medicare for all. I use respondents' positions on these issues to measure policy congruence with a hypothetical member of Congress. Note that I am agnostic about the importance of these particular issues and that, ideally, I would be able to use a variety of policy proposals to measure congruence. As extremely salient, contemporary issues, immigration and healthcare provide a good first test of the relative value of different legislative behaviors. It is possible that these issues are only really important to a relatively small group of people. If this is the case, the effects I present below may in fact be understated. Study 2 uses a different set of issues, and Study 3 takes issue importance into account.

After respondents answered other demographic and unrelated questions in the survey, they were presented with the conjoint design. Two profiles of fictional members of Congress, Congress member A and Congress member B, were presented side by side in a table (see the appendix to this chapter for an example of what respondents saw). I randomly varied the legislator's sex (male, female), party (Democrat, Republican), race/ethnicity (white, African American, Hispanic), latest tweet, and constituent relations (answers more than 90 percent of constituent mail, answers less than half of constituent mail). "Latest tweet" was randomized so that respondents saw a statement expressing animosity toward the out-party or signaling support or opposition for increasing border security or Medicare for all. The exact wording of the statements to signal policy (in)congruence are shown in the appendix of Costa (2021). The statement expressing negative partisan affect was always manipulated so that it referenced the legislator's out-party and read: "[Democrats/Republicans] are CORRUPT and IMMORAL. I will not sit silent while they lie to Americans and steer us in the wrong direction."

While this wording was crafted to be a fairly strong treatment, it does mirror how partisan incivility often plays out on social media. According to a list of every insult tweeted by President Trump since he declared his candidacy, the word "corrupt" has been tweeted at least 85 times, "lie" or "liar" has been tweeted 200 times, and "Democrats" as an entire group are one of his top targets (Lee and Quealy 2019). While President Trump's Twitter account may be exceptional due to his brash use of the platform, it is not uncommon for political elites to take to social media to publicly rile their opponents. Of tweets by members of the 116th Congress that specifically mention the other party, the word "lie" appears 3,592 times, the word "corrupt" appears 306 times, and references to "morality" appear 137 times.

For this treatment, respondents see a legislator who either agrees with them on one of the policy issues, disagrees with them, or expresses negative rhetoric against the other party. Policy congruence and negative rhetoric are not independently randomized as they are in the next two studies. I also use only out-party rhetoric for Study 1 due to the focus on *negative* partisanship and evidence that one's negational partisan identities are stronger than one's affirmational partisan identities. In the next two studies, *positive* partisan treatments are also included to examine the difference between out-party and in-party rhetoric.

On the same screen as the member profiles, respondents were asked: "If you had to choose, which member of Congress would you prefer to have as your representative?" This forced-choice design resembles political decision-making in the "real world," where voters evaluate public officials who vary on multiple dimensions. Respondents completed this task for six pairs; each time, the attributes were fully randomized in every legislator profile.

OVERALL PREFERENCES FOR REPRESENTATION

I estimate the effects of each representative characteristic by treating each profile presented as the unit of analysis. Across the 1,506 respondents, this results in 18,012 observations. The outcome of interest is whether the legislator profile was selected or not in a simple linear regression with indicators for each attribute level on the right-hand side of the equation. The average marginal component effect (AMCE) can therefore be interpreted as the effect of a given attribute level (relative to the excluded baseline level) on the probability a legislator will be selected, averaged across all other possible combinations of the other attributes. Because multiple choice outcomes exist for each respondent in the survey, I use cluster-robust standard errors at the respondent level to correct for the possibility that individuals base choices between latter pairs on profiles they saw earlier in the set of tasks.

Figure 8.1 presents the AMCE and 95 percent confidence intervals for each attribute level on the probability of a profile being selected as the preferred representative compared to the baseline attribute level. Starting from the top, neither sex nor race/ethnicity had a statistically significant effect on the probability of a legislator being selected. Because we are interested in shared partisanship rather than partisan affiliation per se, I include a covariate for whether the respondent is of the same or opposite party as the legislator (true independents and "not sure" responses are used as the baseline category). Unsurprisingly, legislators are more likely to be selected when they share respondents' partisanship and less likely to be selected when they are of the opposite party.

The bottom two panels show the results for attributes regarding legislator behavior. For "latest tweet," I do not distinguish between policy-focused statements having to do with healthcare and those having to do with immigration. Rather, I collapse together all policy statements that align with the respondent's preferences (agree policy) and those that do not align with the respondent's preferences (disagree policy). Using "disagree policy" as

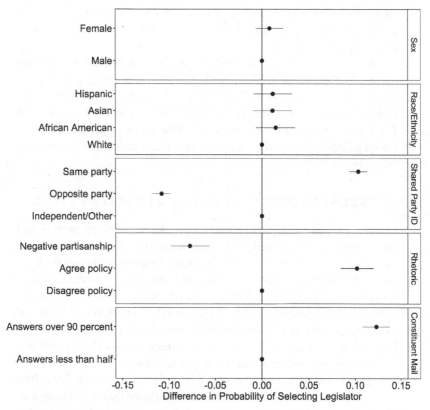

Figure 8.1. Effects of legislator traits on preferences for representation

Note: Average marginal treatment effect estimates using cluster-robust standard errors by subjects. Horizontal lines represent 95 percent confidence intervals.

the baseline category, I isolate the independent effects of policy congruence and expressions of negative partisanship, while also controlling for shared partisanship.

Compared to when legislators have opposing policy views, legislators who share respondents' policy views are 10.2 percentage points more likely to be selected. If legislators insult the out-party, respondents are less likely (by 7.7 percentage points) to select them than if they disagreed on policy. The last panel shows how constituency service compares. Compared to answering less than half of constituent mail, legislators who provide quality service responsiveness are 12.5 percentage points more likely to be selected. The difference between agree on policy and answers 90 percent of constituent mail (–2 points) is not statistically significant, but the differences between disagree on policy and negative partisanship (–7.7 points) *and* answers less than half of constituent mail and negative partisanship (–5 points) are. In other words, on average, individuals reward quality service responsiveness and policy congruence about the same, but they penalize partisan animosity *more* than the other unfavorable behaviors of policy incongruence and poor constituency service. Except when noted otherwise, all of the differences are significant at the $p < 0.001$ level.

RESULTS CONDITIONAL ON SHARING PARTY IDENTIFICATION

As the party of the representative was randomized, the results presented above obscure what happens when legislators target the party opposite the respondent's. Figure 8.2 presents the effects of the latest tweet attribute conditional on whether respondents and legislators have the same party identification. For out-party individuals, legislators who support respondents' policy positions are 11 percentage points more likely to be selected than legislators who do not support the same policy positions ($p < 0.001$). If the legislator expresses negative partisanship, on the other hand, out-party respondents are 18.4 percentage points less likely to select them than if they disagreed on policy ($p < 0.001$). In other words, if someone is a Republican, they would much rather have a Democratic legislator disagree with them

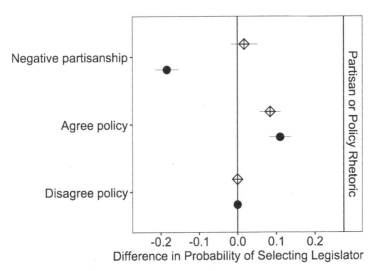

Figure 8.2. Effects of rhetoric on preferences for representation by shared partisan affiliation

Note: Average marginal treatment effect estimates using cluster-robust standard errors by subjects. Circles show treatment effects for out-party subjects; diamonds show treatment effects for in-party subjects. Horizontal lines represent 95 percent confidence intervals. Leaners coded as partisans. True independents and "not sure" responses removed from analysis.

on policy than call Republicans "corrupt" and "immoral," and vice versa for Democrats. To be sure, absent policy information, it is possible that respondents assume that out-party legislators already do not support their policy preferences. One possible way to interpret this result is that respondents penalize out-party legislators when those legislators oppose their substantive interests, but even more when the legislators are assumed to oppose their substantive interests *and* insult the respondent's party.

Turning to in-party respondents, legislators are 8.5 percentage points more likely to be selected when they share rather than oppose policy positions ($p < 0.001$). The difference between disagreeing on policy and expressing negative partisanship (+1.7) is not substantively or statistically significant. Out-party and in-party respondents react in roughly the same way to legislators who agree with them on policy. This indicates that individuals do not give policy-congruent legislators a boost just because they are co-partisans.

Overall, not only do respondents not favor negative partisanship over policy congruence, as recent research and contemporary narratives suggest; they also dislike it just as much as they dislike policy *incongruence* and poor constituency service. This is even true when the representative is attacking the party the respondent does not affiliate with. Respondents much prefer having representatives who agree with them on policy over having representatives who express animosity toward the out-party.

STUDY 2: THE INDEPENDENT EFFECTS OF NEGATIVE PARTISANSHIP AND POLICY CONGRUENCE

To further investigate the findings from Study 1, I present results from a similar experiment with a few adjustments. The experiment was fielded to 1,000 respondents in the 2018 pre-election wave of the Cooperative Congressional Election Study (CCES), the nationally representative online survey of American adults administered by YouGov. First, I adjust specifications of the attribute levels, namely the issues used to measure policy congruence and the wording of the partisan statements, to see if the main findings remain consistent. Selecting policies different from those used in Study 1 allows me to check whether those effects are generalizable to other issue contexts. Moreover, by adding "partisan cheerleading" that boosts the in-party as opposed to denigrating the other party, I can empirically test the widespread notion that people loathe the other party more than they support their own party, suggesting that out-party affect is stronger than in-party affect.

Another benefit of this study is that partisanship tweets were randomized independent of policy congruence. In Study 1, it is possible that respondents assumed that legislators who express strong negative affect against the out-party also share their own policy positions. By randomizing these attributes separately, I can simultaneously measure and compare the independent effects of these behaviors.

As in the first conjoint, respondents were shown a member of Congress profile that contained several randomized attributes, but were not asked to make a choice between two profiles. Instead, one profile was shown and respondents indicated their approval of the Congress member on a five-point scale. They completed this task three times; each time, a new randomized profile was shown. This design more closely resembles a "rating-based conjoint" where respondents evaluate one profile, as opposed to designs where respondents are asked to choose between two.

I randomized legislators' sex (male, female), race/ethnicity (white, Black, Latino, Asian), latest tweet, constituent relations (answers over 90 percent of constituent mail, answers less than half of constituent mail), and voting record on two issues. The legislator's partisan affiliation varied, but always with the party of the respondent. Democrats always evaluated a Democratic legislator and Republicans a Republican legislator. Party was randomized for true independents (individuals who do not lean toward a particular party) and those who selected "not sure" for party identification. For the two issues, legislators randomly either voted for or against (1) banning assault rifles and (2) increasing the tax rate for high-income people. Using two different issues that are randomized independent of one another allows me to measure *strength* of policy congruence: respondents can agree with the legislator on both, one, or neither of the two issues.[4]

"Latest tweet" was randomized so respondents saw a statement emphasizing in-party support or out-party animosity. There were three variations of the tweet expressing in-party support (e.g., "We [Democrats/ Republicans] are working hard to solve the nation's problems") and of the tweet expressing out-party animosity (e.g., "I am disgusted at today's [Democrats/ Republicans]. They are dishonest, dangerous, and bad for America"). The negative/positive partisanship statements were therefore not always symmetrical across profiles. This asymmetry does not affect the estimates because each statement had the same probability of being randomly assigned to a member profile.

POLICY AGREEMENT MATTERS MORE THAN PARTISAN RHETORIC

Figure 8.3 shows the effect of each randomized attribute level on change in approval (rescaled from 0 to 1). Overall, the results support the conclusions from Study 1. Sex and race/ethnicity did not significantly affect approval,

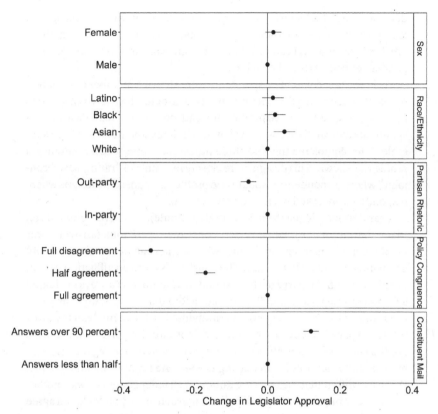

Figure 8.3. Effects of legislator traits on evaluation of representative

Note: Average marginal treatment effect estimates using cluster-robust standard errors by subjects. Horizontal lines represent 95 percent confidence intervals.

with the exception that Asian legislators get a 4.6-point boost in approval compared to white legislators ($p < 0.001$).

Legislators were penalized for negative partisanship, policy incongruence, and poor constituency service. Specifically, compared to when the legislator expressed in-party cheerleading, insulting the out-party decreased approval by 5.2 points. Importantly, the more policy positions respondents and legislators share, the higher respondents' approval; this relationship is nearly linear. When there is full agreement on policy (2/2 positions are shared) compared to full disagreement (0/2 positions), approval increases by 32 points. When there is "half agreement" (1/2 positions are shared), approval increases 15 points. Finally, legislators that provide quality constituency service (by answering over 90 percent of constituent mail) have an approval rating 12 points higher than those who provide poor constituency service. All of these results are statistically significant at the 0.001 level.

Recall that in this experiment the legislator's party always matched that of the subject. Thus, these findings show that people dislike expressions of negative partisanship *even when they are delivered by a politician from their own party*, and the degree of policy congruence is a much more powerful predictor of approval.

STUDY 3: TESTING ISSUE IMPORTANCE AND ELECTORAL-BASED RHETORIC

The previous two experiments suggest that individuals, even primary voters, are not fans of harsh, negative partisan affect compared to policy congruence or even positive partisan affect. However, there are three features of the previous designs that deserve further investigation. First, as discussed earlier, two different types of negative partisanship persist in American politics: (1) incivility driven by negative affect, including the trend for partisans to express hateful rhetoric against out-party citizens in surveys; and (2) a shift in electoral strategy or focus, where partisans care more about the other side losing than about their own side winning. Study 1 and Study 2 focus on what happens when elites engage in the first type of negative partisanship. Yet it is possible that individuals, especially in an artificial survey context, react negatively to incivility compared to more substantive legislative behaviors, but still favor electoral losses for the other party over electoral victories for their own party.

Second, while a variety of issue areas were used to measure congruence (immigration, healthcare, gun control, income tax rates), it is unclear whether issue importance plays a role. In frameworks that treat voters' propensity to support a candidate as involving rational calculations regarding policy, voters especially consider issues that are personally important to them. What is the impact of negative partisanship compared to the impact of policy representation on issues that constituents do not prioritize? Do people still strongly prefer substantive representation over negative representation when it is an issue they do not particularly care about?

Finally, while not impossible, excluding information for some attributes is uncommon in conjoints because it can complicate the interpretation of results; when respondents see multiple profiles across several tasks, the "missing" information is perceived in different ways.[5] Thus, there was not a true baseline category of no policy nor partisan affect in either of the previous two studies. Recall that *either* policy information or partisan affect was shown in Study 1 (the effect of "no policy information" was also the effect of partisan affect). Study 2 differed in that partisan affect and policy information were randomized independently, but both were always shown. For this experiment, I am able to combine these approaches: partisan affect and issue importance are independently randomized *and* include a true baseline category of no information shown. Because respondents see just one legislator profile, attributes are not flagged as "missing," which avoids some of the complications that occur with excluding attribute information in other types of conjoints. This enables me to estimate the effects of issue importance and partisan affect compared to when information about those qualities is absent.

The survey was conducted using Lucid in February 2019. In total, 3,030 individuals completed the survey. First, I gathered information on which policy issues respondents care about. Respondents were asked to rank a set of issue areas in order of importance to them. The list of issues respondents could choose from was order-randomized and included national security, healthcare, education, jobs, crime, immigration, drug addiction, social security, terrorism, and the environment.

The design of the experiment resembles a conjoint in that multiple treatment components were randomized independently to test their relative explanatory power. However, respondents did not complete multiple tasks, unlike in many conjoint experiments (though not all—see for example Carnes and Lupu 2016). In order to distract from the study's purpose and provide more information about the legislator, the profile contained static, nonrandomized information about the legislator's name (Rep. Stevens), family (married, two children), and how long the representative served in Congress (2015–present). As in Study 2, political party was always the same as the respondent's or was randomized for true independents.

The profiles then varied randomly along two dimensions. First, respondents saw a "member quote" that referenced the other party losing in the next election, one that referenced their own party winning the next election, or no quote at all. The out-party statement read: "We should do everything it takes to make sure [Democrats/Republicans] lose the next election," and the in-party statement read: "We should do everything it takes to make sure [Democrats/Republicans] win the next election." Note that the electoral focus of these statements differs from the uncivil, more expressive rhetoric in the previous two studies. The second randomized component was the legislator's "issue priority." This attribute listed either the issue respondents previously ranked as their most important issue or their third most important issue, or it did not show the issue priority category at all. On the same screen as the legislator profile, respondents indicated their approval of the member on a five-point scale.

ISSUE PRIORITIES OVER ELECTORAL WINS

Figure 8.4 plots coefficients and 95 percent confidence intervals from an ordinary least squares regression model estimating the effect of each

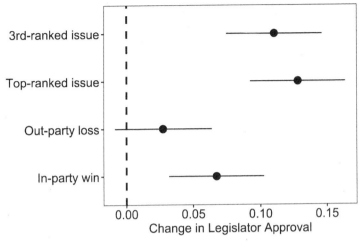

Figure 8.4. Effect of partisan quote and issue priority on evaluation of representative

Note: Change in legislator approval by experimental condition compared to the control group of no issue and no quote. Horizontal lines represent 95 percent confidence intervals.

condition, compared to the control, on respondent approval of the hypothetical member of Congress (rescaled 0–1). If respondents' third most important issue was listed as the member's issue priority, approval increased by 11 points ($p < 0.001$) compared to no issue priority being shown. If respondents' *top* issue was the member's top priority as well, approval increased by 12.8 points ($p < 0.001$). The difference between these coefficients is not statistically distinguishable from 0 ($p = 0.32$), indicating that while respondents favor legislators who list a policy priority over those who do not mention policy at all, they do not distinguish between issues that are more or less important to them personally.

Moving to partisan affect, recall that the profile could include a quote prioritizing the other party's loss or their own party's win in the next election, and that the legislator's party always matched the respondent's. Compared to the baseline of no quote shown, there was no statistically significant effect on approval when the legislator used the negative partisan rhetoric of making sure the other side loses ($p = 0.13$). On the other hand, when the quote focused on their side winning, approval increased by 6.7 points ($p < 0.001$).

As this study contains a true control category in that some people saw *neither* partisan communication nor policy information, I am also able to explore how policy and/or partisan information, regardless of the content, influences evaluations compared to showing none of this information. As demonstrated in prior chapters, partisan rhetoric often, but not always, co-occurs with policy language. Figure 8.5 shows the mean approval when the representative (from left to right): (1) expressed partisan rhetoric without an issue priority, (2) indicated an issue priority without expressing any partisan rhetoric, (3) both expressed partisan rhetoric and indicated an issue priority, or (4) neither expressed partisan rhetoric nor indicated an issue priority. People who saw just an issue priority, regardless of whether it was their most important issue, had significantly higher evaluations ($p < 0.05$) than people who saw just partisan rhetoric. But adding partisan rhetoric to a legislator who already references a policy priority does nothing to increase approval. Referencing a partisan win/loss in an election does increase approval over not referencing any partisan or policy information at all, but it is enough for legislators to *only* invoke an issue priority to receive the maximum approval.

Together, these findings provide further evidence that respondents care the most about policy and that they even prefer in-party "cheerleading" over out-party rhetoric. Respondents showed greater approval for legislators who prioritized an electoral win for their party than for those who prioritized a loss for the other party (+4 points, $p = 0.02$), but prioritizing an important issue increases approval even more than prioritizing an electoral win (+5.9 points, $p = 0.01$). Looking at the impact of the presence of

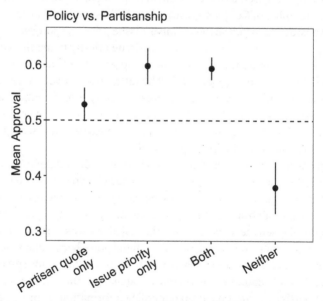

Figure 8.5. Mean representative approval across pooled conditions

Note: Plot shows average approval rating for people seeing just a partisan quote (in either quote condition), just an issue priority (in either issue condition), both a partisan quote and an issue priority, or neither a partisan quote nor an issue priority. Vertical lines represent 95 percent confidence intervals.

partisan/policy information per se regardless of the content of that information, the mere presence of policy information increases approval just as much as the presence of *both* policy information and partisan rhetoric. These results challenge the widespread notion that making sure the other party loses is more important than one's own side winning.

CONCLUSION

Across three experiments, I find that citizens penalize representatives for negative partisanship compared to substantive representation. Respondents reacted as negatively when same-party representatives insulted the out-party as when they had incongruent policy positions. While contemporary narratives would have us expect that out-party loathing is more motivating than in-party loyalty, respondents across multiple studies also preferred positive rhetoric about their own party to negative rhetoric about the out-party. Taken together, the findings suggest that individuals overall prefer representation that is focused on constituency service and policy agreement rather than on partisan affect.

This research has several important implications. First, it highlights the need to explore the limits of mass-level affective polarization. Druckman and Levendusky (2019) insightfully note that it is not clear who survey respondents think of when they are asked to evaluate the other party: ordinary voters or elected officials? While they find that most people think of representatives when denigrating the out-party, the results here show that does not necessarily translate into preferences for representation itself.

Second, politicians are strategic in their public behavior, acting in ways that are presumed to be electorally beneficial. While the external rewards and benefits of negative representation were analyzed elsewhere in this book, my results here suggest that such behavior may turn off citizens. Moreover, politicians are accurate in their perceptions of what citizens want. A great deal of research in legislative studies examines whether elites have accurate perceptions about their constituents' preferences. Most often, this work finds that elites misperceive the policy positions of the public, which has detrimental effects on the quality of representation (Broockman and Skovron 2018; Butler and Dynes 2016). My research offers a new contribution in this line of work analyzing whether elites have accurate perceptions of public's attitudes. In chapter 5, I showed that the candidates and political leaders think that using strong partisan rhetoric (either affective or electoral) will decrease candidates' chances of winning elections. Instead, ideological congruence with voters was perceived as being important for gaining support. The findings from my mass public samples analyzed in this chapter suggest that these perceptions in the aggregate are accurate.

That there are examples of politicians engaging in this behavior and sometimes even being rewarded for it does not mean that these experiments lack external or ecological validity. A particular strategy may work with some voters some of the time, but here I have discerned whether we can expect such a strategy to work on average across a sample of Americans. The findings across all five elite and mass public experiments show that these appeals are not thought by politicians to garner support *and* that they do not lead to more favorable evaluations by voters.

Overall, the implications of this chapter are hopeful for the health of American representative democracy. Claims that Americans are only (or even primarily) driven by partisan animus when evaluating elite behavior may be overblown. To be sure, scholars are right to be troubled by the extent to which people are willing to express negative affect toward their fellow citizens. However, when it comes to representation, these expressions are more symbolic than instrumental. People may welcome opportunities to inflame partisan negativity in surveys, but such emotional proclivities fall by the wayside when they are asked what they actually prefer for political representation.

9. SELECTIVE TOLERANCE: THE SUBGROUPS THAT TURN A BLIND EYE

Americans want representation based on the issues that matter to them. Even though people are less likely to trust and associate with members of the other party, they are turned off when elected officials denigrate the other side. While social-psychological theories about partisan identities may explain why people view members of the other party so negatively, that does not mean they want elites who invoke their partisan identities at the expense of focusing on policy or quality service responsiveness.

This evidence offers an important correction to current narratives about affective polarization and negative partisanship. Negative partisanship is considered a powerful and consistent motivating force in American politics. Even though the first section of this book demonstrated the ubiquity of negative representation, chapter 5 showed little support for the voter-driven hypothesis, which posited that politicians use this representational style to court voters. Using original survey experiments on samples of political candidates and elected officials, I found that elites believe negative partisanship is a losing electoral strategy. The analysis of the (null) relationship between vote share and negative representation suggested that these perceptions are accurate. The experiments in chapter 8 add more evidence that affective partisan rhetoric is not favored by the public and, in most cases, leads citizens to evaluate legislators much more critically.

The implications for what it would mean if people really do disfavor negative representation are profound. Partisanship may very well be a social identity that drives an emotional type of polarization that cannot be explained by issues alone (e.g., Iyengar, Sood, and Lelkes 2012). But if the public prioritizes policy and constituency service over partisan rhetoric, then politicians who often take part in expressive partisanship are *intentionally* acting against their constituents' preferences. People in general disapprove of negative representation, and politicians know it. It may make sense to go as far as to say that negative representation is therefore poor representation. As examined earlier in the book, elites are responding to other incen-

172 CHAPTER NINE

tives when they engage in such partisan behavior, such as media exposure and out-of-state donations, not to mention their own personal, psychological motivations. But they do not seem to be giving their constituents what they want most. The data also demonstrate that the representatives who do this the most are also the least effective lawmakers at advancing important pieces of legislation in Congress. Not only are politicians engaging in negative representation misaligned with their constituents' preferences; they also exhibit legislative inefficacy. How do they get away with it?

OPPORTUNITIES FOR LEEWAY

An important gap remains in understanding how people respond to the negative representational styles they seem to dislike so much. I have so far shown that (1) negative representational styles are distinct from representational styles based on policy, (2) elites think that voters *in general* dislike negative representation and instead prefer policy representation, and (3) that perception is spot on: voters *in general* dislike negative representation and much prefer policy-based representation. Are there certain influential subsets of the electorate who respond favorably to, or at least tolerate, negative representation? Under what conditions might negative representation *not* be penalized? How people in general react, and how elites (mis)perceive these reactions, is an important contribution on its own to understanding the impact of representational styles on democracy. For a more complete picture, we need to look specifically at the groups who are most likely to respond favorably or, at the least, look the other way. Even if the public in the aggregate is turned off by negative partisanship, perhaps there is a smaller, more engaged constituency that reacts positively to either partisan cheerleading or hatred toward the opposition. For example, perhaps party activists do not disfavor negative representation to the extent that other, more apathetic citizens do. If so, this would offer an opportunity for leeway. Politicians may be able to engage in negative representation for other incentives, like gaining media exposure, without compromising support from voters to such a degree that they would lose elections.

Indeed, research shows that politicians have leeway in many aspects of their jobs. There are situations in which legislators can act on their own accord without obvious electoral repercussions. For example, constituents are aware of legislators' positions and hold them accountable for voting out of step with individual preferences (Ansolabehere and Jones 2010; Canes-Wrone, Brady, and Cogan 2002). However, incumbents almost always win reelection, and when they do lose it is often due to a larger national trend, like the "Republican Revolution" in 1994 led by Newt Gingrich or the 2006 "Blue Wave" when Democrats took back over both chambers. On the rare occasions when an incumbent loses without the influence of these broader national swings in control, the reason is most often not simply a direct consequence of their voting record.

It is instructive to consider the abundant research showing that there is little evidence that moneyed interests have influence over roll call votes (e.g., Milyo 2015). After all, votes are easily monitored by constituents and opponents, difficult to change, and constrained by previous decisions. There are opportunities for politicians to respond to donors at other stages in the legislative process in ways that would be less traceable by constituents. For example, in a classic study on the influence of money on legislator behavior, Hall and Wayman (1990) argue that PAC money is more effectively spent at the committee and subcommittee level because legislators' efforts at this stage of the process are hidden from constituent scrutiny and provisions incorporated at this stage have a better chance of surviving. Similarly, Kalla and Broockman (2016) show that members of Congress are much more likely to take meetings with a political organization that has previously donated to the legislator. Overall, the research in this area has focused on these voter "blind spots"—when behavior is not visible to the public, there is potentially leeway for politicians to act without being held accountable for their actions.

In the case of negative representation, however, rhetoric is necessarily more visible. Indeed, it is the whole point. If there is significant variation among Americans in their evaluations of partisan rhetoric, politicians can use that rhetoric without necessarily turning off enough voters to lose elections. Additionally, people may give legislators leeway to use this rhetoric (even if they dislike it) as long as they are receiving good representation in other ways. This allows legislators to respond to both internal and external motivations to engage in partisan rhetoric without worrying about the potential negative consequences. In other words, if negative representation has a null effect on perceptions under some conditions, constituents may turn a blind eye to such behaviors, allowing politicians more room to engage in rhetoric that may be more polarizing than they would otherwise consider prudent.

In this chapter, I examine whether preferences for negative partisanship differ along several dimensions. First, we need to know which individuals feel the most negatively toward the other party and are thus most likely to reward or tolerate elites who engage in negative partisanship. I analyze out-party affect across several subgroups. The findings are generally consistent with arguments in the literature about the types of people most susceptible to affective party attachments. People who are highly politically interested or ideologically extreme, who have donated money to political candidates or campaigns, and/or who vote in primaries have high levels of out-party animus. I break down out-party animus along other lines as well, such as party identification, race, and gender, to understand how different segments of the public may respond to negative representational styles.

Second, I further tease out the experimental evidence about the effects of negative partisan rhetoric compared to issue representation. Do primary voters or political donors reward partisan attacks in a way that other constituents do not? What about strong ideologues or Trump supporters? Despite the fact that these (and others) are the groups most likely to be motivated by negative partisanship, I do not find a single one that favors expressions of negative partisanship by elites. At the same time, the effects of negative representation are, in some cases, statistically indistinguishable from zero. While some people do not favor such expressions, they do not penalize them either, which may offer elites leeway to use such language in a targeted way without losing support.

Over and over again I will show that, even though many groups have above-average levels of negative partisan identity, they generally do not support negative partisan rhetoric from elites. These findings highlight how persistent, widespread, and robust negative reactions to negative representation really are. So much of the current narrative about American politics would have us believe that at least some, if not all, citizens not only favor this behavior from representatives, but actively seek it out. Yet this is not borne out empirically. Even though Americans do not actively favor negative representation, they also passively accept it in some circumstances. I find that when expectations for policy representation are met, politicians have leeway to express negative partisanship without severe consequences. However, the overall negative reaction to negative partisanship has a counterintuitive flip side: when choosing between two styles of representation, constituents would actually prefer a representative who disagrees with them on policy issues over a representative who eschews position-taking on issues in favor of denigrating the other party. In other words, when the political environment is characterized by negative partisan rhetoric rather than policy, poor substantive representation is accepted. Since partisan rhetoric does not take place in a vacuum and is often in response to polarizing discourse from the other side, negative representational styles may have more negative downstream effects for democracy than previously thought. If there is no obvious electoral mechanism to stop such behavior, politicians can reap the benefits of using it (such as garnering attention and exposure in the media) and further reinforce the feedback loop of perceived polarization. Overall, the findings in this chapter suggest a set of conditions that allow for maximum negative representation and minimum substantive policy representation, which has significant implications for democracy in an era of negative partisanship.

WHICH CONSTITUENTS ARE NEGATIVE PARTISANS?

Reactions to negative representation are conditioned, theoretically, by voters' feelings toward out-partisans. People who strongly dislike members of the other party should agree with elite sentiments denigrating the out-party. While the main treatment effects for the experiments in chapter 8 were negative, meaning that elite negative partisanship is disliked on average, the effects may be different for people who strongly loathe other-partisans and have high levels of negative partisan affect.

So who dislikes the other side? First, political engagement and interest is correlated with strength of partisanship (Campbell et al. 1960). The highly engaged or active therefore have high levels of (positive or negative) partisan identity (Bankert 2021; Iyengar and Westwood 2015; Klar, Krupnikov, and Ryan 2018). Both political donors and primary voters are not only more engaged and interested in politics (by definition); they are also often more ideologically extreme (Barber 2016; Fiorina and Abrams 2012; Hill 2015). Other demographics may also influence someone's level of negative partisanship. The growing racial divide between Republicans and Democrats has contributed significantly to affective polarization (Abramowitz and Webster 2018). As the parties have increasingly sorted along lines of race, a distinct group-oriented "white identity politics" has emerged along with affective polarization (Jardina 2019). Gender is also an important factor that contributes to affective attachments. Women respond less favorably to political incivility and animosity (Deckman 2022; Phillips 2019). At the same time, women are more likely to identify strongly with a party (Norrander 1997, 1999; Ondercin 2018), are more ideologically extreme (Norrander and Wilcox 2008), have lower ratings of both parties overall (Greene and Elder 2001), and are more affectively polarized than men (Ondercin and Lizotte 2021). In summary, those predicted to report particularly negative ratings of the out-party are: individuals highly engaged or interested in politics, primary voters, political donors, extreme ideologues, white conservatives, and women.

Before I turn to these groups' reactions to elite expressions of negative partisan representation, I analyze whether they do in fact express negative ratings of the other party. I use the 2020 American National Election Study, which includes interviews with 8,280 American adults, to detect which people have above-average negative partisan animus.[1] The survey included standard feeling thermometer questions to capture ratings of both parties.[2] Respondents were asked to rate each party on a 0- to 100-point scale, with lower values representing less favorable evaluations. All figures shown in the next section plot the probability density distributions for each group across feeling thermometer ratings for the other party (Democrats' ratings for Republicans and Republicans' ratings for Democrats) on the 0- to 100-point scale. Higher values on the x-axis mean respondents rate out-partisans favorably and thus have low partisan animus. Lower values on the x-axis mean respondents rate out-partisans unfavorably and thus have high partisan animus. For this analysis, I rely on just the ratings of out-partisans. The difference between in-party loyalty and out-party loathing is important for exploring the *gap* in affective feelings about the parties, but here we are primarily interested in feelings toward opposite partisans given the theoretical framework about differential treatment effects. People who strongly dislike members of the other party might reward negative partisan attacks, regardless of how they feel about their own party. Later, I also estimate associations between these individual-level characteristics and ratings of the out-party, ratings of the in-party, and the difference between these ratings in a regression analysis for a more complete picture of these relationships.

In chapter 6 I compared ratings of the other party by the public and by political leaders to examine the hidden elite-driven layer of polarization, and found that elites have even more negative affect toward the other party than do ordinary citizens. As a starting point for analyzing subgroups, figure 9.1 again shows the distribution of partisan animus for the entire mass public sample. The distribution is heavily skewed to the right; the unweighted mean is 18.7 (denoted by the vertical dashed line) and the median is 15 with a standard deviation of 20.8. Forty percent of respondents gave the other party the lowest possible rating of zero. In figure 9.2, if a distribution has a mean out-party rating (denoted by a solid line) to the left of the dashed vertical line, it means they rate the other party *less favorably* than the average rating for the full sample and have relatively high levels of partisan animosity. If the mean (solid line) is to the right of the dashed line, the group rated the other party *more favorably* on average and have relatively low levels of partisan animosity.

Race and Ethnicity. White respondents were the only group with a below-average rating of opposite partisans (17.3). White respondents' feelings toward the other party are significantly lower than those of Black, Hispanic, Asian, and Native American respondents ($p < 0.001$), which generally follows the literature on race and affective polarization (e.g., Abramowitz and Webster 2018).

Gender. Men have more animus toward the out-party than women. Women have an out-party rating of 19.5; men are slightly more negative toward the out-party (17.8, difference significant at $p < 0.001$).

News Interest.[3] People who are highly interested in politics have substantially lower ratings of the other party (11.5) compared to people who do not indicate a high interest in politics (21.1, difference significant at $p < 0.001$). This is one of the largest differences we see.

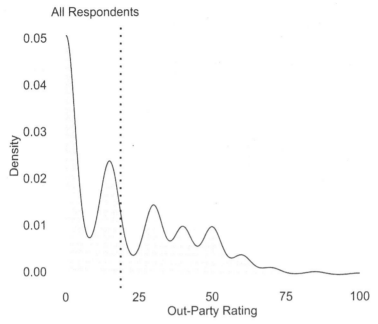

Figure 9.1. How Americans feel about the other party

Note: Plot shows the density probability distribution of feeling thermometer ratings for opposite partisans. Vertical dotted line shows the mean for the full ANES sample.

Primary Voters. Primary voters also feel much less favorably toward outpartisans compared to nonprimary voters. Primary voters give the other party a rating of 15.6 compared to 22.2 for people who did not vote in the primary ($p < 0.001$).[4]

Political Donors. Political donors have one of the lowest ratings of the outparty. Their rating of the other party is almost a full 10 points lower than people who have never donated to a political candidate or campaign ($p < 0.001$).

Party Affiliation. Party identification is only weakly related to partisan affect. Republicans loathe Democrats slightly more than Democrats loathe Republicans. Their rating is only 1.9 points lower than Democrats' rating, though this small difference is statistically significant ($p < 0.01$).

Trump Supporters. What matters more than partisan affiliation is whether someone is a strong supporter of Donald Trump. The survey asked respondents whether they approve or disapprove of the way Trump is handling his job as president. Those who answered "strongly approve" gave the other party an average rating of only 12.8 on the 0- to 100-point scale, while those who did not strongly approve of Trump gave an average rating of 21.6 ($p < 0.001$). This suggests the presence of a "Trump Effect," the phenomenon

178 CHAPTER NINE

that Trump's neglect of norms of civility leads people to tolerate and express more uncivil rhetoric themselves (Schaffner 2020).

Ideologues. Liberals and conservatives, overall, feel about the same level of partisan animus. As expected, the real difference is between strong ideologues and everyone else. People who identify on either polar end of the ideological scale, whether on the left or the right, rate the other side about the same. That is, the difference between people who selected "extremely liberal" and "extremely conservative" is not statistically significant. But these groups are significantly more negative toward the out-party than are their less extreme ideological counterparts. People who identify as "liberal" are 5 points more favorable toward out-partisans than those who identify as "very" liberal ($p < 0.001$), and "conservatives" are over 5.5 points more favorable than those who identify as "very" conservative ($p < 0.001$). Non-ideologues, on the other hand, feel much warmer toward the other side. People who are not sure of their ideology give other-partisans a rating of 24, and ideological moderates have the highest rating of other-partisans of any group in the graph at 27.8.

Of course, while the results in figure 9.2 are instructive, they cannot give us a clear sense of which of these traits matter the most. For example, do people who are more interested in politics loathe the other party more because of how much political news they consume, or is it because these people also tend to vote in primaries, or donate to candidates, or identify as ideologues? To sort out which identities matter the most in predicting how much an individual dislikes the opposing party, I estimated three separate ordinary least squares regression models—one predicting assessments of the out-party, one predicting assessments of the in-party, and one predicting the difference in how a respondent rated both parties. The results from these regression models can help us to sort out which traits are most predictive of one's level of negative (and positive) partisanship.

The first set of results, given in table 9.1, show whether a particular variable is associated with more positive or more negative feelings toward the out-party. For example, Asian Americans and Hispanic Americans rate the out-party 5 and 3 points (respectively) more positively than white Americans do. Notably, Republicans rate Democrats about 6 points more favorably than Democrats rate Republicans, indicating that after controlling for other factors, Democrats are the more vehement negative partisans. The results also reflect what we saw in the distributions—namely, that moderates rate the opposing party much more favorably (nearly 8 points more warmly) than do liberals or conservatives. Several traits produce considerably more negative sentiments toward the out-party. People who have high interest in politics and political donors rate the other party about 5 points more negatively (compared to people who are not interested in politics and people

Selective Tolerance 179

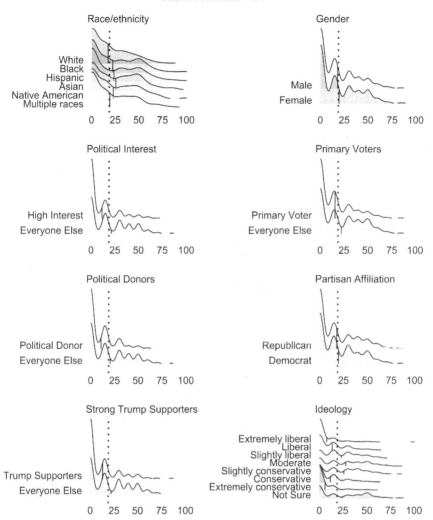

Figure 9.2. Negative partisanship across different constituency groups

Note: Plot shows the density probability distribution of feeling thermometer ratings for opposite partisans by individual-level characteristics. Vertical dotted line shows the mean for the full sample; solid line shows the mean for each subgroup.

who have not donated to a political campaign, respectively). Primary voters are about 3.5 points more negative toward the out-party than are people who did not vote in that year's primary election. The largest single coefficient in the first column is for Trump supporters. People who strongly approve of Trump rated the other party about 12.6 points lower than those who were not strong approvers.

Table 9.1. Regression Analysis Estimating Ratings of the Parties

Predictors	OUT-PARTY RATING Coef. (s.e.)	IN-PARTY RATING Coef. (s.e.)	IN-PARTY– OUT-PARTY Coef. (s.e.)
(Intercept)	21.21 * (0.60)	68.67 * (0.60)	47.51 * (0.93)
Male	−0.88 (0.48)	−4.25 * (0.48)	−3.38 * (0.74)
Asian	5.10 * (1.36)	1.71 1.34)	−3.42 (2.09)
Black	0.04 (0.89)	7.33 * (0.89)	7.27 * (1.37)
Hispanic	3.00 * (0.88)	2.79 * (0.87)	−0.28 (1.35)
Multiple races	0.23 (1.39)	−1.68 1.38)	−2.01 (2.14)
Native American	1.87 (1.87)	−2.29 (1.86)	−3.26 2.89)
Republican	6.23 * (0.84)	−10.37 * (0.83)	−16.73 * (1.29)
Conservative	0.23 0.87)	0.44 (0.86)	0.28 (1.34)
Moderate/not sure	7.91 * (0.67)	−1.43 * (0.67)	−9.35 * (1.03)
Trump supporters	−12.59 * (0.71)	19.86 * (0.71)	32.62 * (1.09)
High news interest	−5.25 * (0.57)	2.62 * (0.57)	7.88 * (0.88)
Primary voter	−3.53 * (0.50)	2.61 * (0.50)	6.11 * (0.77)
Political donor	−4.97 * (0.62)	1.88 * (0.61)	6.88 * (0.95)
Observations	6377	6374	6352
R^2 / R^2 adjusted	0.156 / 0.155	0.152 / 0.150	0.209 / 0.207

Note: * $p < 0.05$

Many of these same traits are also related to how one feels about one's own party. However, these associations are typically weaker, which speaks to the point that negative partisan affect is stronger than positive affect for one's own party. For example, interest in politics, primary voting, and political donating are all associated with feeling more positive about the in-party, but the magnitude of these effects is only about half as large as for out-party ratings. It is also worth noting that Black and Hispanic Americans feel considerably warmer toward their own party than white Americans do. Additionally, while there were no gender differences in terms of negative partisanship, men do feel significantly less positive about their own party compared to women. And, finally, it is striking that Republicans rate their own party about 10 points less favorably than Democrats rate the Democratic Party.

The final column in the table combines both measures to get the net affect—that is, the difference between how one rates their own party and how they rate the opposing party. Here we see patterns that fit well with what we observed in the first two models. Trump supporters, donors, primary voters, and those with high levels of political interest like their own party over the other party even more than the typical American does. The large negative coefficient for Republicans also underscores what we've already seen from the first two models—once we control for other factors, Republicans in this survey seem to be less affectively polarized than Democrats.

HOW DO DIFFERENT GROUPS REACT TO NEGATIVE PARTISAN REPRESENTATION?

Several patterns emerge from the preceding analyses. The groups with the highest ratings of the other party, controlling for other characteristics, are (1) people who are ideologically moderate or unsophisticated, (2) people who are not highly interested in politics, and (3) Asian and Hispanic Americans. Others, such as Democrats, women, and people who do not donate to political candidates or vote in primaries, are not particularly favorable toward out-partisans. If having unfavorable views of the other party is a mechanism for preferring negative partisanship as a representational style, then we are interested in the groups that had above-average levels of partisan animus. These are people who are highly politically interested, political donors, primary voters, strong Trump supporters, and ideological extremists. In this section, I examine each of these groups (and a few others) with regard to how they react to elite expressions of partisan affect.

Two of the experiments from chapter 8 are best suited to this purpose. First, Study 1 contained the same feeling thermometer measure of partisan animosity used above. Using this pre-treatment measure, I can directly analyze the theoretical mechanism at play: do people who feel very negatively toward the other party reward negative representation compared to policy representation? Second, I use the pre-election survey fielded as part of the CCES (Study 2) to analyze specific differences across subgroups. Since the CCES draws on a large, nationally representative sample and includes a variety of other questions as part of the survey, I can investigate whether evaluations vary by respondents' political engagement and other characteristics in a way that is not possible with the other experiments. For both conjoint experiments, the randomization of each politician profile enables a causal interpretation of estimates. Randomizing gender, race, partisan rhetoric, policy representation, and constituency service simultaneously enables me to estimate the causal effect of any one of these attributes averaged across all combinations of the others. To compare subgroups, I present the marginal means for any given attribute to estimate descriptive differences across groups (Leeper, Hobolt, and Tilley 2020).

DO NEGATIVE PARTISANS FAVOR NEGATIVE REPRESENTATION?

I first examine whether people high in negative partisanship themselves favor expressions of negative partisanship from elites. In this experiment, negative partisan rhetoric was not randomized independently of policy congruence. Rather, respondents selected between politicians who either attacked the other party, agreed with the respondent on policy, or disagreed with the respondent on policy. I show only the estimates for the partisan or policy rhetoric attribute, but the models include terms for all randomized attributes including race, gender, and quality of constituency service. The x-axis can be interpreted as the mean outcome across all appearances of the given conjoint levels. If an estimated marginal mean is above 0.5, then that type of rhetoric increased a politician's probability of being selected as the preferable representative. If an estimated marginal mean is below 0.5, then that type of rhetoric decreased a politician's probability of being selected.

Figure 9.3 shows how people extremely high in negative partisanship evaluate negative partisan rhetoric compared to policy representation. The plot on the top uses individuals' out-party ratings to measure negative partisanship (defined as giving members of the other party the lowest score of 0 on the feeling thermometer) and the plot on the bottom uses the difference between in-party and out-party ratings to measure net partisan affect (defined as having a net score of over 90 indicating a very high gap in how one feels about their own party compared to the opposite party). On average, representatives who express out-party affect are preferred only 40 percent of the time by people who do not have high negative partisanship. This is

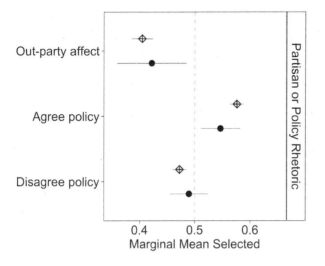

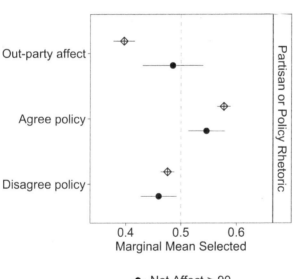

Figure 9.3. How negative partisans evaluate negative representation

Note: Plot shows estimated marginal means for partisan or policy rhetoric conjoint attribute across level of partisan animus. Model includes terms for other attributes not shown here: race, gender, party, and quality constituency service. Horizontal bars represent 95 percent confidence intervals. Cluster-robust standard errors by subject.

consistent with my earlier conclusions that elite out-party affect is penalized by voters especially compared to quality substantive representation (agreeing on policy). But what about people who actively loathe members of the opposite party? It turns out that negative partisan rhetoric does not appeal to these voters either. Representatives are selected at roughly the same rate by people with the most negative partisan affect (42 percent of the time). Looking at the plot on the bottom, when we take in-party attachments also into account, candidates were selected about 48 percent of the time when they denigrated the other party only by people who are affectively polarized—who have strong in-party loyalty and strong out-party animosity. The difference between individuals who are affectively polarized and everyone else is statistically significant at $p < 0.01$. While these people do not penalize partisan attacks quite as severely as everyone else, negative representation is still not rewarded. In contrast, policy congruence is rewarded by both groups at about the same rate. Politicians who share the respondents' policy positions are selected about 55 percent of the time by negative partisans using either measure, while politicians who oppose the respondents' policy positions are selected only 46–49 percent of the time.

These findings offer important insights about the consequences of affective polarization. Theories offered in the literature are very clear that these are exactly the types of people who will respond to partisan insults, attacks, and "othering" by politicians. If the American public is affectively polarized, then elites are thought to be held accountable based on the extent to which they denigrate the opposition. Instead, I find that even among voters who themselves dislike the opposition, denigrating the opposition is not a favored style of representation.

INVESTIGATING OTHER SEGMENTS OF THE ELECTORATE

To be clear, citizens with high negative partisanship do not reward negative representation, but when considering the gap between negative partisanship and positive partisanship, they do not necessarily penalize it either, and they are more likely to select politicians who use out-party rhetoric than are people who do not feel strongly about the parties. It is therefore important to examine the other groups who have overall high levels of partisan animosity. While people who hate the other side in general do not reward negative partisanship, maybe people who hate the other party and are political donors or extreme ideologues (for example) do. In the following sections, I estimate reactions from other subgroups: primary voters, political donors, people who contact their elected officials, highly interested voters, political activists, social media "activists," Republicans, Democrats, independents, liberals, conservatives, moderates, extreme ideologues, whites, Blacks, Hispanics, men, and women. I do not find a single one of these groups that responds favorably to negative partisanship.

Recall that the CCES experiment was a rating-based conjoint in which respondents indicated their overall approval for a single representative rather than choosing between two. The x-axis can still be interpreted as the mean outcome across all appearances of a particular conjoint level (such as out-party rhetoric or in-party rhetoric) averaged across all other features, but the outcome here is approval (on a 0 to 1 scale) rather than whether the representative was selected in a matchup against another representative. The vertical dashed line shows where the average approval is for the whole sample (54.4). If the marginal mean for any group is to the right of this dashed line, then that group has an above-average rating of politicians who had that attribute level. Also note that partisan rhetoric and policy congruence were randomized independently to enable me to simultaneously measure and compare the independent effects of these behaviors. Two different issues were randomized so that respondents could agree with the legislator on both, one, or neither of the two issues. "Full agreement" means that the legislator shared 2 out of 2 policy positions; "half agreement" means that the legislator shared 1 out of 2 policy positions; "full disagreement" means that the legislator shared 0 out of 2 policy positions. Respondents in this experiment always evaluated a politician of their own party, so the analyses estimate how people view expressions of negative/positive partisanship delivered by a politician from their own party and the relative importance of policy congruence in comparison.

PRIMARY VOTERS, POLITICAL DONORS, ENGAGED ACTIVISTS

Earlier in this book, I showed that elites do not think negative partisanship will help them win general or primary elections. In general elections, candidates have to appeal to a wider swath of voters, more of whom may be turned off by some extreme partisan styles. In primary elections, candidates seek to defeat opponents in the same party, so focusing on the out-party may be perceived as wasted energy. At the same time, it is possible that people who vote in primaries comprise a more engaged constituency that reacts positively to this type of rhetoric. The same logic applies for political donors or people who are politically engaged in other ways. Even if elites do not think negative partisanship wins elections overall, it may help them attract resources if people who contribute their money and time to campaigns are mobilized by partisan animus.

The 2018 CCES matched respondents to the voter file to validate whether they voted in that year's primary election for the midterms. Figure 9.4 shows the mean approval for primary voters (top plot) and political donors (bottom plot) compared to everyone else. There are few differences between primary voters and people who did not vote in the primary. Most notably, primary voters penalize legislators more than 10 points more than nonprimary voters do for disagreeing with them on both issues ($p < 0.001$). Legislators have an approval rating of 0.75 (on a scale from 0 to 1) among primary voters when there is agreement on both issues. Among nonprimary voters, approval is about 0.68. While both groups significantly reward legislators for sharing their policy positions, policy (in)congruence matters much more for primary voters than for nonprimary voters. As for partisan rhetoric, primary voters have an about average evaluation (0.53) of legislators who express negative partisan rhetoric, indicating that they do not favor these expressions but do not penalize them either. Expressing negative partisanship does not do anything to decrease primary voters' ratings of representatives, as it does for everyone else. Among nonprimary voters, politicians who use in-party rhetoric have a significantly higher rating (0.57) than politicians that use out-party rhetoric (0.517), but this difference is not statistically significant among primary voters. That is, partisan cheerleading is evaluated about the same as negative partisanship for primary voters, but partisan cheerleading is favored *more than* negative partisanship for nonprimary voters.

The patterns are similar for political donors. Donors also care strongly about policy congruence, and (dis)agreeing on more (fewer) issues results in a more (less) favorable evaluation among donors than among non-donors. Again, neither donors nor non-donors reward out-party rhetoric. The mean approval among political donors for out-party rhetoric (.496) is actually significantly *lower* than the overall mean, while the mean approval among non-donors is not (though the difference between donors and non-donors is not statistically significant).

As a robustness check, I examine people who report high political engagement in a multitude of other ways: writing to one's elected official, following political news, engaging in other political activities like putting up a yard sign or attending a rally, or posting about politics on social media. The results are similar. In no cases did these more engaged individuals report higher than average evaluations of a representative who used out-party affect. People who reported recently doing two or more political activities (whom I consider "activists") actually had below-average evaluations of representatives who used out-party affect, compared to their less engaged counterparts. In a few cases (e.g., for people who said they follow political news often), partisan affect neither increased nor decreased evaluations. This again highlights that while constituents penalize polarizing rhetoric from elites on average, individuals who are the most likely to pay attention to representatives' behavior are unaffected by such rhetoric, and rely

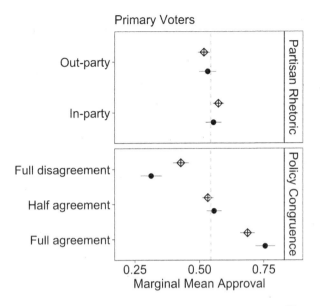

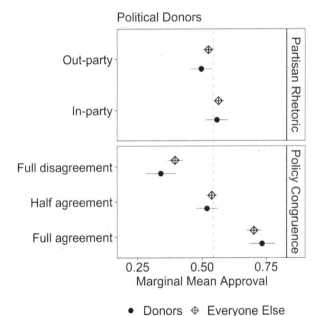

Figure 9.4. How primary voters and political donors evaluate partisan rhetoric and policy congruence

Note: Plot shows estimated marginal means for partisan rhetoric and policy congruence attributes across primary voters and everyone else (*top*) and political donors and everyone else (*bottom*). Model includes terms for other conjoint attributes not shown here: race, gender, and quality constituency service. Horizontal bars represent 95 percent confidence intervals. Vertical dashed line shows mean approval for full sample. Cluster-robust standard errors by subject.

instead on other dimensions to evaluate representation, such as how well they are represented on policy issues.

Overall, these are surprising results that are critical for understanding the effects and implications of affective polarization. Ample research suggests that as highly informed and engaged partisans, primary voters are exactly the type of people who would place partisan interests above all else (e.g., Bakker, Lelkes, and Malka 2019; Huddy, Mason, and Aarøe 2015; Lavine, Johnston, and Steenbergen 2012). Klar and Krupnikov (2016) show that there is a small portion of the mass public that does not support vitriolic cross-party disagreement, and t suggest that claims of affective polarization are overstated. The results shown here take this argument even further. Not only are party "leaners" turned off by negative partisan affect—so are the most loyal members of a party's base.

Social media facilitates uncivil, negative political communication. As seen in chapter 3, members of Congress use out-group appeals and attacks toward the other party on Twitter often *without* substantive underpinnings about policy. It follows that people who use social media to discuss politics are more desensitized to hearing such rhetoric from politicians. "Hobbyists" view politics as a spectator sport, something to win or lose, rather than a tool to actually enact policy change (Hersh 2020). Yet I find that these "armchair activists" who share political news on social media still do not respond favorably to their own party's politicians denigrating the other party on social media. At the same time, the analyses in chapter 7 showed that these types of tweets from members of Congress receive the most online engagement and are more likely to go viral than in-party or positive tweets. Even if people do not reward representatives with their votes or expressions of approval for negative representation, they reward them indirectly by giving them attention and boosting the exposure of these messages by causing them to be distributed more widely. If the people most likely to see and consume messages of partisan affect from representatives are not turned off by such messages, then representatives have leeway to follow the internal and external motivations for using a negative representational style without having to worry too much about losing support for their indulgence.

PARTY IDENTIFICATION AND THE TRUMP EFFECT

Previous scholarship suggests that partisan incivility is asymmetrical. Partisan identities have become wrapped up in other forms of identification, such as race and religion. The more any given individual sees their partisanship as a central form of identity, the more they are affected by partisan animosity. As the Republican Party is more socially homogeneous than the Democratic Party, Republicans are more prone to incivility and more sensitive to negative partisanship (Mason 2018a; Mason and Wronski 2018;

Roccas and Brewer 2002). Many self-identified conservatives actually prefer liberal policies (Mason 2018b), but they embrace symbolic—rather than concrete, policy-oriented—victories for the party in the name of "ideological purity" (Barber and Pope 2019; Grossmann and Hopkins 2016). In general, some sources find that conservatives have a more unfavorable view of Democrats than liberals have of Republicans (Pew Research Center 2014), but my analysis in table 9.1 showed that when controlling for other factors, liberals and conservatives have similar ratings of the other party. What really set people apart is whether they were moderate and whether they were a strong Trump supporter.

First, I test the hypothesis that Republicans and Democrats respond differently to negative partisanship; I show the results using the CCES experiment in the top plot in figure 9.5. As in the pooled analysis, both Democrats and Republicans have higher approval ratings for in-party rhetoric compared to out-party rhetoric. Unlike the pooled analysis, Democrats and Republicans have about average ratings for representatives who use out-party rhetoric, suggesting that the negative effect described in chapter 8 may be primarily driven by individuals who do not affiliate with a political party. Independents and people who are unsure of their partisan affiliation have significantly lower evaluations for representatives who express negative representation. This pattern fits with work by Klar and Krupnikov (2016) showing that many independents are turned off by partisan fighting among elites. However, this difference is also likely explained by the fact that the party of the legislators was randomized for nonpartisans, whereas partisans always evaluated the same-party legislators. Independents' baseline levels of approval were thus lower for all legislators, regardless of partisan rhetoric. The results are similar across ideology: liberals and conservatives do not penalize out-party rhetoric on average, but ideological moderates do (see the appendix to this chapter). Even though the distribution of out-party affect is different for ideologues on the extreme end of the left–right scale, the reactions to partisan rhetoric do not differ. We might expect that people who identify as "very" liberal or conservative reward out-party rhetoric, but I find that they give approximately average ratings for representatives who engage in this behavior.

Importantly, analyzing Study 3 from chapter 8 yields slight but important differences between Democrats and Republicans (see the bottom plot in figure 9.5). This experiment included two dimensions: a representative's out-party or in-party electoral-based rhetoric and a representative's policy issue priority. In the pooled sample, I found that out-party electoral-based rhetoric did not harm nor improve evaluations of the representative, but in-party rhetoric, as in the other experiments, improved evaluations. Listing an issue priority, regardless of whether or not it was the respondent's top issue priority, significantly improved evaluations. Analyzing Republicans

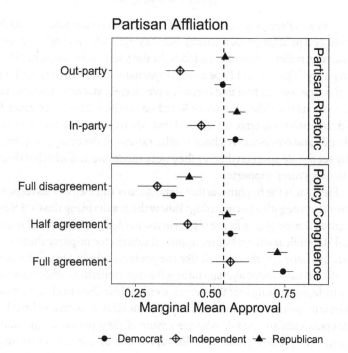
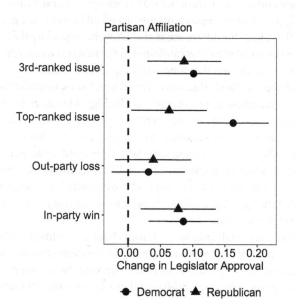

Figure 9.5. How Democrats and Republicans evaluate partisan rhetoric and policy congruence

Note: Plot shows estimated marginal means for partisan rhetoric and policy congruence attributes across party affiliation (Study 1 on the top; Study 3 on the bottom). Model includes terms for other conjoint attributes not shown here: race, gender, and quality constituency service. Horizontal bars represent 95 percent confidence intervals. Vertical dashed line shows mean approval for full sample. Cluster-robust standard errors by subject.

Selective Tolerance   191

alone shows a similar pattern across conditions, but the treatment effects for issue priorities and partisan rhetoric are very similar and not statistically distinguishable from one another. Legislators who talk about issues are not rewarded more by Republicans than those who focus on partisan wins/losses in an election.

On the other hand, Democrats not only approve more of legislators who prioritize an issue area over electoral negative partisanship or partisan cheerleading, but also take into account issue importance. Listing respondents' third most important issue as their issue priority boosted approval by 10 points, while prioritizing respondents' most important issue boosted approval by 16.3 points (+6.3 points, $p < .05$). On average, Democrats prefer representatives who focus on their issue priorities over those who engage in partisan rhetoric. For Republicans, the differences are smaller and not statistically significant. These results suggest that Democrats in particular are motivated by policy congruence and issue importance. While Republicans did not reward negative partisanship, they also did not reward policy congruence as much as Democrats and did not distinguish between issues that were more or less important to them.

Finally, we look at the results for Trump supporters (figure 9.6). Recall that being a Trump supporter had the strongest association with evaluating the other party negatively. No other variable predicted negative out-party sentiment as strongly as this single indicator. Thus, if there is any one group where we would expect *positive* reactions to negative partisanship, this is it. Nevertheless, the patterns in figure 9.6 once again show no strong differences—Trump supporters reacted to the out-party and in-party rhetoric in about the same way that all other adults reacted. Not even Trump's strongest supporters reward a legislator who employs out-party rhetoric.

In the appendix to this chapter, I also show the results by gender and race. While I did not find meaningful differences in partisan affect between men and women, some research suggests that women in particular are turned off by incivility and anger in politics. Moreover, as negative partisanship differs along lines of race, we might think there are heterogeneous effects in responses to negative rhetoric for white constituents. But I do not find any meaningful differences in reactions to negative representation across gender, race, or ethnicity.

POLICY REPRESENTATION PROVIDES LEEWAY FOR
NEGATIVE REPRESENTATION (AND VICE VERSA)

The previous analyses reveal a complex landscape of representational preferences. While some groups (like people who vote in primary elections and Trump supporters) harbor more negative feelings about the other party, expressions of negative or positive partisanship by representatives did not

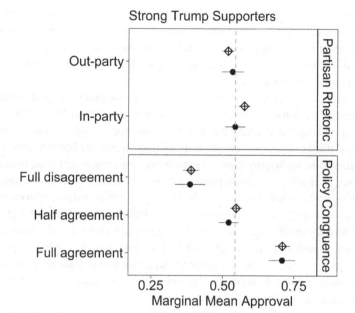

Figure 9.6. How Trump supporters evaluate partisan rhetoric and policy congruence

Note: Plot shows estimated marginal means for partisan rhetoric and policy congruence attributes across whether or not respondents "strongly approve" of Trump's performance as president. Model includes terms for other conjoint attributes not shown here: race, gender, and quality constituency service. Horizontal bars represent 95 percent confidence intervals. Vertical dashed line shows mean approval for full sample. Cluster-robust standard errors by subject.

shift their evaluations of those representatives. For others (like people who donate to political campaigns) negative partisanship by elites still had a negative effect on evaluations. Policy representation instead was the most important factor for these constituents. This underscores the importance of substantive representation, and also opens a window for what can be termed selective tolerance for negative representation, depending on policy alignment.

What is the interaction between policy representation and negative representation? Affective polarization has foundations in ideological polarization (see Iyengar et al. 2019). The more someone agrees with co-partisan leaders on policy, the more they tend to dislike the opposing party. Since policy agreement and partisan affect were independently randomized in this experiment, I can investigate approval for out-party and in-party rhetoric *across levels of policy agreement*.

Selective Tolerance 193

For the first time, out-party rhetoric has a statistically significant *positive* estimate. Figure 9.7 shows that representatives who agreed with the respondents on both policy issues have a higher-than-average approval rating (0.69 on the 0 to 1 scale when they use negative partisan rhetoric and 0.73 when they use positive partisan rhetoric). Representatives that share "half" policy agreement (1 out of 2 issues) and out-partisan rhetoric receive a statistically significant below-average evaluation (0.51), while in-partisan rhetoric slightly improves evaluations for half agreement (0.57). Finally, when representatives are in full disagreement (0 out of 2 issues shared) with respondents on policy, both out-partisan and in-partisan rhetoric receives very unfavorable evaluations.

The takeaway from this analysis is that policy-congruent respondents rate legislators higher overall *even if* they express negative partisanship. Negative rhetoric is not favored *compared* to positive rhetoric or policy

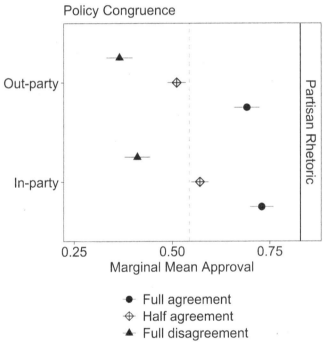

Figure 9.7. Partisan rhetoric is evaluated favorably if representative agrees on policy

Note: Plot shows estimated marginal means for partisan rhetoric conjoint attribute by level of policy agreement. Model includes terms for other attributes not shown here: race, gender, and quality constituency service. Horizontal bars represent 95 percent confidence intervals. Vertical dashed line shows overall mean approval for full sample. Cluster-robust standard errors by subject.

194 CHAPTER NINE

agreement, but when legislators agree with their constituents on policy they still receive very favorable evaluations, even when attacking the other party. These findings highlight the importance of substantive representation over negative representation, and also show that politicians may not be penalized for using a negative representational style in certain circumstances. When politicians are able to meet the policy expectations of their constituents, they can maintain high levels of constituent support even if they invoke negative partisanship. Negative representation is otherwise not a desired style of elite communication, but constituents are unlikely to hold their representatives accountable for it as long as substantive representation occurs.

When I dig deeper into the relationship between substantive representation and negative representation, I find that this leeway afforded by policy agreement goes the other way as well. In Study 1, representatives were evaluated side by side, so I can analyze the effect of partisan rhetoric depending on what the "opponent" (in the matchup to evaluate representation, not in an election) focuses on. I find that politicians are selected as the preferred representative less often if they focus on attacking the other party while their opponent focuses on policy, even if the policy focus is *incongruent* with the respondent's own positions (see the appendix to this chapter for these results). That is, respondents preferred a representative who *disagreed with them on policy* over a representative who used negative partisan rhetoric.

This is a counterintuitive flipside of negative representation being disfavored to such an extreme extent. When comparing two styles of representation, citizens almost always prefer a focus on policy over a focus on affective partisanship. But this means they are willing to sacrifice *agreement* on policy if it means not having a representative who is focused on affective partisanship. Of course, representation does not happen in a vacuum. As demonstrated earlier in the book, representatives focus on *both* policy and partisanship, often in the same newsletter or tweet. These findings suggest that the continued focus on partisanship has the power to amplify the positive effect of communication around policy, while at the same time diminishing the importance of actual policy responsiveness and representation. In short, in the contemporary environment where partisan rhetoric is so ubiquitous, people are willing to tolerate imperfect policy representation simply to avoid having to listen to yet another partisan attack.

* * *

Taken together, the findings from this chapter and previous chapters suggest a clear set of cases that allow for negative representation without penalties:

When policy representation is present. Constituents do not penalize legislators who engage in negative representation if the legislator indicates an issue priority or shares their policy positions.

Among certain segments of the electorate. Negative representation does not lead to lower favorability ratings or support among people who have high in-party attachment and high out-party animosity, highly engaged partisans, and people who strongly approve of Trump.

On social media. Negative representation receives positive engagement on Twitter, where out-party posts and posts that contain more negative words are retweeted and liked significantly more than in-party posts and posts that contain more positive words. Negative representation on Twitter also increases the amount of out-of-state money representatives fundraise for their campaigns.

Overall, this paints a complicated picture of the role negative representation plays in contemporary politics. Most people, even the most politically engaged partisans, would prefer that their representatives focus on policy instead of partisan attacks. But many people are willing to tolerate these attacks when legislators also focus on advertising their policy views. In particular venues, partisan rhetoric clearly generates more interest (clicks, retweets, and donations) than policy statements. We are therefore ultimately stuck in an environment where the public seems to have a clear preference for legislators who do not engage in partisan attacks, yet tolerates and sometimes even rewards negative representation.

10. THE PERCEPTION GAP

The lack of civility is very unproductive and it makes life miserable. Some people seem to like all this conflict, but I don't.

FORMER SEN. LARRY PRESSLER (R-SD), September 21, 2022

Scholars, journalists, and voters alike decry the state of partisan polarization in the United States. For at least the past ten years, Americans see more conflict between Democrats and Republicans than they do between other "divided" groups in society, such as rich and poor, Black and white people, young people and older people, and people who live in cities versus those who live in rural areas (Schaeffer 2020). Polarization has been studied by political scientists in terms of the actual divide between the parties, and also the *perceived* (by voters) divide between the parties (Armaly and Enders 2021; Chambers, Baron, and Inman 2006; Chambers and Melnyk 2006; Lee 2022; Lees and Cikara 2021; Levendusky and Malhotra 2016b; Stone 2020; Yang et al. 2016). These perceptions of polarization are important because they have real consequences for other attitudes and behaviors. Perceived polarization can exacerbate actual polarization because when people assume the other side is more extreme, they reciprocate by taking more extreme positions themselves and expressing more dislike for the other side (Ahler 2014; Westfall et al. 2015; Wojcieszak and Price 2012). Though scholars have examined how people perceive the extremity of opposite partisans' views on policy issues, we do not know how people perceive opposite partisans' views on representatives who exacerbate polarization through partisan rhetoric. Even though people do not themselves desire negative partisan representation at the expense of policy representation, do they think members of the other party do?

The difference between people's perceptions of reality and the actual state of reality is called *a perception gap*. Perception gaps have long been studied in social psychology (e.g., Robinson et al. 1995), political science (e.g., Levendusky and Malhotra 2016b), risk management and assessment (e.g., Ropeik 2012), and marketing and consumer behavior (Luk and Layton 2002). In chapter 6, I tested whether elites who have particularly low evaluations of the other party experience a "false consensus bias," in that they assume voters would desire a candidate who attacks the other party. However, my analysis found no evidence of such a bias. Even politicians who registered the most extreme dislike of the other party acknowledged that negative representation would not be a successful strategy for winning votes.

While the false consensus effect occurs when individuals overestimate the extent to which others agree with their own beliefs and attitudes, a false *uniqueness* effect occurs when people *underestimate* the extent to which others agree with their own beliefs and attitudes (Pope 2013). For example, an individual may think they are unique in having moderate political views while believing everyone else to be extremists. Both false consensus and false uniqueness result in a perception gap—a gap between people's beliefs about what others believe and what others in fact believe. In chapters 8 and 9 I showed how people overall do not personally support a negative representational style that focuses on out-partisan identities. In this chapter, I investigate whether partisans think *others* want negative representation. I also look at how variables like media consumption and educational level might expand or shrink the perception gap between these groups. Do Americans accurately perceive that people, even in the other party, generally dislike negative partisanship from elites? Or do they exhibit a false uniqueness bias in which they think others like negative partisanship from elites, even when they themselves do not? What is the gap, if any, between people's perceptions about what others want and what others actually want? The false uniqueness effect may be an important part of the story about why we get negative representation. Even if people do not themselves like negative representation, they might be more likely to tolerate such a representational style from their own side if they think most people on the *other* side welcome it.

MISPERCEPTIONS ABOUT OTHERS' BELIEFS

Throughout this book, I have drawn from social identity theory to help understand the phenomenon of negative representation. That same framework also helps us to understand how people form biased and inaccurate perceptions of in-groups and out-groups. In a classic study on in-group-out-group relationships, Tajfel (1970) argued that the mere act of categorizing people as "us" and "them" can itself produce negative intergroup affect and even discrimination. Categorizations then also lead to stereotypes and biased judgments about the traits, attitudes, and behaviors of the out-group. The area of metacognition more specifically considers people's perceptions about how others think. In one of the earliest studies in this area, Robinson et al. (1995) presented pro-choice and pro-life students with multiple scenarios about abortion. The students were asked to indicate how sympathetic they felt toward the person in the scenario getting an abortion and how sympathetic they thought someone with the opposite view would feel. Perceptions by both pro-life and pro-choice camps were greatly exaggerated. The subjects in the study thought their own views were motivated by practical, evidence-based concerns while the "other" group was motivated by ideology. People assumed that those who did not agree with them on the issue were naturally more ideological, more extreme, and less rational.

Most political science research on metacognition has similarly focused on (mis)perceived polarization along ideological lines—that is, the extent to which people perceive the other side as having more extreme issue positions than they actually do (Sherman, Nelson, and Ross 2003; Yang et al. 2016). In one such study, Levendusky and Malhotra (2016b) asked voters to place themselves on a set of issue scales and then to indicate where they thought the typical Democratic and Republican voter would fall on those scales. On average, people perceived partisans as being about twice as far apart on the issue positions as they actually were. People also overestimate the percentage of members of a political party who belong to certain groups. For example, in a 2018 study, people estimated that 38 percent of Republicans make over $250,000 per year, when in reality the figure was only 2 percent (Ahler and Sood 2018).

These misperceptions are not limited to how people perceive the other party's traits or issue positions; they also extend to how they think members of the other party behave. Both Democrats and Republicans report that the other side dehumanizes their own party more than is actually the case. Since they think they are dehumanized by members of the other party, they in turn express more dislike and dehumanization of the other side (Landry et al. 2021). Other research shows how perception gaps about political disagreement fuel partisan conflict, obstructionism, and support for anti-democratic behaviors (Lees and Cikara 2020; Moore-Berg et al. 2020; Pasek et al. 2022). For example, in a recent study by Pasek and colleagues (2022), both Democrats and Republicans valued democratic characteristics such as fair elections, yet they underestimated how much the other side valued the same characteristics. The more people underestimated support for democratic characteristics from the other party, the more accepting they were of practices to undermine democratic principles. Overall, misperceptions about what the other side thinks increase actual polarization, feelings of social distance, endorsement of political violence, dehumanization, and democratic erosion.

MISPERCEPTIONS ABOUT DESIRES FOR NEGATIVE REPRESENTATION

Perceptions about what the other side thinks about policy issues are of course different from perceptions about what the other side thinks about how politicians should speak about the parties. In a 2019 Pew Research Center survey, Democrats and Republicans both emphasized the importance of political civility, compromise, and respect. Eighty-five percent of the public, almost equally across both parties, said that political debate has become too disrespectful, and 67 percent said it is very important for "elected officials to treat opponents with respect." This is consistent with the results in this book, which indicate that Americans on both sides do not support politicians' use of negative partisan rhetoric, especially compared to policy-based rhetoric.

Yet the Pew survey uncovered some hypocrisy and a double standard in both parties. Seventy-five percent of Republicans said it was very important for *Democratic* elected officials to treat Republican elected officials with respect, compared to only 49 percent who said it was very important for *Republican* elected officials to treat Democratic elected officials with respect. Similarly, 78 percent of Democrats said it was very important for *Republican* elected officials to treat Democratic officials with respect, compared to only 47 percent who said it was very important for Democratic officials to treat Republican officials with respect. In simpler terms, partisans think it is more important for the other side to be civil than for their own side to be. At the same time, increasing numbers of people on both sides have negative views of each other, calling their partisan opponents "close-minded," "dishonest," and "immoral" (Pew Research Center 2022). Similar patterns showed up in questions about compromise; people thought it was more important for politicians from the other side to compromise than for politicians from their own side to do so.

These patterns give us some valuable insights into how partisans perceive each other and the importance of civil and compromising (as opposed to polarizing) rhetoric from representatives. The double standard observed suggests that partisans may be less inclined to pressure their own party's representatives to engage in more civil discourse and positive or policy-based representation. If people think representatives on the *other* side need to be more respectful and compromising, they may also think that voters in the other party are not placing enough pressure on their representatives to behave in this way, possibly because this is not what those voters want to see from their representatives. Individuals may believe voters in the opposing party actually *prefer* more combative and confrontational behavior from their own politicians. Empirical evidence about this type of metaperception is lacking.

Do people have accurate perceptions about the extent to which other-partisans desire negative representation? To answer this question, I fielded a set of questions with Social Research Surveys in December 2022 on a representative sample of 2,117 American voters. To get a baseline rate of the public's *actual* desire for negative representation, I first asked people whether they themselves would want members of Congress in their own party to talk about the other party rather than about policy issues. After answering several unrelated questions in the survey, I then asked these same respondents to estimate the percentage of voters in the opposite party who want the same thing from their own members of Congress. For example, Democratic voters were asked, "If you had to guess, what percent of Republican voters think that Republican members of Congress should talk about the Democratic Party rather than talk about policy issues?" I used survey weights for the analyses below to make more generalizable inferences about the population of American voters.

Figure 10.1 shows the results. The first circle on the left represents the *actual* percentage of Republicans and Democrats who said that they want negative representation, and the circle on the right represents the *estimated* percentage of Republicans and Democrats who want negative representation by members of the other party. About 23 percent of Democrats and 24 percent of Republicans answered that members of Congress in their respective parties should spend time talking about the other party rather than about policy issues. However, in each case, partisan respondents vastly overestimated these numbers. Republican respondents on average estimated that almost 58 percent of Democrats want their representatives to talk about Republicans rather than policy, and Democratic respondents on average estimated that over 55 percent of Republicans want the same of their own representatives. This results in a perception gap of about 31 percentage points among Democrats (about Republicans' desires) and 35 percentage points among Republicans (about Democrats' desires), and a pooled perception gap of 33 percentage points across all partisans. Put another way, people perceive that the other side's demand for negative representation is more than twice as large as it actually is.

As a point of reference, the perception gap in negative representation is larger in magnitude than the perception gap in ideology. Levendusky and Malhotra (2016a) estimated that the perception gap between estimated ideological polarization and actual polarization is about 20 percentage points, measuring issue stances on taxes, immigration, trade, and public

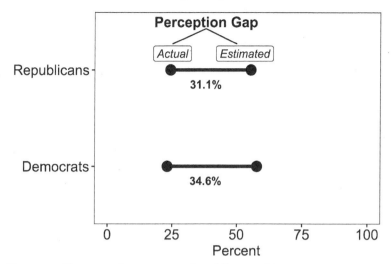

Figure 10.1. The perception gap among Republicans and Democrats
Note: Plot shows the actual (left dot) and estimated (right dot) percentage of Republicans and Democrats who said they desire negative representation.

financing. In 2019, the research organization More in Common asked a nationally representative sample about their perceptions on others' views, such as Democrats' agreement with the statement "most police are bad people" and Republicans' agreement with the statement "properly controlled immigration can be good for America." For these statements, More in Common estimated the out-group perception gap to be 37 percent and 33 percent respectively. In both of these studies, much as I've shown here, both Democrats and Republicans believed the other side held more extreme views than they actually did. Estimating out-partisans' views about policy or social issues, however, can be explained by availability heuristics that coarsely (though in many ways accurately) link issue positions with the two parties. More Democrats than Republicans have favorable views on immigration, so it is understandable that Democrats might assume Republicans would generally think immigration is bad for America, and vice versa regarding Republicans' views about the police. Perceptions about desires for negative representation, however, cannot so obviously be explained by cognitive connections to how the parties have sorted along ideological lines. Neither party is generally associated with negative representation or partisan rhetoric more than the other, and the analyses in chapter 3 confirm that both Democrats and Republicans frequently talk about the other party.

Figure 10.2 shows people's metaperceptions based on their own desire

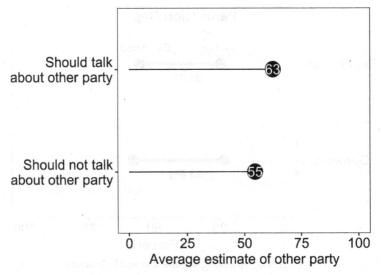

Figure 10.2. Average estimate of out-partisans based on own views
Note: Plot shows the estimated percentage of out-partisans that said they desire negative representation based on respondents' own answer to that question.

for negative representation. On average, Americans who themselves think members of Congress should talk about the other party estimate that 63 percent of out-partisans share that view. Americans who themselves think members of Congress should *not* talk about the other party estimate that 55 percent of out-partisans share the opposite view. The difference between these two groups is statistically significant at the $p < 0.001$ level, suggesting that a false consensus bias is more prominently at play than a false uniqueness bias. While everyone was likely to overestimate other-partisans' desires by a very large and significant amount, the extent of the overestimations trended in the direction of their own views.

In the next sections, I show how the perception gap—the difference between actual and estimated desires for negative partisan representation—differs (or does not differ) across various individual-level characteristics.

FAVORABILITY OF THE OTHER PARTY

To what degree are these misperceptions driven by affective polarization? Some research suggests that affective polarization fuels perceived ideological polarization. For example, using nationally representative panel data, Armaly and Enders (2021) show that as voters feel less favorably toward the other party, their perceptions of the distance between the parties on issue positions increases. The idea is that affective evaluations of the out-group help form further evaluations about the political world, like the distance between parties in ideology. The more people dislike the other political party, the more they tend to think the two parties are very different in their beliefs and agendas. Accordingly, we might expect that it is mostly people who strongly dislike the other party who think out-partisans are the ones exacerbating affective polarization and egging their respective political leaders on to wield partisan attacks. On the other hand, given other analyses in this book regarding the extent to which negative representation is amplified by the media, it would follow that *everyone* is under the impression that people are more motivated by partisanship than by policy. Headlines like "How Hatred Came to Dominate American Politics"[1] and "Negative Partisanship Explains Everything"[2] emphasize the idea that negative affect is widespread. These narratives persist despite research showing that a large portion of the American electorate is just not that interested in politics, let alone driven by hatred for the other side (Krupnikov and Ryan 2022). It is therefore important to understand how negative affect conditions the perception gap in negative representation.

The survey asked respondents for their level of favorability toward each party. Of course, not many respondents reported that they have a favorable view of the opposite party. About 12 percent of Democrats said they have a "somewhat" or "very" favorable opinion of the Republican Party, and 9 percent of Republicans said the same about the Democratic Party. Figure 10.3 shows that the perception gap among Democrats and Republicans is similar regardless of whether they have a favorable or unfavorable view of the other party. The only significant and meaningful difference is between partisans who answered that they have not heard enough about each party to say whether they have an unfavorable or favorable opinion about them. These respondents still overestimated the extent to which other-partisans desire negative representation, but significantly less on average than did people who expressed an evaluation of the other party. This follows Krupnikov and Ryan's (2022) findings about differences between people who are "deeply involved" in politics and everyone else. People who expressed a favorable view of the other party were just as likely as people who expressed an unfavorable view of the other party to think that other-partisans desired negative representation over policy representation.

Importantly, disliking the other party increases misperceptions that the other side holds extreme ideological views and vice versa (Armaly and Enders 2021). Here, disliking the other party is not associated with increased misperceptions. Perception of support for negative representation is categorically different from perception of issue positions. These results suggest that everyone is generally under the impression that the other side

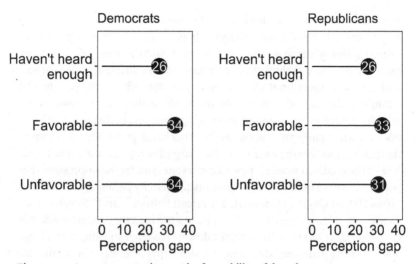

Figure 10.3. Average perception gap by favorability of the other party
Note: Plot shows average gap between actual and estimated percentage of out-partisans who desire negative representation by favorability of the other party.

contributes to partisan discourse, regardless of whether they themselves experience negative partisanship.

MEDIA SOURCES

Another potential driving factor for the perception gap might be how news sources portray the other side and the extent to which people are exposed to negative partisanship from these various sources. In chapter 7 I showed how negative partisanship from members of Congress on Twitter results in more retweets and likes on Twitter than positive partisanship. Moreover, I found that when members of Congress engage in partisan attacks on Twitter, it is more likely to be covered on Fox News and MSNBC than when members of Congress talk about compromise and bipartisanship. Partisan television news outlets have in recent years become more likely to cover the other party; Fox News mentions Democrats more than Republicans, and MSNBC mentions Republicans more than Democrats. If people consume certain media sources that promote and cover partisan division, they may be more likely to believe that out-partisans are fueled by negative partisanship.

The survey asked people to indicate whether they have in the last week gotten news about government and politics from various sources. Figure 10.4 shows average perception gaps by each source of news. Note that people could select multiple sources of news, so these categories are not mutually exclusive; some people who selected CNN as a source of news may also be part of the group identified as receiving news from Twitter, Facebook, or any of the other sources.

Perhaps unsurprisingly, people who received news from OANN or Newsmax, both far-right media companies, had the highest perception gap at 37 percent. These are, after all, news outlets that most actively engage in pushing misperceptions about Democrats. Notably, however, Twitter and the *New York Times* followed at 36 percent. The people with the lowest perception gap were those who received news from broadcast networks like ABC, CBS, or NBC (32 percent), and CNN, local television news, and MSNBC (33 percent). It is important to note, though, that the differences between these groups are relatively small. Nevertheless, it is perhaps significant that the perception gap is smallest among those who receive their news from broadcast networks and the largest gaps are for those who follow far-right news outlets and Twitter.

EDUCATION

In their study of perceptions about ideological polarization, Levendusky and Malhotra (2016a) found that the more educated people were, the more they overestimated polarization. More in Common found that this was only the case for Democrats; as Democrats' level of education increased, they expressed a larger perception gap between estimated positions of Republicans

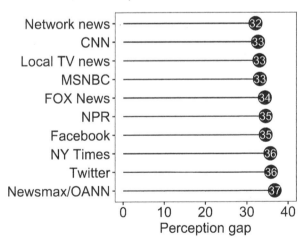

Figure 10.4. Average perception gap by news source consumption

Note: Plot shows average gap between actual and estimated percentage of out-partisans who desire negative representation by sources respondent received news from in the last week.

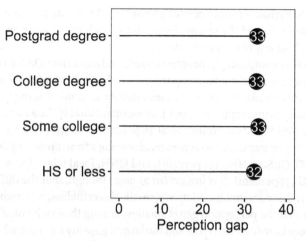

Figure 10.5. Average perception gap by education level
Note: Plot shows average gap between actual and estimated percentage of out-partisans who desire negative representation by education level.

and the reality of those positions. When it comes to estimations about desires for negative representation, I find that there is no meaningful association between level of education and one's perception gap (figure 10.5). People who did not pursue education after high school misestimated desires for negative representation by 32 percent, and everyone else misestimated desires by 33 percent. There are no meaningful differences by education between Democrats and Republicans.

VOTE CHOICE

Finally, voting behavior is a strong indicator of people's views of the political world. Even though I did not find evidence in chapter 9 that people who are strong supporters of Donald Trump (a president known for hostility toward out-groups) were favorable toward representatives who use negative partisan rhetoric, it is possible that these voters tolerate Trump's partisan attacks because they think the other side is to blame for such behavior. If this were the case, we might see a higher perception gap among people who voted for Trump. By the same token, people who voted for Joe Biden in 2020 were strongly motivated by anti-Trump sentiments (Albert 2022; Rakich and Mehta 2019; Sheffield 2019). We might then see a higher perception gap among Biden voters as well if they perceive Trump's rhetoric as reflective of or responding to the GOP's electorate.

I find some support for this in figure 10.6, which shows that people who voted for Donald Trump or Joe Biden in 2020 both overestimate how much the other side desires negative representation over policy by 33 percent, compared to people who voted for someone else at 30 percent and people who did not vote in the presidential election at 27 percent. These differences are not large, but they show that voting for one of the two major party candidates in 2020 is generally associated with thinking the other party's voters care less about policy than about partisan discourse. The fact that non-voters have smaller misperceptions is also noteworthy, especially if we recall that this was also true of people who did not rate the other party favorably or unfavorably. This is consistent with the notion that partisans who are less engaged in politics do not have the same strength of misperceptions as those who participate more in the political system.

CONCLUSION

Most people do not want politicians to focus on partisanship over policy. While I showed in chapter 9 that some groups, like strong Trump supporters and people who are especially politically engaged, do not actively express disapproval of representatives who do so, I also showed that practically *everyone* wants representation based on advancing a policy agenda. My findings in this chapter provide evidence for that as well. Yet Twitter timelines and television news media would have us believe not only that politicians spend a great deal of time expressing negative partisanship (which,

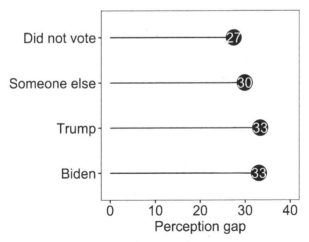

Figure 10.6. Average perception gap by 2020 presidential vote choice

Note: Plot shows average gap between actual and estimated percentage of out-partisans who desire negative representation by 2020 presidential vote choice.

in chapter 3, I found to be only partly true—in fact, they talk more about bipartisanship, compromise, and policy-related topics on average), but also that people in the mass public respond favorably to such expressions. Affective polarization, driven by politicians and the media, creates the perception that everyone is in on this game. Like the quote opening this chapter by former senator Larry Pressler, people think, "*I* may not thrive on partisan hostility, but others surely do."

People substantially overestimate the extent to which members of the other party think their representatives in Congress should talk about the opposing party rather than focusing on policy. The gap between perceptions and reality is large for all groups analyzed (the highly educated, people who consume network news, people who consume news on social media, people who voted for Trump in 2020, people who voted for Biden in 2020, and so on), which shows that it is not just a small subset of people who have wildly inaccurate perceptions. Thinking that people in the other party care more about partisanship and less about policy is a misperception that runs deep for broad segments of the population. While people who indicated they do *not* desire negative representation themselves had a significantly smaller perception gap than people who do desire negative representation, they still overestimate other-partisans' desires by over 30 percentage points.

Of course, as with all survey research on capturing accurate beliefs, this study is not without its limitations. First, it is possible that, due to social desirability bias, most people did not accurately answer the question about their own desire for negative representation over substantive representation in rhetoric. That would mean that the "actual" estimate (that is, what people said when asked if they themselves want negative representation) is biased downward and that more people *do* want their politicians to talk about the other party rather than policy. Yet the findings from several conjoint experiments (which have been shown to reduce social desirability bias and elicit more truthful preferences) presented in earlier chapters provide strong evidence that this is not the case. Across several studies and experiments, I find that most people do not prefer representatives who talk about the parties rather than policy. Moreover, this aligns with other surveys about the perceived importance and desire for more civility and compromise in politics (e.g., Tyson 2019).

Some may argue that the "estimated" estimate (that is, what people said when asked how many other-partisans want negative representation) is biased upward. This might be the case if respondents give an estimate that is larger than what they actually think as an artifact of the survey. Once explicitly primed to think about whether members of the other party want representatives to talk partisanship instead of policy, they may give an exaggerated estimate in response to the prime. Of course, the potential for such priming is almost always a possibility in survey research. Yet what people report when explicitly asked, even if primed, is important on its own and is a critical first step to understanding metacognition in this area. Even if people exaggerate their estimates, it is important to consider why. We know from other studies that people already do perceive deepening polarization and negativity in American politics. Giving a high estimate of out-partisans who desire polarizing rhetoric from representatives, even if it is exaggerated, is a signal that people sense that political discourse from the other side is focused too much on partisanship at the expense of policy.

When individuals have inaccurate perceptions of the beliefs of others, it can lead to further conflicts and misunderstandings. Democrats and Republicans may express support for political violence (see Kalmoe and Mason 2022) or obstructionist tactics (see Lees and Cikara 2020), for example, because they believe members of the opposite party want the same. This could further polarize society as well as make it more difficult for politicians to work together to address important policy issues. Likewise, a similar process may occur when it comes to negative representation. Even though people do not like it when their representatives engage in partisan rhetoric (particularly if they do so instead of talking about policy), they may be more willing to tolerate such an approach if they think the other side is pushing for it. Such a dynamic may promote a reinforcing cycle. In the concluding chapter, I consider this possibility further and propose some ways we might be able to push against these misperceptions and break out of the cycle of negative representation.

11. THE RACE TO THE BOTTOM (AND THE WAY BACK UP)

You become what you give your attention to.

EPICTETUS

Politicians polarize. They exploit real or manufactured concerns to make the other side out to be a bogeyman who is to blame. In an age when partisanship is a divisive identity, separating people into "us" and "them" camps, political leaders can represent their constituents by "othering" the opposing party. After losing an election, members of Congress talk about the other party more, and in a more explicitly negative way on social media. When the opposition responds to polarizing rhetoric with similarly divisive rhetoric, they contribute to a cycle that entrenches polarization in society. Ideological extremists in both parties are the most likely to invoke the out-party, presumably to critique their opponents. These extremists are also less likely to talk about policy and compromise. The more time representatives dedicate to the other party in their communications to constituents to discuss the other party, the less they advance legislation in the chamber. While people do not on average desire negative partisan rhetoric from representatives, they often turn a blind eye to it under certain conditions. People on Twitter are more likely to engage with posts from members of Congress who share negative, partisan attacks rather than positive posts or messages focused on policy. The news media rewards out-party negative rhetoric with more attention, so people in the mass public perceive more polarization than actually exists and consequently tolerate more divisive rhetoric from representatives, solidifying the cycle.

THE FUTURE OF REPRESENTATION IN THE AGE OF NEGATIVE PARTISANSHIP

The issue of representation in an era of heightened political polarization extends beyond mere rhetoric—it raises serious questions about the core functions of a democracy. One of the basic premises of representative democracy is that politicians act as conduits for the will of their constituents. High levels of affective polarization can hinder productive political discourse and make it more difficult for politicians to represent the needs and interests of their constituents. It is striking that lawmakers engage in negative representation despite having accurate perceptions of what voters want. Much of the foundational research on representation posits that politicians act according to constituents' preferences (Erikson, MacKuen, and Stimson 2002; Erikson 2013; Tausanovitch and Warshaw 2014). Other studies suggest that politicians sometimes do not know what constituents want and thus do not act accordingly (Arnold 1990; Broockman and Skovron 2018; Butler and Dynes 2016; Miler 2010). When it comes to negative versus policy representational styles, politicians are aware of what constituents desire but do *not* act accordingly, likely due to the array of other benefits and influence that accrue from negative representation.

This disparity raises critical questions for future research on representation. There is an urgent need to examine in greater detail what the consequences are when lawmakers consciously choose a path that contrasts with Americans' preferences despite being fully aware of what their constituents desire. This book shows that this dissonance leads to a perception gap, where people think the other side favors negative representation over policy more than they do in reality. What are other downstream effects? The consequences could manifest in declining voter turnout, reduced faith in governmental institutions, and an erosion of social cohesion. These adverse effects may not be immediately visible but could become pronounced over time, eroding the very foundation of a democratic society.

One significant factor that allows this behavior to persist is the electoral environment in which lawmakers at the federal level operate. Legislators from districts that are overwhelmingly partisan find themselves somewhat immune to electoral pressures. They engage in negative partisanship the most frequently and fervently, as the ideological uniformity of their constituency often shields them from backlash. This immunity emboldens them to perpetuate polarizing rhetoric without facing substantial political costs. As we contemplate the future of partisan rhetoric and negative representation, understanding the implications of this electoral stability becomes crucial. There is little incentive for politicians to adjust their behavior if the penalty for negative representation is not large enough to even threaten their incumbency. With minimal turnover in Congress, the future could very well see an amplification of the trends outlined in this book. Future research should focus on primary elections as well, which serve as the initial gatekeeping event that dictates the type of candidates who will proceed to general elections. Understanding the dynamics in these contests could shed light on how extreme or moderate candidates are elected in the first place.

There are other long-term implications of role model effects and candidate entry. The "role model effect" refers to the phenomenon in which the presence of political figures from certain groups—based on gender, race, sexual orientation, or other categories—inspires individuals from that group to become more politically engaged or aspire to political office themselves. This effect serves as a mechanism for fostering political inclusion and could lead to increased diversity in political systems over time (e.g., Ladam, Harden, and Windett 2018). But the flip side is true as well: if only a certain type of politician or legislative behavior is visible, this may decrease engagement and political ambition on the part of other types of candidates. The type of representation citizens observe sets a standard or norm for what is acceptable. If potential future leaders are constantly exposed to a divisive, polarizing style of governance, this could influence the next generation of political figures to adopt similar tactics. In general, other research has documented how some candidates opt out of the field as partisan polarization increases (Hall 2019; Thomsen 2017). The cumulative effect could lead to an even more fractured and divided political environment, further shaping the ideological contours of political representation and influencing the quality of democratic representation in the long term. For instance, as lawmakers increasingly adopt polarizing tactics, the potential for bipartisan policymaking may decline further, resulting in legislative stagnation. These trends may also cultivate an environment conducive to democratic backsliding, where norms and institutions that sustain democracy are systematically eroded.

The findings presented in this book thus have broader implications that extend far beyond the current state of affairs. They challenge us to think more deeply about the nature of representation, the institutional structures that encourage or inhibit polarizing behavior, and the long-term consequences of negative representation on the future of democracy. The challenge ahead is not just understanding these dynamics, but also devising strategies to rectify the deficiencies in our current system of representation.

How do we find our way back up from the race to the bottom? Of course, I have no single or straightforward answer to this—it is a topic for other scholars to consider. Here I briefly discuss four considerations based on social science research that are important for understanding the current moment, which also have the potential to lead others to design concrete solutions to the vicious cycle of negative representation. These considerations are: keeping perspective of the ways in which affective polarization has *not* ruined democratic representation, valuing the benefits of partisanship and polarization, identifying interventions to reduce mass-level partisan animosity, and addressing the attention economy and negativity biases.

THE WAY BACK UP

Keeping Perspective

This book presented several worrisome findings regarding how partisan rhetoric is associated with a decline in substantive representation and results in public disillusionment with elected officials and out-partisans. At the same time, there are several important silver linings. Policy language still dominates in legislative communications, above and beyond partisan language. Calls for bipartisanship and compromise have actually *increased* over time. Political elites think focusing on partisan rhetoric is not a successful electoral strategy. Instead, ideological congruence with voters is viewed as the most important way to win elections. This is borne out in what actually happens in elections: the number of times a legislator invokes out-partisan language in their communications is not associated in any meaningful way with the number of votes they receive in the next election. Despite being affectively polarized, voters prefer representational styles focused on policy agreement and do not want to sacrifice substantive representation for negative representation.

Of course, the problem is when an "us versus them" dynamic becomes an integrated part of representation and all that Americans think they can expect out of their leaders. Deepening polarization escalates interpersonal conflict (Kalmoe and Mason 2022), increases tolerance for undemocratic measures to defeat the other side (Lees and Cikara 2020; Moore-Berg et al. 2020; Pasek et al. 2022), and erodes citizens' faith in government (Pew Research Center 2022). Parties and politicians become more focused on scoring symbolic partisan victories than on working together to advance a legislative agenda that reflects the needs and interests of their constituents (Lee 2009). For these reasons, it is important to consider ways out of this race to the bottom, but such considerations must keep in perspective the ways affective polarization and negative partisanship do *and do not* necessarily wreak havoc on American democracy. In this book, I have presented ways in which it does, but also ways in which it does not. Accounts of affective polarization and its destructive effects for representation must be based in evidence, rather than panic.

The Benefits of Partisanship and Polarization

We also must not overstate the harms of partisanship (or even polarization) itself. Partisanship and polarization are not inherently or always bad. Political disagreement is an expected and necessary part of any healthy, functioning democracy. People with different views need to compete and negotiate with one another to make progress on shared concerns. Without its corrupting pathologies, partisanship itself helps people make sense of issues, organize complex information, and make more informed decisions (e.g., Aldrich 1995; Kam 2005; Page and Shapiro 1992). Consequently, elections without party labels have lower turnout and citizen participation than do partisan elections (e.g., Schaffner, Streb, and Wright 2001).

Political scientists have long recognized that having two strong yet diverging political parties is good for American democracy. E. E. Schattschneider (1960) argued that a competitive party system expands the scope of conflict in politics, bringing the public into the policymaking process. Only through strong competitive parties can representative democracy live up to its name without being corrupted by special interests. Parties govern for the common good, bringing together many fragmented interests to hold politicians accountable. La Raja and Schaffner (2015) provide evidence that polarization and gridlock stem from a system that is candidate-centered, rather than party-centered. If party organizations had more resources, they would support more moderate candidates and promote pragmatist legislative behavior that appealed to the most voters. The political theorist Russ Muirhead argues in *The Promise of Party in a Polarized Age* (2014) that "what politics needs is not less partisanship, but better partisanship." Part of Muirhead's argument is that the parties have real disagreements about the approach to politics and the role of government that should not be ignored in favor of nonpartisan deliberation. Parties offer a useful way to legitimately adjudicate between these disagreements.

While most political scientists agree that partisanship itself is constructive, not as many seem to think that the increasing separation and division between the parties is beneficial, especially when that division bleeds into other social cleavages. Since partisanship overlaps with racial, religious, and other cultural identities, more partisan polarization also means more *social* polarization, which makes it more challenging to work toward the "better partisanship" based on good-faith disagreements and compromise that Muirhead endorses. However, some scholars argue that affective polarization does not have the significant downstream effects on democratic norms and accountability that some claim it does (Broockman, Kalla, Westwood 2023). Moreover, incivility in politics has the power to activate emotions that stimulate engagement and action (Gervais 2017; Marcus, Neuman, and MacKuen 2000; Valentino et al. 2011). Many citizens are turned off by the vitriol of partisan politics (Klar, Krupnikov, and Ryan 2018; Krupnikov and Ryan 2022), but if wielded appropriately, polarizing rhetoric can be an antidote to a disillusioned and apathetic public. It is no coincidence that turnout in American elections has increased significantly during the past couple of polarizing decades.

How to Reduce Partisan Animosity

While we must resist exaggerating the harms of polarization and conflating healthy levels of partisanship with severe partisan animosity, it is also important to identify solutions to problematic levels of affective polarization. The rising panic about our polarizing electorate and its associated consequences had led scholars in recent years to investigate interventions that successfully reduce political conflict (e.g., Landry et al. 2023; Mernyk et al. 2022; Santos et al. 2022). In an effort to synthesize this research, the recent Stanford University "Strengthening Democracy Challenge" issued a call for research proposals for interventions to reduce partisan animosity and strengthen democratic attitudes. Of over 250 submissions, 25 were selected and fielded in a survey on a large sample of American adults.

The results were promising. Nearly all of the studies selected (23 of 25) successfully reduced individuals' reported feelings of partisan animosity, and several others also reduced anti-democratic attitudes and support for political violence. The principal investigators of the project identified two strategies that were the most effective at reducing partisan animosity: "highlighting relatable, sympathetic exemplars with different political beliefs" and "highlighting a common cross-partisan identity" (Voelkel et al. n.d.). These most effective interventions had survey respondents watch videos about reconciling interpersonal differences, read about how the media distorts and exaggerates political division, and learn about how most Americans do actually support democracy and share a common identity.

At the end of the day, the solution for negative rhetoric from political elites will have to come from elites, not from voters. The research in this book shows that even if Americans do have high levels of partisan animosity, they do not reward representational styles that reflect such animosity. So why should we focus on reducing mass-level affective polarization? Partisan animosity weakens the stability of our personal relationships (Chen and Rohla 2018) and has a number of other detrimental effects outside the political realm (Chopik and Motyl 2016; Huber and Malhotra 2017). The strategies that have been found to be successful at reducing voters' partisan animosity might offer insight about what might work to, at the least, lessen the power such rhetoric has over the electorate. Whether that would also work to lessen the extent to which politicians use such rhetoric is an open question. But lessening affective polarization at the mass level is a worthy goal in its own right.

216 CHAPTER ELEVEN

The Attention Economy and Negativity Bias

The media plays a vital role in shaping our understanding of the world around us. In the digital age, we are constantly exposed to an abundance of information from a diverse array of sources. Sifting through this deluge of information can be challenging, and the way in which we focus our attention plays a significant role in how we make sense of it all. Political scientists have long studied whether Americans are informed enough to participate meaningfully in the political process (e.g., Converse 1964), but experts in cognitive processing suggest that the question is not one of information, but of attention (Davenport and Beck 2001; Simon 1971).

The media often portrays negative images of polarization and focuses more on partisan fights than on compromise. Ironically, this coverage uses tactics similar to those they criticize—pushing sensational headlines and emphasizing conflict to attract viewers. Democrats and Republicans consume very different forms of media, political and otherwise (Young 2020). And our political identities increasingly overlap with other social identities (Mason 2018a), which means that consuming partisan news scratches more than one itch. The economics of attention scarcity and information surplus therefore encourages and rewards the amplification of these already existing divisions. Social media algorithms additionally take advantage of these differences and continue to push us toward more biased information that further entrenches perceptions of polarization.

The solution must be two-sided. First, social media companies can implement safeguards on technological platforms for disinformation, hate speech, and imbalanced feeds. Tromble and McGregor (2019) advocate for a social-science-based agenda for improving social media platforms that have social consequences. They argue that tech giants like Facebook and Google need to integrate social science thinking and evidence into their operations to design more informed solutions and theoretical perspectives of their potential impact. In short, engineers and programmers need to be cognizant of the social implications of their technology and actively bring more social scientists on board to help design solutions to these multifaceted problems. Of course, social media platforms are not the only culprit bleeding our attention and fueling polarization. Traditional news outlets also amplify perceptions of polarization and provide incentives for politicians to engage in partisan warfare. To be sure, there are many instances of journalists pushing back against disinformation (e.g., flagging Trump's false statements) and centering stories that are important to cover in a democracy (e.g., the January 6 insurrection and the ensuing investigation). I do not mean to suggest that the media should not cover newsworthy stories and important threats to democracy or instances of partisan violence. But when our television anchors incessantly share stories of Twitter-fights between members of Congress, we become blind to the reality that members of Congress more commonly talk about legislation, bipartisanship, and compromise.

The second solution must be consumer- and viewer-driven. After all, out-partisan tweets by members of Congress go further on Twitter because users retweet them more than they do policy-based tweets. The negativity bias in individuals is, in part, evolutionary, and it is not a phenomenon limited to the United States (Soroka, Fournier, and Nir 2019). Approaches that simply inform individuals of their implicit negativity biases and make them aware of the problem can be effective in reducing partisan animosity or perceptions of polarization (Voelkel et al. 2022). These approaches, however, are likely not enough on their own to alter cognitive biases that determine long-standing media selection habits (e.g., Devine et al. 2012; Santos and Gendler 2014). Individuals must deliberately apply new strategies to their behavior and actively flex their reflective muscles (Arceneaux and Vander Wielen 2017).

SUMMING UP

There is a lot more to be examined about the role of partisan rhetoric in political representation. This book shows that members of Congress use partisan language more often on social media than in newsletters where they have more space to communicate. Politicians and candidates themselves express high levels of partisan animosity, but they do not believe negative partisanship is an effective way to win votes, especially compared to ideological representation. Congress members who talk a lot about the other party, often in negative terms, are also less effective at their more central representative duties. The more representatives focus on negative partisanship, the less actual legislation they sponsor and pass in Congress. Strikingly, the American public is critical of partisan warfare and wants politicians to focus on policy instead, but is not dissatisfied enough to vote representatives out of office. Thus, even though it is not what constituents say they want, representatives have leeway to follow both instrumental and expressive motivations to denigrate the other side at the expense of actual policy representation. These findings have important implications for both future research and political practice, as they suggest that politicians who prioritize policy discussions may be more likely to appeal to voters. Insecure majorities have incentives to inflame partisan negativity given the reward system of the media environment, but perhaps less than originally thought.

We must keep in mind the ways affective polarization is handed down by politicians, not just driven by preexisting divisions in society. Elected officials both reflect and create these divisions. By choosing to focus on policy-based messaging and avoiding divisive language, politicians have the power to set norms and expectations for political representation.

ACKNOWLEDGMENTS

This book was made possible through the collective effort, wisdom, and support of many people and organizations. The following acknowledgments offer a modest attempt to express my gratitude to them.

I have been very fortunate to work with an amazing team at the University of Chicago Press and I am extremely grateful for their confidence in this project. My two editors, Sara Doskow at Chicago and Frances Lee with the series Chicago Studies in American Politics, were indispensable in helping me think big about the questions and problems posed in this book, and each of them offered invaluable feedback. Special acknowledgment is due the two anonymous peer reviewers, whose excellent suggestions made this book infinitely better than it could have been otherwise. Thank you to Evan Young, Rosemary Frehe, Lindsy Rice, Michaela Luckey, and the rest of the team at Chicago.

Institutional support from Dartmouth College was critical for the success of this book. Thank you to the administration and my colleagues there for offering a professional home that made this project feasible. Thank you as well to Harvard University's Center for American Political Studies, which for two years provided me with a space to write and to bring this project to completion.

I owe special thanks to many incredible scholars who offered helpful feedback on various parts of this book, including Zack Albert, Steve Ansolabehere, Jason Barabas, Austin Bussing, Dan Butler, Ivelisse Cuevas-Molina, Ryan Enos, Jeff Friedman, Anne Hannusch, Michael Herron, Mike Kowal, Devin Judge Lord, Nick Miller, Russ Muirhead, Thomas Nelson, Brendan Nyhan, Jeremy Pope, Katy Powers, Brian Schaffner, and Wouter van Erve (thanks especially to Zack for coming up with the much simpler, more intuitive "negative representation" to replace the alternatives I was considering). David Broockman, Michael Gauger, Christian Grose, Nathan Kalmoe, Laura Moses, and Katelyn Stauffer all served as discussants for this project at one point or another, and their careful reading and incisive

220 *Acknowledgments*

comments greatly improved the research. I am also grateful for conversations with David Eckles, Ray La Raja, Tatishe Nteta, and Brian Schaffner for helping me to sort through my thinking and refine presentations of concepts that appear in this book.

I also benefited from insightful dialogue and feedback from participants at multiple venues, including conferences hosted by the American Political Science Association, the Midwest Political Science Association, the Southern Political Science Association, Women in Legislative Studies, the Cooperative Election Study, Dartmouth Program in Quantitative Social Science, Dartmouth Department of Government, the Rockefeller Center at Dartmouth, the Elite Experiments mini-conference, and the Junior Americanist Workshop series. In addition, I was fortunate to have the opportunity to present this research at Harvard University, Yale University, State University of New York at New Paltz, Washington University at St. Louis, the University of Toronto, the University of Notre Dame, and the Centre Universitaire de Norvège à Paris with the Roots of Inequality Workshop. My gratitude extends to the participants and audience members at these institutions for their comments, which enriched the quality of this work.

Thank you to three anonymous reviewers at the *American Journal of Political Science* and the journal's editors Kathleen Dolan and Jen Lawless for their constructive feedback on the article "Ideology, Not Affect: What Americans Want from Political Representation," which forms the basis for one of the chapters in this book. This article was really the starting point for the entire project. I was not planning on writing this book, or any book at all, until the response to that article made me realize there was a lot more story to tell. For other extremely helpful advice as I navigated the book-writing and publishing process, I am grateful to Nathan Kalmoe, Katy Powers, Alice Kang, Jenn Jerit, Tali Mendelberg, and Nazita Lajevardi.

The legislative communication analyses in this book were made possible thanks to Lindsey Cormack, who runs the DCInbox project, an invaluable source of data and public service to the scholarly community and beyond. Thanks as well to Runxin Gao for helping to access and compile that data. And many thanks to Steve Rathje, Jay Van Bavel, and Sander van der Linden for sharing their congressional Twitter data, which are used in the book. Thank you to Annelise Russell for also sharing congressional Twitter data, and to Carlos Algara for sharing and updating Gary Jacobson's election returns data. John Cho, Holland Bald, Erin Parker, Hayley Piper, and Felix Davis provided exceptional research assistance. Emily Lukas and Felix Davis, students in my American Political System class at Dartmouth, helped with proofreading and caught an embarrassing number of typos.

Special thanks to Duygu Akdevelioglu, Anne Hannusch, Lindsey Novack, and "Coach" Maggie Andersen for unwavering and irreplaceable support, both personal and professional, from the beginning of this journey. I am grateful to Jackie Pedowicz for cheering on "Poli Sci & I" throughout the last few years, and for conversations with Chris Shanky that made all of this feel easier than it actually is.

Finally, I am grateful to my family, including Andrea Costa, Angelo Costa, Lisa Costa, Alex Costa, Brian Schaffner, Karen Schaffner, John Schaffner, and Fonzie Costa-Schaffner for their encouragement. Thank you especially to Brian, who has already received three different mentions in these acknowledgments for his varied forms of support. It is still not quite enough, so thank you, Brian, repeatedly and infinitely.

APPENDIX TO CHAPTER 3

LIST OF POLICY WORDS FOR DICTIONARY

abortion; agricultural; agriculture; amendment; appropriation; bicameral; bill; budget; business; citizenship; climate; committee; consumer; consumers; corporation; corporations; crime; debt; defense; deficit; drugs; economic; economy; education; employment; energy; environment; finance; firearms; fiscal; fossil; gdp; gun; guns; health; healthcare; housing; immigration; incarceration; issues; jobs; justice; labor; legislation; legislative; Medicaid; Medicare; nuclear; penalty; petition; policing; policy; pollution; poverty; prison; prisons; reform; refugee; regulation; renewable; resolution; rights; rule; science; security; sustainability; sustainable; tax; taxation; taxes; taxing; technology; terrorism; terrorists; trade; trafficking; unemployment; veto; wage; wages; warming; welfare

POLICY, PARTISAN, AND IDENTITY MENTIONS IN CONGRESSIONAL NEWSLETTERS AND TWEETS

Table A3.1. Average Counts per Legislator (with 116th Congress and Race and Gender Terms)

	ALL CONGRESSES		116TH CONGRESS	
	Avg. total in newsletters	Avg. total in tweets	Avg. total in newsletters	Avg. total in tweets
Out-party	17.066	35.577	27.464	60.747
In-party	16.074	18.953	21.032	30.35
Policy	770.297	570.778	841.523	897.685
Bipartisan	21.043	28.663	33.37	49.418
Election	7.461	12.62	17.532	22.451
Race	6.986	14.866	11.723	28.063
Black	4.451	10.257	7.832	19.392
Latino	1.648	3.576	2.777	6.731
Women	16.566	28.882	18.076	47.438

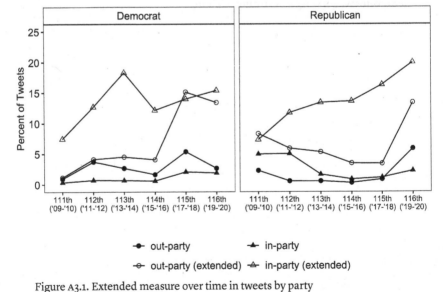

Figure A3.1. Extended measure over time in tweets by party

Note: Percentage of tweets that contain mention of this book's measure of out-party and in-party compared to the "extended" measure (including terms such as liberal, conservative, and names of high-profile party members).

EXTENDED PARTISAN RHETORIC MEASURE

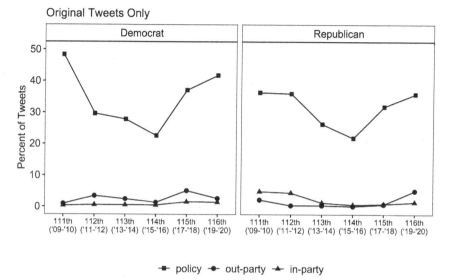

Figure A3.2. Policy, out-party, and in-party mentions in tweets excluding retweets

Note: Percentage of tweets that contain mention of policy, out-party, and in-party, excluding retweets.

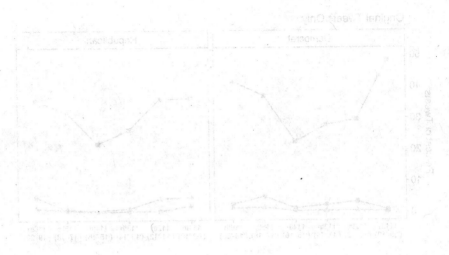

APPENDIX TO CHAPTER 4

REGRESSION MODELS PREDICTING LANGUAGE IN NEWSLETTERS AND TWEETS

Table A4.1. OLS Regression Predicting Partisan and Policy Language in Newsletters

| Predictor | DEPENDENT VARIABLE: MENTIONS IN NEWSLETTERS | | | |
| | Out-party | In-party | Bipartisanship | Policy |
	Coef. (s.e.)	Coef. (s.e.)	Coef. (s.e.)	Coef. (s.e.)
(Intercept)	−5.27	−4.90	26.07 ***	411.45 ***
	(3.93)	(3.41)	(4.01)	(99.66)
Male	0.35	−1.95	−5.14	−21.66
	(2.59)	(2.28)	(2.73)	(59.18)
African American	−5.76	−3.29	−4.69 *	−72.48
	(3.61)	(2.67)	(2.28)	(75.50)
DW Nominate	27.24 **	18.51 **	−50.34 ***	−439.96 *
	(9.01)	(7.04)	(7.60)	(221.12)
Republican	6.24 *	13.11 ***	7.17 ***	428.25 ***
	(2.69)	(1.79)	(2.16)	(60.45)
Seniority	0.43	0.15	−0.40	−7.15
	(0.23)	(0.19)	(0.23)	(5.42)
Party leader	10.29 *	15.00 **	6.89	149.29
	(4.56)	(5.21)	(4.26)	(123.37)
Legislative effectiveness	−2.03 **	0.33	1.50 *	45.46
	(0.78)	(0.78)	(0.64)	(23.34)
112th Congress	7.00 ***	8.23 ***	11.54 ***	380.49 ***
	(1.36)	(1.09)	(0.86)	(31.02)
113th Congress	3.91 *	6.10 ***	17.24 ***	318.89 ***
	(1.52)	(1.39)	(1.40)	(40.88)
114th Congress	1.22	4.21 **	17.02 ***	321.18 ***
	(1.80)	(1.38)	(1.63)	(43.79)
115th Congress	12.03 **	6.98 ***	23.33 ***	448.06 ***
	(3.97)	(1.85)	(1.99)	(53.95)
116th Congress	19.13 ***	12.77 ***	31.56 ***	447.56 ***
	(2.58)	(2.03)	(2.36)	(51.24)
Observations	2881	2881	2881	2881
R^2 / R^2 adjusted	0.045 / 0.041	0.081 / 0.077	0.132 / 0.128	0.095 / 0.092

Note: * $p < 0.05$; ** $p < 0.01$; *** $p < 0.001$

Table A4.2. OLS Regression Predicting Partisan and Policy Language in Tweets

Predictor	DEPENDENT VARIABLE: MENTIONS IN TWEETS			
	Out-party	*In-party*	*Bipartisanship*	*Policy*
	Coef. (s.e.)	Coef. (s.e.)	Coef. (s.e.)	Coef. (s.e.)
(Intercept)	−35.80 *	3.77	84.13 ***	902.08 ***
	(18.11)	(6.23)	(7.02)	(96.10)
Male	10.09	0.96	−6.35	−153.74 **
	(11.19)	(3.85)	(4.34)	(59.39)
African American	−25.72	−8.49	−15.75 **	−204.83 *
	(15.04)	(5.18)	(5.83)	(79.85)
DW Nominate	168.93 ***	58.29 ***	−61.14 ***	792.24 ***
	(35.43)	(12.19)	(13.74)	(188.04)
Republican	20.20	−8.82 *	−12.39 **	−528.67 ***
	(11.39)	(3.92)	(4.42)	(60.47)
Seniority	0.39	0.67	−1.18 **	−12.88 *
	(1.06)	(0.37)	(0.41)	(5.63)
Party leader	126.98 ***	57.23 ***	14.16	328.81 **
	(23.79)	(8.18)	(9.23)	(126.27)
Legislative effectiveness	0.53	0.34	2.95	24.58
	(4.89)	(1.68)	(1.90)	(25.95)
Observations	404	404	404	404
R^2 / R^2 adjusted	0.171 / 0.156	0.183 / 0.169	0.160 / 0.145	0.264 / 0.251

Note: $p < 0.05$; ** $p < 0.01$; *** $p < 0.001$

APPENDIX TO CHAPTER 7

REGRESSION MODELS PREDICTING FUNDRAISING

Table A7.1. OLS Regression Estimating Effect of Rhetoric on Twitter on Total Fundraising Dollars

	DEPENDENT VARIABLE: TOTAL DOLLARS FUNDRAISED (IN THOUSANDS)			
	Twitter		Newsletters	
Predictors	Coef. (s.e.)	Coef. (s.e.)	Coef. (s.e.)	Coef. (s.e.)
Out-party mentions	6.16 ** (1.98)		−15.82 *** (3.62)	
In-party mentions	8.81 (6.93)		38.18 *** (5.29)	
Policy mentions	−1.17 ** (0.40)	−0.70 (0.36)	−0.81 *** (0.25)	−0.07 (0.20)
Bipartisanship mentions	7.94 (4.70)	9.22 (4.71)	8.46 * (3.92)	6.18 (4.00)
Out-party–In-party		8.08 *** (1.84)		−19.53 *** (3.63)
Republican	−543.23 (499.15)	−426.78 (501.39)	−113.00 (332.21)	44.31 (339.40)
Male	−1041.16 *** (323.66)	−912.29 ** (322.42)	−621.71 (320.82)	−571.77 (329.23)
African American	−261.70 (468.40)	−238.64 (472.43)	−594.18 (427.84)	−577.60 (439.28)
DW Nominate	−4369.39 *** (1117.45)	−3975.53 *** (1116.26)	−3805.55 *** (1071.78)	−3112.16 ** (1090.19)
Previous vote share (D)	−5.94 (14.88)	−3.76 (14.98)		
Seniority	−128.48 *** (33.17)	−113.13 *** (32.90)	−88.42 ** (30.34)	−87.63 ** (31.15)
Party leader	1597.81 * (744.93)	1978.42 ** (735.94)	4449.86 *** (709.11)	5330.91 *** (702.66)
Legislative effectiveness	229.67 (153.13)	228.24 (154.47)	41.92 (141.84)	−0.86 (145.35)
Observations	316	316	407	407
R^2 / R^2 adjusted	0.221 / 0.190	0.204 / 0.175	0.249 / 0.230	0.249 / 0.230

Note: $* p < 0.05$; $** p < 0.01$; $*** p < 0.001$

Appendixes 233

Table A7.2. OLS Regression Estimating Effect of Rhetoric in Newsletters on Out-of-State Fundraising Dollars

	DEPENDENT VARIABLE: OUT-OF-STATE FUNDRAISING (IN THOUSANDS)			
	Twitter		Newsletters	
Predictors	Coef. (s.e.)	Coef. (s.e.)	Coef. (s.e.)	Coef. (s.e.)
Total fundraising (in thousands)	0.66 *** (0.01)	0.66 *** (0.01)	0.75 *** (0.01)	0.75 *** (0.01)
Out-party mentions	1.23 ** (0.43)		−0.75 (0.89)	
In-party mentions	0.88 (1.47)		2.79 * (1.35)	
Policy mentions	−0.10 (0.09)	−0.03 (0.08)	−0.03 (0.06)	0.04 (0.05)
Bipartisanship mentions	0.14 (1.00)	0.30 (1.00)	−0.53 (0.94)	−0.77 (0.94)
Out-party–In-party		1.48 (0.40)		−0.99 (0.88)
Republican	270.99 * (105.77)	288.66 ** (105.55)	211.84 ** (79.40)	225.90 ** (79.20)
Male	−135.90 (69.61)	−115.06 (68.68)	−56.86 (77.24)	−49.52 (77.33)
African American	230.35 * (99.12)	234.29 * (99.38)	198.29 (102.83)	202.66 * (103.06)
DW Nominate	−325.91 (242.23)	−258.78 (239.56)	240.58 (260.70)	318.60 (257.55)
Previous vote share (D)	7.70 * (3.15)	8.02 * (3.15)		
Seniority	18.17 * (7.19)	20.66 ** (7.05)	31.23 *** (7.35)	31.73 *** (7.36)
Party leader	225.31 (158.74)	273.26 (156.57)	337.78 (178.37)	392.02 * (176.13)
Legislative effectiveness	−89.62 ** (32.51)	−90.49 ** (32.60)	−63.70 (33.98)	−67.55 * (34.00)
Observations	316	316	410	410
R^2 / R^2 adjusted	0.928 / 0.925	0.927 / 0.924	0.934 / 0.932	0.933 / 0.931

Note: * $p < 0.05$; ** $p < 0.01$; *** $p < 0.001$

APPENDIX TO CHAPTER 8

STUDY 1 EXAMPLE CONJOINT SCREEN

Table A8.1. Study 1 Example Conjoint Screen

	CONGRESSMEMBER A	CONGRESSMEMBER B
Sex	Female	Male
Party	Democrat	Republican
Race/ethnicity	African American	Hispanic
Latest tweet	"Providing Medicare for all Americans is NOT the right solution to fix health care in this country."	"Increasing spending on border security between the US and Mexico would NOT fix immigration policy in this country."
Constituent relations	Answers over 90 percent of constituent mail	Answers less than half of constituent mail

STUDY 2 EXAMPLE CONJOINT SCREEN

Table A8.2. Study 2 Example Conjoint Screen

Gender	Female
Party	Democrat
Race/ethnicity	White
Latest tweet	"Listening to Republicans makes me so angry and fearful for this country. What a disgrace."
Constituent relations	Answers over 90 percent of constituent mail
Ban assault rifles	Voted *for* banning assault rifles
Increase income tax rate for high-income people by 3 percent	Voted *against* increasing tax rate for high income people

STUDY 3 EXAMPLE CONJOINT SCREEN

Name: Rep. Stevens
Party: Democratic
Served: 2013–present
Family: Married, two children
Member quote: "We should do everything it takes to make sure Republicans lose the next election."
Issue priority: Environment

APPENDIX TO CHAPTER 9

RESULTS BY IDEOLOGY

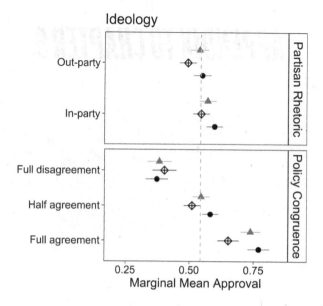

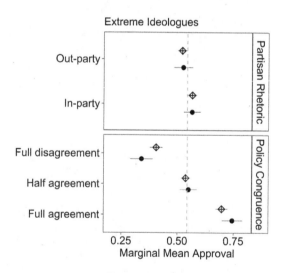

Figure A9.1. How ideologues evaluate partisan rhetoric and policy congruence

Note: Plot shows estimated marginal means for partisan rhetoric and policy congruence attributes across ideology (*left*) and ideological extremity (*right*). Model includes terms for other conjoint attributes not shown here: race, gender, and quality constituency service. Horizontal bars represent 95 percent confidence intervals. Vertical dashed line shows mean approval for full sample. Cluster-robust standard errors by subject.

RESULTS BY GENDER AND RACE

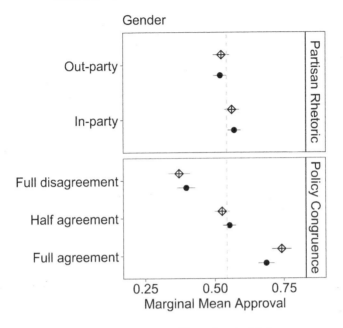

Figure A9.2. How men and women evaluate partisan rhetoric and policy congruence

Note: Plot shows estimated marginal means for partisan rhetoric and policy congruence attributes across gender. Model includes terms for other conjoint attributes not shown here: race, gender, and quality constituency service. Horizontal bars represent 95 percent confidence intervals. Vertical dashed line shows mean approval for full sample. Cluster-robust standard errors by subject.

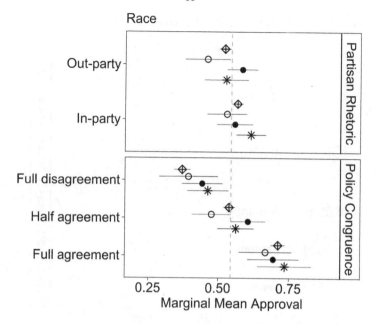

Figure A9.3. How different racial/ethnic groups evaluate partisan rhetoric and policy congruence

Note: Plot shows estimated marginal means for partisan rhetoric and policy congruence attributes across race/ethnicity. Model includes terms for other conjoint attributes not shown here: race, gender, and quality constituency service. Horizontal bars represent 95 percent confidence intervals. Vertical dashed line shows mean approval for full sample. Cluster-robust standard errors by subject.

RESULTS CONDITIONAL ON OPPONENT'S RHETORIC

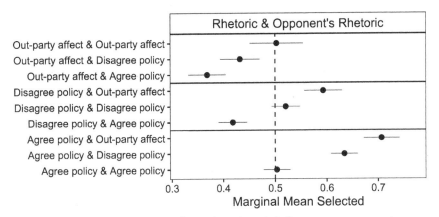

Figure A9.4. How (the opponent's) partisan rhetoric influences voter perceptions
Note: Plot shows estimated marginal means for a legislator's rhetoric and their opponent's rhetoric. Model includes terms for other attributes not shown here: race, gender, and political experience. Horizontal lines represent 95 percent confidence intervals. Cluster-robust standard errors by subject.

NOTES

CHAPTER ONE

1. See https://memory.loc.gov/cgi-bin/query/r?ammem/hlaw:@field(DOCID+@lit (hj025175)).

2. Since the writing of this book, there have been two additional instances of censure among Democratic members of Congress. The first was Rashida Tlaib, who was censured for comments made in relation to the 2023 Israel-Hamas conflict. The second was Jamaal Bowman, who faced censure over allegations by Republicans of disrupting congressional proceedings by pulling a fire alarm before a critical vote to avoid a government shutdown.

CHAPTER TWO

1. Newport 2022.
2. Vesoulis 2021.
3. Benen 2021.

CHAPTER THREE

1. See, for example, the recent founding of the *Journal of Quantitative Description: Digital Media* and related articles within.

2. See "Voteview: Congressional Roll-Call Vote Database," compiled by Jeffrey Poole et al., accessed July 2, 2024, https://www.voteview.com.

3. The raw dataset of tweets was generously provided by Rathje, Van Bavel, and van der Linden—see Rathje, Van Bavel, and van der Linden 2021.

4. See "Partisan Language in Congressional Outreach," Pew Research Center, February 23, 2017, http://www.people-press.org/2017/02/23/partisan-language-in -congressional-outreach/.

5. Because the 116th Congress is the only time period for which I have full coverage of tweets for every legislator, we can more directly compare newsletters and tweets during that session. See the Appendix for table 2.1 reproduced with additional columns just for the 116th Congress, as well as for average counts per legislator for more social identity group terms, such as the number of times legislators mention gender and race.

6. "How President Trump's Rhetoric Has Affected US Politics," NPR, January 19, 2021, https://www.npr.org/2021/01/19/958472423/how-president-trumps-rhetoric -has-affected-u-s-politics.

7. Many words in the English language are considered "neutral" and therefore not given a "positive" or "negative" coding in the lexicon; these words are dropped from the sentiment analysis.

8. This method is less informative for large bodies of text like email newsletters that often contain several paragraphs. However, general patterns can still be informative.

CHAPTER FOUR

1. For the sake of space, I show the results for newsletters here since these data contain observations across different legislators across different years. The results for Twitter follow similar patterns but are less pronounced and have larger standard errors due to the smaller sample size.

2. See https://thelawmakers.org/methodology for more information on how these scores are calculated.

CHAPTER FIVE

1. Gallup News, "Presidential Approval Ratings—Donald Trump," accessed July 2, 2024, https://news.gallup.com/poll/203198/presidential-approval-ratings -donald-trump.aspx.

2. For example, see "How Popular/Unpopular Is Donald Trump?" Five-Thirty-Eight, updated January 20, 2021, https://projects.fivethirtyeight.com/trump-approval -ratings/.

3. Stefonek 2021.

4. For more on surveying and experimenting on political elites, see Kertzer and Renshon 2022.

5. As of 2020, the Cooperative Congressional Election Study (CCES) dropped the "Congressional" from its name to become the Cooperative Election Study (CES).

6. Note that while my interest is in substantive representation rather than ideological or partisan asymmetries per se, it is interesting that I find greater penalties for "very liberal" candidates compared to others (when disregarding the ideology of the district). Future research should examine how ideological labels alone influence perceptions of electoral viability and partisan attacks.

7. Note that the confidence intervals get larger as distance increases. This is because the number of elites who answered in the pre-treatment that Democratic primary voters in their district are "somewhat conservative" or "very conservative" is relatively small.

8. See "In-State vs. Out-of-State," OpenSecrets.org, accessed July 2, 2024, https:// www.opensecrets.org/elections-overview/in-state-vs-out-of-state; and "Blue Wave of Money Propels 2018 Election to Record-Breaking $5.2 Billion in Spending," OpenSecrets .org, October 29, 2018, https://www.opensecrets.org/news/2018/10/2018-midterm -record-breaking-5-2-billion/.

CHAPTER SIX

1. Respondents were instructed: "Ratings between 50 degrees and 100 degrees mean that you feel favorable and warm toward the group. Ratings between 0 degrees and 50 degrees mean that you don't feel favorable toward that group and that you don't care

too much for them. You would rate the group at the 50 degree mark if you don't feel one way or the other about them."

2. There are no significant differences between Democratic (16.5) and Republican elites (15.3).

3. Using survey weights. In the mass sample, there is a small but statistically significant difference between Democrats (20.5) and Republicans (18.0).

4. In addition to Democrats and Republicans, I also asked about scientists, journalists, and social media influencers to distract respondents from the purpose of the question and to elicit more truthful responses. The order of the groups was randomized.

5. Unlike in chapter 3, I show marginal means instead of average marginal component effects in order to avoid misestimating subgroup preferences (Leeper, Hobolt, and Tilley 2020). I also combine the different types of partisan statements (electoral and affect) considering the small differences between these found in chapter 5 to retain statistical power after conditioning on negative affect.

6. Because I am analyzing the joint effect of statements made by both candidate profiles, I only estimate the marginal means for selecting the first candidate. The marginal means of selecting the second candidate would simply be the inverse of what is presented in the graph.

CHAPTER SEVEN

1. Nelson 2020.

2. What makes the Porter example even more striking is that she actually represents one of the most competitive districts in the country.

3. Examining "likes" only and excluding retweets does not markedly alter these results; see the Appendix.

4. I used the Television Explorer tool powered by the TV 2.0 API by the GDELT project. See https://api.gdeltproject.org/api/v2/summary/summary?d=iatv.

5. Searches for phrases that span the boundary between two clips are counted for the first clip, ensuring there is no double counting.

6. Segments were characterized as "attack" if they were in the context of the following words: attack, attacked, criticized, criticize, condemned, condemn. Segments were characterized as "compromise" if they were in the context of the following words: bipartisan, bipartisanship, compromise.

CHAPTER EIGHT

1. This research and portions of this chapter were previously published in the *American Journal of Political Science* (Costa 2021).

2. Recent work has argued that because the average marginal component effect measures the direction and intensity of voters' preferences, it is not always ideal for making reliable inferences about matchups in an electoral contest (Abramson, Koçak, and Magazinnik 2022). This study largely avoids this problem because the outcome of interest is the overall effect of attributes on representational preferences rather than vote choice, thus the intensity of such preferences is quite relevant to the question at hand. Nonetheless, interpretation of the results should be done with caution so as not to overstate what types of legislators are likely to win elections. See the Appendix of Costa 2021

for marginal means for all three studies. I also follow the recommendation of Abramson, Koçak, and Magazinnik (2022) and provide these results in context of other experiments designed to recover individuals' priorities. Study 2 and Study 3 are rating-based instead of forced-choice designs, which avoids this misinterpretation of the AMCE altogether.

3. Coppock and McClellan (2018) find that demographic characteristics and experimental treatment effects on Lucid track well with other popular convenience samples, like Mechanical Turk, as well as with national benchmarks. For other examples of studies conducted on Lucid, see Flores and Coppock 2018, Graham 2020, and Pennycook and Rand 2019.

4. Respondents indicated their position on banning assault rifles earlier in the CCES as part of the Common Content, so I am able to measure whether their stance is the same as the hypothetical legislator's. The question on increasing tax rates for high-income people ended up being dropped for the full sample from the CCES Common Content. In order to measure congruence for this issue, I imputed support using a probit model on the subsample of 1,262 respondents who did answer the question. The model includes their position on six other related tax rate questions, as well as 7-point party identification, family income level, an indicator for stock ownership, and approval of President Trump. From this I generated predicted probabilities for the remaining 984 respondents for which I did not have a self-report measure. As the model correctly predicts respondents' answers on this question 74 percent of the time, considerable measurement error is introduced. The results presented in the next section are likely understating the importance of policy congruence.

5. For example, see the discussion in Kivetz and Simonson 2000 and Yates, Jagacinski, and Faber 1978; also Auspurg and Hinz 2014 and Wallander 2009.

CHAPTER NINE

1. "ANES 2020 Time Series Study Full Release" [dataset and documentation], accessed July 19, 2021, https://www.electionstudies.org/.

2. Note that the feeling thermometers used here ask for ratings of the "Democratic Party" and "Republican Party." See Druckman and Levendusky 2019 for more on the important differences between measures and how respondents may call to mind groups of partisans in the mass public versus party institutions.

3. I use a standard "news interest" question which captures how often people self-report paying attention to what's going on in government and public affairs. People could answer "most of the time," "some of the time," "only now and then," "hardly at all," or "don't know." I compare people who answer "most of the time" with everyone else to discriminate high-interest individuals since almost a quarter of respondents (23.5 percent) selected this category.

4. The ANES only includes self-reports of voting in the primary. For the main analyses below, I use validated voter turnout in the primary election from the CCES.

CHAPTER TEN

1. Drutman 2020.
2. Abramowitz and Webster 2017.

REFERENCES

Abramowitz, Alan. 2010. *The Disappearing Center: Engaged Citizens, Polarization, and American Democracy.* New Haven, CT: Yale University Press.

Abramowitz, Alan, and Jennifer McCoy. 2019. "United States: Racial Resentment, Negative Partisanship, and Polarization in Trump's America." *The ANNALS of the American Academy of Political and Social Science* 681 (1): 137–56.

Abramowitz, Alan, and Kyle Saunders. 2005. "Why Can't We All Just Get Along? The Reality of a Polarized America." *The Forum* 3 (2): 000010220215408884076.

Abramowitz, Alan I., and Kyle L. Saunders. 2008. "Is Polarization a Myth?" *Journal of Politics* 70 (2): 542–55.

Abramowitz, Alan I., and Steven W. Webster. 2016. "The Rise of Negative Partisanship and the Nationalization of U.S. Elections in the 21st Century." *Electoral Studies* 41: 12–22.

Abramowitz, Alan I., and Steven W. Webster. 2017. "'Negative Partisanship' Explains Everything." *Politico Magazine*, September/October. https://www.politico.com/magazine/story/2017/09/05/negative-partisanship-explains-everything-215534/.

Abramowitz, Alan I., and Steven W. Webster. 2018. "Negative Partisanship: Why Americans Dislike Parties but Behave Like Rabid Partisans." *Political Psychology* 39: 119–35.

Abramson, Scott F., Korhan Koçak, and Asya Magazinnik. 2022. "What Do We Learn about Voter Preferences from Conjoint Experiments?" *American Journal of Political Science* 66 (4): 1008–20.

Achen, Christopher. 1975. "Mass Political Attitudes and the Survey Response." *American Political Science Review* 69 (4): 1218–31.

Achen, Christopher, and Larry Bartels. 2017. *Democracy for Realists: Why Elections Do Not Produce Responsive Government.* Princeton, NJ: Princeton University Press.

Ahler, D. J. 2014. "Self-fulfilling Misperceptions of Public Polarization." *Journal of Politics* 76 (3): 607–20.

Ahler, D. J., and G. Sood. 2018. "The Parties in Our Heads: Misperceptions about Party Composition and Their Consequences." *Journal of Politics* 80 (3): 964–81.

Akerlof, George A. 1978. "The Market for 'Lemons': Quality Uncertainty and the Market Mechanism." In *Uncertainty in Economics: Readings and Exercises*, ed. Peter Diamond and Michael Rothschild, 235–51. New York: Academic Press.

Albert, Zachary. 2022. "Persistent Factionalism? An Analysis of Endorsements in the 2020 Democratic Primary." In *Polarization and Political Party Factions in the 2020 Election*, ed. Jennifer C. Lucas, Christopher J. Galdieri, and Tauna Starbuck Sisco. Lanham, MD: Lexington Books.

References

Albert, Zachary, and Mia Costa. 2024. "Winning at All Costs? How Negative Partisanship Affects Voter Decision-Making." *Political Behavior*.

Aldrich, J. 1995. *Why Parties?* Chicago: University of Chicago Press.

Amira, K., J. Wright, and D. Goya-Tocchetto. 2021. "In-Group Love versus Out-Group Hate: Which Is More Important to Partisans and When?" *Political Behavior* 43 (2): 473–94. https://doi.org/10.1007/s11109-019-09557-6.

Anderson, Sarah E., Daniel M. Butler, and Laurel Harbridge-Yong. 2020. *Rejecting Compromise: Legislators' Fear of Primary Voters*. Cambridge: Cambridge University Press.

Andrews, Natalie, and Michael Bender. 2019. "Trump Draws GOP Pushback as He Steps Up Attacks on Lawmakers." *Wall Street Journal*, August 2.

Ansolabehere, S., R. Behr, and S. Iyengar. 1993. *The Media Game: American Politics in the Television Age*. New York: Macmillan.

Ansolabehere, S., and S. Iyengar. 1995. *Going Negative: How Political Ads Shrink and Polarize the Electorate*. New York: Free Press.

Ansolabehere, Stephen, Shanto Iyengar, Adam Simon, and Nicholas Valentino. 1994. "Does Attack Advertising Demobilize the Electorate?" *American Political Science Review* 88 (4): 829–38.

Ansolabehere, Stephen, and Philip Jones. 2010. "Constituents' Responses to Congressional Roll-Call Voting." *American Journal of Political Science* 54 (3): 583–97.

Ansolabehere, S., J. Rodden, and J. M. Snyder. 2008. "The Strength of Issues: Using Multiple Measures to Gauge Preference Stability, Ideological Constraint, and Issue Voting." *American Political Science Review* 102 (2): 215–37.

Arbour, B. 2014. "Issue Frame Ownership: The Partisan Roots of Campaign Rhetoric." *Political Communication* 31 (4): 604–27.

Arceneaux, Kevin, and Ryan J. Vander Wielen. 2017. *Taming Intuition: How Reflection Minimizes Partisan Reasoning and Promotes Democratic Accountability*. Cambridge: Cambridge University Press.

Armaly, M., and A. Enders. 2021. "The Role of Affective Orientations in Promoting Perceived Polarization." *Political Science Research and Methods* 9 (3): 615–26. https://doi.org/10.1017/psrm.2020.24.

Arnold, R. Douglas. 1990. *The Logic of Congressional Action*. New Haven, CT: Yale University Press.

Augoustinos, M., and S. De Garis. 2012. "'Too Black or Not Black Enough': Social Identity Complexity in the Political Rhetoric of Barack Obama." *European Journal of Social Psychology* 42 (5): 564–77.

Auspurg, Katrin, and Thomas Hinz. 2014. *Factorial Survey Experiments*. Quantitative Applications in the Social Sciences 175. Thousand Oaks, CA: Sage Publications.

Baker, Anne E. 2022. "Out-of-State Contributions Provide Non-Incumbent House Candidates with a Competitive Edge." *American Politics Research* 50 (5): 668–81.

Bakker, Bert, Yphtach Lelkes, and Ariel Malka. 2019. "Understanding Partisan Cue Receptivity: Tests of Predictions from the Bounded Rationality and Expressive Utility Perspectives." *Journal of Politics* 49: 1045–69.

Ballard, Andrew O., et al. 2022. "Dynamics of Polarizing Rhetoric in Congressional Tweets." *Legislative Studies Quarterly* 48 (1).

Banda, Kevin K., and John Cluverius. 2018. "Elite Polarization, Party Extremity, and Affective Polarization." *Electoral Studies* 56: 90–101.

References 249

Bankert, Alexa. 2020. "The Origins and Effect of Negative Partisanship." In *Research Handbook on Political Partisanship*, ed. Henrik Oscarsson and Sören Holmberg, 89–101. Cheltenham, UK: Edward Elgar Publishing.

Bankert, Alexa. 2021. "Negative and Positive Partisanship in the 2016 US Presidential Elections." *Political Behavior* 43 (4): 1467–85.

Barber, Michael. 2016. "Donation Motivations: Testing Theories of Access and Ideology." *Political Research Quarterly* 69 (1): 148–59.

Barber, Michael, and Jeremy Pope. 2019. "Does Party Trump Ideology? Disentangling Party and Ideology in America." *American Political Science Review* 113 (1): 38–54.

Barker, David C., and Christopher Jan Carman. 2012. *Representing Red and Blue: How the Culture Wars Change the Way Citizens Speak and Politicians Listen.* Oxford: Oxford University Press.

Bartels, Larry M. 2016. *Unequal Democracy: The Political Economy of the New Gilded Age.* Princeton, NJ: Princeton University Press.

Benen, Steve. 2021. "New Republican Congressman Prioritizes Punditry over Policy." MaddowBlog, MSNBC, January 28. https://www.msnbc.com/rachel-maddow-show /maddowblog/new-republican-congressman-prioritizes-punditry-over-policy -n1255967.

Berry, Jeffrey M., and Sarah Sobieraj. 2013. *The Outrage Industry: Political Opinion Media and the New Incivility.* Oxford: Oxford University Press.

Best, Heinrich, and Lars Vogel. 2014. "The Sociology of Legislators and Legislatures." In *The Oxford Handbook of Legislative Studies*, ed. Shane Martin, Thomas Saalfeld, and Kaare W. Strøm, 57–81. Oxford: Oxford University Press.

Binder, Sarah A. 2003. *Stalemate: Causes and Consequences of Legislative Gridlock.* Washington, DC: Brookings Institution Press.

Black, Duncan. 1958. *The Theory of Committees and Elections.* Cambridge: Cambridge University Press.

Bougher, L. D. 2017. "The Correlates of Discord: Identity, Issue Alignment, and Political Hostility in Polarized America." *Political Behavior* 39 (3): 731–62.

Boxell, L., M. Gentzkow, and J. M. Shapiro. 2017. "Greater Internet Use Is Not Associated with Faster Growth in Political Polarization among US Demographic Groups." *PNAS* 114 (40): 10612–17.

Brady, William J., Ana P. Gantman, and Jay J. Van Bavel. 2020. "Attentional Capture Helps Explain Why Moral and Emotional Content Go Viral." *Journal of Experimental Psychology: General* 149 (4): 746.

Broockman, David E., Joshua L. Kalla, and Sean J. Westwood. 2023. "Does Affective Polarization Undermine Democratic Norms or Accountability? Maybe Not." *American Journal of Political Science* 67 (3): 808–28.

Broockman, David, and Christopher Skovron. 2018. "Bias in Perceptions of Public Opinion among Political Elites." *American Political Science Review* 112 (3): 542–63.

Brooks, Deborah Jordan, and John G. Geer. 2007. "Beyond Negativity: The Effects of Incivility on the Electorate." *American Journal of Political Science* 51 (1): 1–16.

Brown, Nadia, and Sarah Gershon. 2016. "Intersectional Presentations: An Exploratory Study of Minority Congresswomen's Websites Biographies." *Du Bois Review* 13 (1): 85–108.

Brown, Nadia E., and Sarah Allen Gershon. 2017. "Examining Intersectionality and Symbolic Representation." *Politics, Groups, and Identities* 5 (3): 500–505.

Bump, Phillip. 2018. "The Irony of Washington's 'Civility' Debate: Trump Already Proved That Incivility Works." *Washington Post*, June 25.

Burns, Peter, and James Gimpel. 2000. "Economic Insecurity, Prejudicial Stereotypes, and Public Opinion on Immigration Policy." *Political Science Quarterly* 115 (2): 201-25.

Bushman, Brad J., and Craig A. Anderson. 2009. "Comfortably Numb: Desensitizing Effects of Violent Media on Helping Others." *Psychological Science* 20 (3): 273-77.

Butler, Daniel M., and David E. Broockman. 2011. "Do Politicians Racially Discriminate Against Constituents? A Field Experiment on State Legislators." *American Journal of Political Science* 55 (3): 463-77.

Butler, Daniel M., and Adam Dynes. 2016. "How Politicians Discount the Opinions of Constituents with Whom They Disagree." *American Journal of Political Science* 60 (4): 975-89.

Butler, Daniel M., and Jonathan Homola. 2017. "An Empirical Justification for the Use of Racially Distinctive Names to Signal Race in Experiments." *Political Analysis* 25 (1): 122-30.

Butler, Daniel, and David Nickerson. 2011. "Can Learning Constituency Opinion Affect How Legislators Vote? Results from a Field Experiment." *Quarterly Journal of Political Science* 6 (1): 55-83.

Caldeira, Gregory A., and Samuel C. Patterson. 1987. "Political Friendship in the Legislature." *Journal of Politics* 49 (4): 953-75.

Campbell, Angus, Philip Converse, Warren Miller, and Donald Stokes. 1960. *The American Voter*. Chicago: University of Chicago Press.

Canes-Wrone, Brandice. 2015. "From Mass Preferences to Policy." *Annual Review of Political Science* 18: 147-65.

Canes-Wrone, Brandice, David W. Brady, and John F. Cogan. 2002. "Out of Step, Out of Office: Electoral Accountability and House Members' Voting." *American Political Science Review* 96 (1): 127-40.

Cappella, Joseph N., and Kathleen Hall Jamieson. 1997. *Spiral of Cynicism: The Press and the Public Good*. Oxford: Oxford University Press.

Carnes, Nicholas, and Noam Lupu. 2016. "Do Voters Dislike Working-Class Candidates? Voter Biases and the Descriptive Underrepresentation of the Working Class." *American Political Science Review* 110 (4): 832-44.

Carson, J. L., M. H. Crespin, and A. J. Madonna. 2014. "Procedural Signaling, Party Loyalty, and Traceability in the US House of Representatives." *Political Research Quarterly* 67 (4): 729-42.

Cassese, Erin. 2021. "Partisan Dehumanization in American Politics." *Political Behavior* 43: 29-50. https://doi.org/10.1007/s11109-019-09545-w.

Chambers, J. R., R. S. Baron, and M. L. Inman. 2006. "Misperceptions in Intergroup Conflict: Disagreeing about What We Disagree About." *Psychological Science* 17 (1): 38-45. https://doi.org/10.1111/j.1467-9280.2005.01662.x.

Chambers, J. R., and D. Melnyk. 2006. "Why Do I Hate Thee? Conflict Misperceptions and Intergroup Mistrust." *Personality and Social Psychology Bulletin* 32 (10): 1295-311. https://doi.org/10.1177/0146167206289979.

Chen, M. K., and R. Rohla. 2018. "The Effect of Partisanship and Political Advertising on Close Family Ties." *Science* 360 (6392): 1020-24.

Chopik, W. J., and M. Motyl. 2016. "Ideological Fit Enhances Interpersonal Orientations." *Social Psychological and Personality Science* 7 (8): 759-68.

References 251

Christenson, Dino, and Todd Makse. 2015. "Mass Preferences on Shared Representation and the Composition of Legislative Districts." *American Politics Research* 43 (3): 451–78.

Clarke, A. J., J. A. Jenkins, and N. K. Micatka. 2020. "How Have Members of Congress Reacted to President Trump's Trade Policy?" *The Forum* 17 (4): 631–45.

Clinton, Joshua D. 2006. "Representation in Congress: Constituents and Roll Calls in the 106th House." *Journal of Politics* 68 (2): 397–409.

Converse, Philip. 1964. "The Nature of Belief Systems in Mass Publics." In *Ideology and Discontent*, ed. David Apter. New York: Free Press.

Cook, T. 1989. *Making Laws and Making News: Media Strategies in the US House of Representatives*. Washington, DC: Brookings Institution.

Cook, T. 1998. *Governing with the News: The News Media as a Political Institution*. Chicago: University of Chicago Press.

Coppock, Alexander, and Oliver McClellan. 2018. "Validating the Demographic, Political, Psychological, and Experimental Results Obtained from a New Source of Online Survey Respondents." *Research and Politics* 6 (1). https://doi.org/10.1177/2053168018822174.

Cormack, Lindsey. 2016a. "Extremity in Congress: Communications versus Votes." *Legislative Studies Quarterly* 41 (3): 575–603.

Cormack, Lindsey. 2016b. "Gender and Vote Revelation Strategy in the United States Congress." *Journal of Gender Studies* 25 (6): 626–40.

Cormack, Lindsey. 2017. "DCinbox—Capturing Every Congressional Constituent E-newsletter from 2009 Onwards." *The Legislative Scholar* 2 (1): 27–34.

Costa, Mia. 2017. "How Responsive Are Political Elites? A Meta-analysis of Experiments on Public Officials." *Journal of Experimental Political Science* 4 (3): 241–54.

Costa, Mia. 2021. "Citizen Evaluations of Legislator-Constituent Communication." *British Journal of Political Science* 51: 1–8. https://doi.org/10.1017/S0007123419000553.

Costa, Mia, Kaylee Johnson, and Brian Schaffner. 2018. "Rethinking Representation from a Communal Perspective." *Political Behavior* 40 (2): 301–20.

Crockett, Molly J. 2017. "Moral Outrage in the Digital Age." *Nature Human Behaviour* 1 (11): 769–71.

Curry, James M., and Frances E. Lee. 2020. *The Limits of Party: Congress and Lawmaking in a Polarized Era*. Chicago: University of Chicago Press.

Dalton, R. J., and M. P. Wattenberg. 2002. "The Decline of Party Identification in Advanced Industrial Democracies." In *Parties Without Partisans: Political Change in Advanced Industrial Democracies*, ed. R. J. Dalton and M. P. Wattenberg, 1–22. Oxford, UK: Oxford University Press.

Davenport, Thomas, and John Beck. 2001. *The Attention Economy: Understanding the New Currency of Business*. Cambridge, MA: Harvard Business School Press.

de Benedictis-Kessner, Justin. 2022. "Strategic Government Communication about Performance." *Political Science Research and Methods* 10 (3): 601–16.

Deckman, Melissa. 2022. "Civility, Gender, and Gendered Nationalism in the Age of Trump." *Politics, Groups, and Identities* 10 (7): 1–25.

Devine, Patricia G., Patrick S. Forscher, Anthony J. Austin, and William T. L. Cox. 2012. "Long-term Reduction in Implicit Race Bias: A Prejudice Habit-breaking Intervention." *Journal of Experimental Social Psychology* 48 (6): 1267–78.

Dias, Nicholas, and Yphtach Lelkes. 2022. "The Nature of Affective Polarization: Disentangling Policy Disagreement from Partisan Identity." *American Journal of Political Science* 66 (3): 775–90.

Dickson, Eric S., and Kenneth Scheve. 2006. "Social Identity, Political Speech, and Electoral Competition." *Journal of Theoretical Politics* 18 (1): 5–39.

Disch, L. J. 2021. *Making Constituencies: Representation as Mobilization in Mass Democracy.* Chicago: University of Chicago Press.

Doherty, David. 2015. "How Policy and Procedure Shape Citizens' Evaluations of Senators." *Legislative Studies Quarterly* 40 (2): 241–72.

Downs, Anthony. 1957. *An Economic Theory of Democracy.* New York: Harper.

Druckman, James N., Martin J. Kifer, and Michael Parkin. 2010. "Timeless Strategy Meets New Medium: Going Negative on Congressional Campaign Web Sites, 2002–2006." *Political Communication* 27 (1): 88–103.

Druckman, James, and Matthew Levendusky. 2019. "What Do We Measure When We Measure Affective Polarization?" *Public Opinion Quarterly* 83 (1): 114–22.

Druckman, James N., Matthew S. Levendusky, and Audrey McLain. 2018. "No Need to Watch: How the Effects of Partisan Media Can Spread via Interpersonal Discussions." *American Journal of Political Science* 62 (1): 99–112.

Druckman, James N., and Rose McDermott. 2008. "Emotion and the Framing of Risky Choice." *Political Behavior* 30 (3): 297–321.

Drutman, Lee. 2020. "How Hatred Came to Dominate American Politics." FiveThirtyEight, October 5. https://fivethirtyeight.com/features/how-hatred-negative-partisanship-came-to-dominate-american-politics/.

Elkins, Zachary, and Rui de Figueiredo. 2003. "Are Patriots Bigots? An Inquiry into the Vices of In-Group Pride." *American Journal of Political Science* 47 (1): 171–88.

Enders, Adam M. 2021. "Issues Versus Affect: How Do Elite and Mass Polarization Compare?" *Journal of Politics* 83 (4): 1872–77.

Erikson, Robert S. 2013. *Policy Responsiveness to Public Opinion.* Oxford: Oxford University Press.

Erikson, Robert S., Michael B. MacKuen, and James A. Stimson. 2002. *The Macro Polity.* Cambridge: Cambridge University Press.

Eulau, Heinz, and Paul Karps. 1977. "The Puzzle of Representation: Specifying Components of Responsiveness." *Legislative Studies Quarterly* 2: 233–54.

Eulau, Heinz, John C. Wahlke, William Buchanan, and Leroy C. Ferguson. 1959. "The Role of the Representative: Some Empirical Observations on the Theory of Edmund Burke." *American Political Science Review* 53 (3): 742–56.

Feinberg, Ayal, Regina Branton, and Valerie Martinez-Ebers. 2022. "The Trump Effect: How 2016 Campaign Rallies Explain Spikes in Hate." *PS: Political Science & Politics* 55 (2): 257–65.

Fenno, Richard F. 1977. "US House Members in Their Constituencies: An Exploration." *American Political Science Review* 71 (3): 883–917.

Fenno, Richard. 1978. *Homestyle: House Members in Their Districts.* Boston: Little, Brown.

Fine, Jeffrey A., and Megan F. Hunt. 2023. "Negativity and Elite Message Diffusion on Social Media." *Political Behavior* 45: 955–73.

Fiorina, Morris P. 2017. *Unstable Majorities: Polarization, Party Sorting, and Political Stalemate.* Stanford, CA: Hoover Institution Press.

Fiorina, Morris P., and Samuel J. Abrams. 2008. "Political Polarization in the American Public." *Annual Review of Political Science* 11: 563–88.

Fiorina, Morris P., and Samuel J. Abrams. 2012. *Disconnect: The Breakdown of Representation in American Politics*. Norman: University of Oklahoma Press.

Fiorina, Morris, Samuel Abrams, and Jeremy Pope. 2005. *Culture War? The Myth of a Polarized America*. London: Pearson Longman.

Fiorina, Morris P., Samuel A. Abrams, and Jeremy C. Pope. 2008. "Polarization in the American Public: Misconceptions and Misreadings." *Journal of Politics* 70 (2): 556–60.

Flores, Alejandro, and Alexander Coppock. 2018. "Do Bilinguals Respond More Favorably to Candidate Advertisements in English or in Spanish?" *Political Communication* 35 (4): 612–33.

Freedman, P., and K. Goldstein. 1999. "Measuring Media Exposure and the Effects of Negative Campaign Ads." *American Journal of Political Science* 43 (4): 1189–208.

Fridkin, Kim Leslie, and Patrick J. Kenney. 2004. "Do Negative Messages Work? The Impact of Negativity on Citizens' Evaluations of Candidates." *American Politics Research* 32 (5): 570–605.

Furnas, A. C., and T. M. Lapira. 2024. "The People Think What I Think: False Consensus and Unelected Elite Misperception of Public Opinion." *American Journal of Political Science* 00: 1–14. https://doi.org/10.1111/ajps.12833.

Gainous, J., and K. Wagner. 2014. *Tweeting to Power: The Social Media Revolution in American Politics*. Oxford: Oxford University Press.

Geer, John G. 2008. *In Defense of Negativity: Attack Ads in Presidential Campaigns*. Chicago: University of Chicago Press.

Geer, John G. 2012. "The News Media and the Rise of Negativity in Presidential Campaigns." *PS: Political Science & Politics* 45 (3): 422–27.

Gelman, Jeremy. 2019. "In Pursuit of Power: Competition for Majority Status and Senate Partisanship." *Party Politics* 25 (6): 782–93.

Gelman, Jeremy. 2020. *Losing to Win: Why Congressional Majorities Play Politics Instead of Make Laws*. Ann Arbor: University of Michigan Press.

Gerber, Elisabeth R., and Rebecca B. Morton. 1998. "Primary Election Systems and Representation." *Journal of Law, Economics, and Organization* 14 (2): 304–24.

Gervais, Bryan T. 2014. "Following the News? Reception of Uncivil Partisan Media and the Use of Incivility in Political Expression." *Political Communication* 31 (4): 564–83.

Gervais, Bryan T. 2015. "Incivility Online: Affective and Behavioral Reactions to Uncivil Political Posts in a Web-based Experiment." *Journal of Information Technology & Politics* 12 (2): 167–85.

Gervais, Bryan. 2017. "More than Mimicry? The Role of Anger in Uncivil Reactions to Elite Political Incivility." *International Journal of Public Opinion Research* 29 (3): 384–405.

Gervais, Bryan T., and Walter C. Wilson. 2017. "New Media for the New Electorate? Congressional Outreach to Latinos on Twitter." *Politics, Groups, and Identities* 7 (2): 305–23.

Gidron, Noam, James Adams, and Will Horne. 2020. *American Affective Polarization in Comparative Perspective*. Cambridge: Cambridge University Press.

Goldschmidt, Kathy. 2011. "Communicating with Congress: How Citizen Advocacy Is Changing Mail Operations on Capitol Hill." Washington, DC: Congressional Management Foundation. https://www.congressfoundation.org/storage/documents/CMF_Pubs/cwc-mail-operations.pdf.

254 *References*

Goldschmidt, Kathy, and Leslie Ochreiter. 2008. "Communicating with Congress: How the Internet Has Changed Citizen Engagement." Washington, DC: Congressional Management Foundation. https://www.congressfoundation.org/storage /documents/CMF_Pubs/cwc_citizenengagement.pdf.

Graham, Matthew. 2020. "Self-Awareness of Political Knowledge." *Political Behavior* 42: 305–26. https://doi.org/10.1007/s11109-018-9499-8.

Green, Donald, Bradley Palmquist, and Erick Schickler. 2004. *Partisan Hearts and Minds: Political Parties and the Social Identities of Voters*. New Haven, CT: Yale University Press.

Green-Pedersen, C., and P. B. Mortensen. 2010. "Who Sets the Agenda and Who Responds to It in the Danish Parliament? A New Model of Issue Competition and Agenda-setting." *European Journal of Political Research* 49 (2): 257–81.

Greene, S., and L. Elder. 2001. "Gender and the Psychological Structure of Partisanship." *Women & Politics* 22 (1): 63–84.

Griffin, John, and Patrick Flavin. 2011. "How Citizens and Their Legislators Prioritize Spheres of Representation." *Political Research Quarterly* 64 (3): 520–33.

Grimmer, J. 2013. "Appropriators Not Position Takers: The Distorting Effects of Electoral Incentives on Congressional Representation." *American Journal of Political Science* 57 (3): 624–42.

Grimmer, Justin, Solomon Messing, and Sean J. Westwood. 2012. "How Words and Money Cultivate a Personal Vote: The Effect of Legislator Credit Claiming on Constituent Credit Allocation." *American Political Science Review* 106 (4): 703–19.

Grose, C. R., N. Malhotra, and R. Parks Van Houweling. 2015. "Explaining Explanations: How Legislators Explain Their Policy Positions and How Citizens React." *American Journal of Political Science* 59 (3): 724–43.

Gross, Justin H., and Kaylee T. Johnson. 2016. "Twitter Taunts and Tirades: Negative Campaigning in the Age of Trump." *PS: Political Science & Politics* 49 (4): 748–54.

Grossmann, Matthew, and David Hopkins. 2016. *Asymmetric Politics: Ideological Republicans and Group Interest Democrats*. Oxford: Oxford University Press.

Hacker, Jacob S., and Paul Pierson. 2005. *Off Center: The Republican Revolution and the Erosion of American Democracy*. New Haven, CT: Yale University Press.

Haines, Pavielle E., Tali Mendelberg, and Bennett Butler. 2019. "'I'm Not the President of Black America': Rhetorical versus Policy Representation." *Perspectives on Politics* 17 (4): 1038–58.

Hainmueller, Jens, Dominik Hangartner, and Teppei Yamamoto. 2015. "Validating Vignette and Conjoint Survey Experiments against Real-World Behavior." *Proceedings of the National Academy of Sciences* 112 (8): 2395–400.

Hainmueller, Jens, Daniel Hopkins, and Teppei Yamamoto. 2014. "Causal Inference in Conjoint Analysis: Understanding Multidimensional Choices via Stated Preference Experiments." *Political Analysis* 22 (1): 1–30.

Hall, Andrew B. 2019. *Who Wants to Run? How the Devaluing of Political Office Drives Polarization*. Chicago: University of Chicago Press.

Hall, Richard L., and Frank W. Wayman. 1990. "Buying Time: Moneyed Interests and the Mobilization of Bias in Congressional Committees." *American Political Science Review* 84 (3): 797–820.

Harbridge, Laurel. 2015. *Is Bipartisanship Dead? Policy Agreement and Agenda-Setting in the House of Representatives*. Cambridge: Cambridge University Press.

References   255

Harbridge, Laurel, and Neil Malhotra. 2011. "Electoral Incentives and Partisan Conflict in Congress: Evidence from Survey Experiments." *American Journal of Political Science* 55 (3): 494–510.

Harbridge, Laurel, Neil Malhotra, and Brian F. Harrison. 2014. "Public Preferences for Bipartisanship in the Policymaking Process." *Legislative Studies Quarterly* 39 (3): 327–55.

Harbridge-Yong, Laurel, Craig Volden, and Alan Wiseman. 2021. "Are Bipartisan Lawmakers More Effective?" IPR working paper series WP-21-08. Institute for Policy Research, Northwestern University. https://www.ipr.northwestern.edu/documents /working-papers/2021/wp-21-08.pdf.

Harden, Jeffrey J. 2015. *Multidimensional Democracy: A Supply and Demand Theory of Representation in American Legislatures.* Cambridge: Cambridge University Press.

Hare, Christopher, and Keith T. Poole. 2014. "The Polarization of Contemporary American Politics." *Polity* 46 (3): 411–29.

Hawkins, Kirk, and Levente Littvay. 2019. *Contemporary US Populism in Comparative Perspective.* Cambridge: Cambridge University Press.

Hayes, Matthew, and Matthew V. Hibbing. 2017. "The Symbolic Benefits of Descriptive and Substantive Representation." *Political Behavior* 39 (1): 31–50.

Hersh, Eitan. 2020. *Politics Is for Power: How to Move Beyond Political Hobbyism, Take Action, and Make Real Change.* New York: Simon and Schuster.

Hess, Stephen. 1986. *Live from Capitol Hill!* Washington, DC: Brookings Institution.

Hibbing, John R., and Elizabeth Theiss-Morse. 2002. *Stealth Democracy: Americans' Beliefs about How Government Should Work.* Cambridge: Cambridge University Press.

Hill, Seth J. 2015. "Institution of Nomination and the Policy Ideology of Primary Electorates." *Quarterly Journal of Political Science* 10 (4): 461–87.

Hill, Seth, and Chris Tausanovitch. 2015. "A Disconnect in Representation? Comparison of Trends in Congressional and Public Polarization." *Journal of Politics* 77 (4): 1058–75.

Hillygus, D. Sunshine, and Todd G. Shields. 2009. *The Persuadable Voter: Wedge Issues in Presidential Campaigns.* Princeton, NJ: Princeton University Press.

Hitt, Matthew P., Craig Volden, and Alan E. Wiseman. 2017. "Spatial Models of Legislative Effectiveness." *American Journal of Political Science* 61 (3): 575–90.

Hoffman, K. S. 2011. "Visual Persuasion in George W. Bush's Presidency: Cowboy Imagery in Public Discourse." *Congress & the Presidency* 38 (3): 322–43.

Horiuchi, Yusaku, Zachary Markovich, and Teppei Yamamoto. 2022. "Does Conjoint Analysis Mitigate Social Desirability Bias?" *Political Analysis* 30 (4): 535–49.

Hu, Minqing, and Bing Liu. 2004. "Mining and Summarizing Customer Reviews." In *Proceedings of the ACM SIGKDD International Conference on Knowledge Discovery & Data Mining (KDD-2004).* New York: ACM Digital Library.

Huber, G. A., and N. Malhotra. 2017. "Political Homophily in Social Relationships: Evidence from Online Dating Behavior." *Journal of Politics* 79 (1): 269–83.

Huddy, Leonie, Lilliana Mason, and Lene Aarøe. 2015. "Expressive Partisanship: Campaign Involvement, Political Emotion, and Partisan Identity." *American Political Science Review* 109 (1): 1–17.

Huddy, Leonie, and Omer Yair. 2021. "Reducing Affective Polarization: Warm Group Relations or Policy Compromise?" *Political Psychology* 42 (2): 291–309.

Iyengar, Shanto, and Donald Kinder. 1987. *News That Matters: Television and American Opinion*. Chicago: University of Chicago Press.

Iyengar, Shanto, and Masha Krupenkin. 2018. "The Strengthening of Partisan Affect." *Political Psychology* 39: 201–18.

Iyengar, Shanto, Yphtach Lelkes, Matthew Levendusky, Neil Malhotra, and Sean J. Westwood. 2019. "The Origins and Consequences of Affective Polarization in the United States." *Annual Review of Political Science* 22: 129–46.

Iyengar, Shanto, Gaurav Sood, and Yphtach Lelkes. 2012. "Affect, Not Ideology: A Social Identity Perspective on Polarization." *Public Opinion Quarterly* 76 (3): 405–31.

Iyengar, Shanto, and Sean J. Westwood. 2015. "Fear and Loathing Across Party Lines: New Evidence on Group Polarization." *American Journal of Political Science* 59 (3): 690–707.

Jacobs, Lawrence R., and Robert Y. Shapiro. 2000. *Politicians Don't Pander: Political Manipulation and the Loss of Democratic Responsiveness*. Chicago: University of Chicago Press.

Jardina, Ashley. 2019. *White Identity Politics*. Cambridge: Cambridge University Press.

Jerit, Jennifer. 2004. "Survival of the Fittest: Rhetoric during the Course of an Election Campaign." *Political Psychology* 25 (4): 563–75.

Joly, Jeroen K., Joeri Hofmans, and Peter Loewen. 2018. "Personality and Party Ideology among Politicians: A Closer Look at Political Elites from Canada and Belgium." *Frontiers in Psychology* 9: 308852.

Kalla, Joshua L., and David E. Broockman. 2016. "Campaign Contributions Facilitate Access to Congressional Officials: A Randomized Field Experiment." *American Journal of Political Science* 60 (3): 545–58.

Kalla, Joshua L., and David E. Broockman. 2022. "Voter Outreach Campaigns Can Reduce Affective Polarization among Implementing Political Activists: Evidence from Inside Three Campaigns." *American Political Science Review* 116 (4): 1516–22.

Kalmoe, N. P., and L. Mason. 2022. *Radical American Partisanship: Mapping Violent Hostility, Its Causes, and the Consequences for Democracy*. Chicago: University of Chicago Press.

Kam, C. D. 2005. "Who Toes the Party Line? Cues, Values, and Individual Differences." *Political Behavior* 27: 163–82.

Kertzer, Jonathan, and Jonathan Renshon. 2022. "Experiments and Surveys on Political Elites." *Annual Review of Political Science* 25: 529–50.

Kinder, Donald, and Nathan Kalmoe. 2017. *Neither Liberal nor Conservative: Ideological Innocence in the American Public*. Chicago: University of Chicago Press.

Kingdon, John. 1989. *Congressmen's Voting Decisions*. Ann Arbor: University of Michigan Press.

Kirkland, Justin H. 2011. "The Relational Determinants of Legislative Outcomes: Strong and Weak Ties Between Legislators." *Journal of Politics* 73 (3): 887–98.

Kirkland, Justin H., and Jeffrey J. Harden. 2022. *The Illusion of Accountability: Transparency and Representation in American Legislatures*. Cambridge: Cambridge University Press.

Kivetz, Ran, and Itamar Simonson. 2000. "The Effects of Incomplete Information on Consumer Choice." *Journal of Marketing Research* 37 (4): 427–48.

Klar, Samara, and Yanna Krupnikov. 2016. *Independent Politics*. Cambridge: Cambridge University Press.

Klar, S., Y. Krupnikov, and J. B. Ryan. 2018. "Affective Polarization or Partisan Disdain? Untangling a Dislike for the Opposing Party from a Dislike of Partisanship." *Public Opinion Quarterly* 82 (2): 379–90.

Klein, Ezra. 2020. *Why We're Polarized*. New York: Simon and Schuster.

Klein, Ezra, and Alvin Chang. 2015. "'Political Identity Is Fair Game for Hatred': How Republicans and Democrats Discriminate." *Vox*, December 7.

Kowal, Michael. 2023. "The Value of a Like: Facebook, Viral Posts, and Campaign Finance in US Congressional Elections." *Media and Communication* 11 (3): 153–63.

Krupnikov, Yanna, and John Barry Ryan. 2022. *The Other Divide: Polarization and Disengagement in American Politics*. Cambridge: Cambridge University Press.

Ladam, Christina, Jeffrey J. Harden, and Jason H. Windett. 2018. "Prominent Role Models: High-profile Female Politicians and the Emergence of Women as Candidates for Public Office." *American Journal of Political Science* 62 (2): 369–81.

Landry, Alexander P., Jonathan W. Schooler, Robb Willer, and Paul Seli. 2023. "Reducing Explicit Blatant Dehumanization by Correcting Exaggerated Meta-perceptions." *Social Psychological and Personality Science* 14 (4): 407–18.

Lapinski, John, Matt Levendusky, Ken Winneg, and Kathleen Hall Jamieson. 2016. "What Do Citizens Want from Their Member of Congress?" *Political Research Quarterly* 69 (3): 535–45.

La Raja, Raymond, and Brian Schaffner. 2015. *Campaign Finance and Political Polarization: When Purists Prevail*. Ann Arbor: University of Michigan Press.

Lau, Richard R. 1985. "Two Explanations for Negativity Effects in Political Behavior." *American Journal of Political Science* 29 (1): 119–38.

Lau, Richard R., and Gerald M. Pomper. 2002. "Effectiveness of Negative Campaigning in US Senate Elections." *American Journal of Political Science* 46: 47–66.

Lau, Richard R., Lee Sigelman, Caroline Heldman, and Paul Babbitt. 1999. "The Effects of Negative Political Advertisements: A Meta-analytic Assessment." *American Political Science Review* 93 (4): 851–75.

Lau, Richard R., Lee Sigelman, and Ivy Brown Rovner. 2007. "The Effects of Negative Political Campaigns: A Meta-analytic Reassessment." *Journal of Politics* 69 (4): 1176–209.

Lavine, Howard, Christopher Johnston, and Marco Steenbergen. 2012. *The Ambivalent Partisan: How Critical Loyalty Promotes Democracy*. Oxford: Oxford University Press.

Lee, Amber Hye-Yon. 2022. "Social Trust in Polarized Times: How Perceptions of Political Polarization Affect Americans' Trust in Each Other." *Political Behavior* 44 (3): 1533–54.

Lee, Frances E. 2009. *Beyond Ideology: Politics, Principles, and Partisanship in the US Senate*. Chicago: University of Chicago Press.

Lee, Frances E. 2016. *Insecure Majorities: Congress and the Perpetual Campaign*. Chicago: University of Chicago Press.

Lee, Jamine, and Kevin Quealy. 2019. "The 598 People, Places and Things Donald Trump Has Insulted on Twitter: A Complete List." *New York Times*, September 15.

Lee, Nathan. 2022. "Do Policy Makers Listen to Experts? Evidence from a National Survey of Local and State Policy Makers." *American Political Science Review* 116 (2): 677–88.

Lee, Nathan, Michelangelo Landgrave, and Kirk Bansak. 2023. "Are Subnational Policymakers' Policy Preferences Nationalized? Evidence from Surveys of Township, Municipal, County, and State Officials." *Legislative Studies Quarterly* 48 (2): 441–54.

Leeper, Thomas J., Sara B. Hobolt, and James Tilley. 2020. "Measuring Subgroup Preferences in Conjoint Experiments." *Political Analysis* 28 (2): 207–21.

Lees, Jeffrey, and Mina Cikara. 2020. "Inaccurate Group Meta-perceptions Drive Negative Out-group Attributions in Competitive Contexts." *Nature Human Behavior* 4: 279–86.

Lees, Jeffrey, and Mina Cikara. 2021. "Understanding and Combating Misperceived Polarization." *Philosophical Transactions of the Royal Society B* 376: 20200143.

Lelkes, Y. 2018. "Affective Polarization and Ideological Sorting: A Reciprocal, Albeit Weak, Relationship." *The Forum* 16 (1): 67–79.

Lelkes, Y. 2021. "Policy Over Party: Comparing the Effects of Candidate Ideology and Party on Affective Polarization." *Political Science Research and Methods* 9 (1): 189–96.

Lelkes, Yphtach, Gaurav Sood, and Shanto Iyengar. 2017. "The Hostile Audience: The Effect of Access to Broadband Internet on Partisan Affect." *American Journal of Political Science* 61 (1): 5–20.

Lelkes, Yphtach, and Sean Westwood. 2017. "The Limits of Partisan Prejudice." *Journal of Politics* 79 (2): 485–501.

Levendusky, Matthew S. 2009a. *The Partisan Sort: How Liberals Became Democrats and Conservatives Became Republicans.* Chicago: University of Chicago Press.

Levendusky, Matthew S. 2009b. "The Microfoundations of Mass Polarization." *Political Analysis* 17 (2): 162–76.

Levendusky, Matthew S. 2018. "Americans, Not Partisans: Can Priming American National Identity Reduce Affective Polarization?" *Journal of Politics* 80 (1): 59–70.

Levendusky Matthew, and Neil Malhotra. 2016a. "Does Media Coverage of Partisan Polarization Affect Political Attitudes?" *Political Communication* 33 (2): 283–301. https://doi.org/10.1080/10584609.2015.1038455.

Levendusky, Matthew S., and Neil Malhotra. 2016b. "(Mis)perceptions of Partisan Polarization in the American Public." *Public Opinion Quarterly* 80 (S1): 378–91.

Lipinski, Daniel. 2001. "The Effect of Messages Communicated by Members of Congress: The Impact of Publicizing Votes." *Legislative Studies Quarterly* 26 (1): 81–100.

Lombardo, Emanuela, and Petra Meier. 2014. *The Symbolic Representation of Gender: A Discursive Approach.* New York: Routledge.

Lowande, Kenneth, Melinda Ritchie, and Erinn Lauterbach. 2019. "Descriptive and Substantive Representation in Congress: Evidence from 80,000 Congressional Inquiries." *American Journal of Political Science* 63 (3): 644–59.

Lucas, Jack, and Lior Sheffer. 2023. "What Explains Elite Affective Polarization? Evidence from Canadian Politicians." *Political Psychology.* OSF preprints, May 18. https://osf.io/5jgrv.

Lucas, Jack, Lior Sheffer, and Peter J. Loewen. 2022. "Are Politicians Democratic Realists?" OSF Preprints, May 12. https://doi.org/10.31219/osf.io/5buek.

Luk, Sherriff T. K., and Roger Layton. 2002. "Perception Gaps in Customer Expectations: Managers versus Service Providers and Customers." *Service Industries Journal* 22 (2): 109–28.

Luttig, Matthew D. 2017. "Authoritarianism and Affective Polarization: A New View on the Origins of Partisan Extremism." *Public Opinion Quarterly* 81 (4): 866–95.

Maestas, Cherie D., Matthew K. Buttice, and Walter J. Stone. 2014. "Extracting Wisdom from Experts and Small Crowds: Strategies for Improving Informant-based Measures of Political Concepts." *Political Analysis* 22 (3): 354–73.

Malhotra, Neil, Benoît Monin, and Michael Tomz. 2019. "Does Private Regulation Preempt Public Regulation?" *American Political Science Review* 113 (1): 19–37.

Mansbridge, Jane. 1999. "Should Blacks Represent Blacks and Women Represent Women? A Contingent 'Yes.'" *Journal of Politics* 61 (3): 628–57.

Marcus, George E., W. Russell Neuman, and Michael MacKuen. 2000. *Affective Intelligence and Political Judgment.* Chicago: University of Chicago Press.

Marks, Gary, and Norman Miller. 1987. "Ten Years of Research on the False-consensus Effect: An Empirical and Theoretical Review." *Psychological Bulletin* 102 (1): 72.

Martherus, James, Andres Martinez, Paul Piff, and Alexander Theodoridis. 2021. "Party Animals? Extreme Partisan Polarization and Dehumanization." *Political Behavior* 43: 517–40. https://doi.org/10.1007/s11109-019-09559-4.

Martin, Jonathan, and Maggie Haberman. 2020. "Trump Keeps Talking. Some Republicans Don't Like What They're Hearing." *New York Times*, April 9.

Mason, Lilliana. 2016. "A Cross-Cutting Calm: How Social Sorting Drives Affective Polarization." *Public Opinion Quarterly* 80 (S1): 351–77.

Mason, Lilliana. 2018a. *Uncivil Agreement: How Politics Became Our Identity.* Chicago: University of Chicago Press.

Mason, Lilliana. 2018b. "Ideologues Without Issues: The Polarizing Consequences of Ideological Identities." *Public Opinion Quarterly* 82: 280–301.

Mason, Lilliana, and Julie Wronski. 2018. "One Tribe to Bind Them All: How Our Social Group Attachments Strengthen Partisanship." *Political Psychology* 39: 257–77.

Matos, Y., and J. L. Miller. 2021. "The Politics of Pronouns: How Trump Framed the Ingroup in the 2016 Presidential Election." *Politics, Groups, and Identities* 11 (3): 507–25.

Mayhew, D. R. 1974. *Congress: The Electoral Connection.* New Haven, CT: Yale University Press.

McCarty, Nolan. 2019. *Polarization: What Everyone Needs to Know.* Oxford: Oxford University Press.

McCarty, Nolan, Keith T. Poole, and Howard Rosenthal. 2006. *Polarized America: The Dance of Political Ideology and Unequal Riches.* Cambridge, MA: MIT Press.

Meffert, Michael F., Sungeun Chung, Amber J. Joiner, Leah Waks, and Jennifer Garst. 2006. "The Effects of Negativity and Motivated Information Processing during a Political Campaign." *Journal of Communication* 56 (1): 27–51.

Mernyk, Joseph S., Sophia L. Pink, James N. Druckman, and Robb Willer. 2022. "Correcting Inaccurate Metaperceptions Reduces Americans' Support for Partisan Violence." *Proceedings of the National Academy of Sciences* 119 (16): e2116851119.

Michelitch, Kristin, and Stephen Utych. 2018. "Electoral Cycle Fluctuations in Partisanship: Global Evidence from Eighty-Six Countries." *Journal of Politics* 80 (2): 412–27.

Miler, Kristina C. 2010. *Constituency Representation in Congress: The View from Capitol Hill.* Cambridge: Cambridge University Press.

Miller, Warren E., and Donald E. Stokes. 1963. "Constituency Influence in Congress." *American Political Science Review* 57 (1): 45–56.

Milyo, Jeffrey. 2015. "Money in Politics." In *Emerging Trends in the Social and Behavioral Sciences: An Interdisciplinary, Searchable, and Linkable Resource*, ed. Robert A. Scott and Marlis C. Buchmann, 1–9. New York: John Wiley and Sons.

Moore-Berg, S. L., L.-O. Ankori-Karlinsky, B. Hameiri, and E. Bruneau. 2020. "Exaggerated Meta-perceptions Predict Intergroup Hostility between American Political Partisans." *Proceedings of the National Academy of Sciences* 117: 14864.

Morris, Jonathan S. 2001. "Reexamining the Politics of Talk: Partisan Rhetoric in the 104th House." *Legislative Studies Quarterly* 26 (1): 101–21.

Muirhead, Russell. 2014. *The Promise of Party in a Polarized Age*. Cambridge, MA: Harvard University Press.

Mutz, Diana C. 2006. *Hearing the Other Side: Deliberative Versus Participatory Democracy*. Cambridge: Cambridge University Press.

Mutz, Diana. 2015. *In-Your-Face Politics: The Consequences of Uncivil Media*. Princeton, NJ: Princeton University Press.

Mutz, Diana, and B. Reeves. 2005. "The New Videomalaise: Effects of Televised Incivility on Political Trust." *American Political Science Review* 99 (1): 1–15.

Nelson, Rebecca. 2020. "YouTube Sensation. Progressive in a Purple District. Single Mom. What the Democratic Party Could Learn from First-Term Congresswoman Katie Porter." *California Sunday*, March 25. https://story.californiasunday.com/katie-porter-congress/.

Newhagen, John E., and Byron Reeves. 2013. "Emotion and Memory Responses for Negative Political Advertising: A Study of Television Commercials Used in the 1988 Presidential Election." In *Television and Political Advertising, vol. 1: Psychological Processes*, ed. Frank Biocca, 197–220. New York: Routledge.

Newman, Benjamin, Jennifer L. Merolla, Sono Shah, Danielle Casarez Lemi, Loren Collingwood, and S. Karthick Ramakrishnan. 2021. "The Trump Effect: An Experimental Investigation of the Emboldening Effect of Racially Inflammatory Elite Communication." *British Journal of Political Science* 51 (3): 1138–59.

Newport, Frank. 2022. "US Public Opinion and the Role of Government." Polling Matters, Gallup News, November 4. https://news.gallup.com/opinion/polling-matters/404750/public-opinion-role-government.aspx.

Nithyanand, Rishab, Brian Schaffner, and Phillipa Gill. 2017. "Online Political Discourse in the Trump Era." arXiv preprint, Cornell University, November 14. https://doi.org/10.48550/arXiv.1711.05303.

Norrander, Barbara. 1997. "The Independence Gap and the Gender Gap." *Public Opinion Quarterly* 61 (3): 464–76.

Norrander, Barbara. 1999. "The Evolution of the Gender Gap." *Public Opinion Quarterly* 63 (4): 566–76.

Norrander, B., and Wilcox, C. 2008. "Uniform versus Proportional Voting Systems and Voter Turnout." *American Politics Research* 36 (1): 108–28.

Norris, P. 2004. *Electoral Engineering: Voting Rules and Political Behavior*. Cambridge: Cambridge University Press.

Norwood, F. Bailey, and Jayson L. Lusk. 2011. "Social Desirability Bias in Real, Hypothetical, and Inferred Valuation Experiments." *American Journal of Agricultural Economics* 93 (2): 528–34.

Ondercin, H. L. 2018. "Is It a Chasm? Is It a Canyon? No, It Is the Gender Gap." *The Forum* 16 (4): 611–29.

Ondercin, Heather Louise, and Mary Kate Lizotte. 2021. "You've Lost That Loving Feeling: How Gender Shapes Affective Polarization." *American Politics Research* 49 (3): 282–92.

Orr, Lilla, and Gregory Huber. 2020. "The Policy Basis of Measured Partisan Animosity in the United States." *American Journal of Political Science* 64 (3): 569–86.

Osnabrügge, Moritz, Sara B. Hobolt, and Toni Rodon. 2021. "Playing to the Gallery: Emotive Rhetoric in Parliaments." *American Political Science Review* 115 (3): 885–99.

Page, B. I., and R. Y. Shapiro. 1983. "Effects of Public Opinion on Policy." *American Political Science Review* 77 (1): 175–90.

Page, B. I., and R. Y. Shapiro. 1992. *The Rational Public: Fifty Years of Trends in Americans' Policy Preferences*. Chicago: University of Chicago Press.

Parker, David, and Craig Goodman. 2009. "Making a Good Impression: Resource Allocation, Home Styles, and Washington Work." *Legislative Studies Quarterly* 34 (4): 493–524.

Pasek, M. H., L. O. Ankori-Karlinsky, A. Levy-Vene, et al. 2022. "Misperceptions about Out-partisans' Democratic Values May Erode Democracy." *Scientific Reports* 12: 16284. https://doi.org/10.1038/s41598-022-19616-4.

PBS/NPR. 2017. "National Public Radio/PBS NewsHour Poll: November 2017, Question 17." USMARIST.112117NP.R17, Marist College Institute for Public Opinion. Ithaca, NY: Roper Center for Public Opinion Research.

Pennycook, Gordon, and David Rand. 2019. "Fighting Misinformation on Social Media Using Crowdsourced Judgments of News Source Quality." *Proceedings of the National Academy of Sciences* 116 (7): 2521–26.

Pereira, Miguel M. 2021. "Understanding and Reducing Biases in Elite Beliefs about the Electorate." *American Political Science Review* 115 (4): 1308–24.

Peterson, Jordan Carr, and Christian R. Grose. 2021. "The Private Interests of Public Officials: Financial Regulation in the US Congress." *Legislative Studies Quarterly* 46 (1): 49–84.

Pew Research Center. 2014. "Political Polarization in the American Public." Pew Research Center Report, June 12. https://www.pewresearch.org/politics/2014/06/12/political-polarization-in-the-american-public/.

Pew Research Center. 2022. "As Partisan Hostility Grows, Signs of Frustration with the Two-Party System." Pew Research Center, August 9. https://www.pewresearch.org/politics/2022/08/09/as-partisan-hostility-grows-signs-of-frustration-with-the-two-party-system/.

Phillips, Justin Bonest. 2019. "Negative Political Communication on Social Media and the Gender Gap: A Study of Men's and Women's Reactions to Presidential Candidate Attacks on Facebook in 2012 and 2016." *Politics & Gender* 17 (3): 1–29.

Pitkin, Hanna Fenichel. 1967. *The Concept of Representation*. Berkeley: University of California Press.

Poole, Keith, and Howard Rosenthal. 1984. "The Polarization of American Politics." *Journal of Politics* 46 (4): 1061–79.

Pope, J. W. 2013. "False Uniqueness Effect." In *The Encyclopedia of Cross-Cultural Psychology*, ed. Kenneth D. Keith. New York: Wiley-Blackwell.

Prior, Markus. 2007. *Post-broadcast Democracy: How Media Choice Increases Inequality in Political Involvement and Polarizes Elections*. Cambridge: Cambridge University Press.

Prior, Markus. 2013. "Media and Political Polarization." *Annual Review of Political Science* 16: 101–27.

Rakich, Nathaniel, and Dhrumil Mehta. 2019. "Democrats Care More about Winning Than Usual." Five-ThirtyEight, March 8. https://fivethirtyeight.com/features/democrats-care-more-about-winning-than-usual/.

Rathje, Steve, Jay J. Van Bavel, and Sander Van Der Linden. 2021. "Out-group Animosity Drives Engagement on Social Media." *Proceedings of the National Academy of Sciences* 118 (26): e2024292118.

Reingold, Beth. 1996. "Conflict and Cooperation: Legislative Strategies and Concepts of Power Among Female and Male State Legislators." *Journal of Politics* 58 (2): 464–85.

Rhodes, J. H., and Z. Albert. 2017. "The Transformation of Partisan Rhetoric in American Presidential Campaigns, 1952–2012." *Party Politics* 23 (5): 566–77.

Rigby, Elizabeth, and Gerald C. Wright. 2013. "Political Parties and Representation of the Poor in the American States." *American Journal of Political Science* 57 (3): 552–65.

Robinson, R. J., D. Keltner, A. Ward, and L. Ross. 1995. "Actual versus Assumed Differences in Construal: 'Naive realism' in Intergroup Perception and Conflict." *Journal of Personality and Social Psychology* 68 (3): 404.

Roccas, Sonia, and Marilynn Brewer. 2002. "Social Identity Complexity." *Personality and Social Psychology Review* 6 (2): 88–106.

Rogers, N., and J. J. Jones. 2021. "Using Twitter Bios to Measure Changes in Self-identity: Are Americans Defining Themselves More Politically Over Time?" *Journal of Social Computing* 2 (1): 1–13.

Rogers, Steven. 2017. "Electoral Accountability for State Legislative Roll Calls and Ideological Representation." *American Political Science Review* 111 (3): 555–71.

Rogowski, Jon, and Joseph Sutherland. 2017. "How Ideology Fuels Affective Polarization." *Political Behavior* 38 (2): 485–508.

Romney, Mitt. 2016. "Full Transcript: Mitt Romney's Remarks on Donald Trump and the 2016 Race." *Politico*, March 3. https://www.politico.com/story/2016/03/full-transcript-mitt-romneys-remarks-on-donald-trump-and-the-2016-race-220176.

Ropeik, D. 2012. "The Perception Gap: Recognizing and Managing the Risks That Arise When We Get Risk Wrong." *Food and Chemical Toxicology* 50 (5): 1222–25. https://doi.org/10.1016/j.fct.2012.02.015. Epub February 21, 2012. PMID: 22381258.

Ross, L., D. Green, and P. House. 1977. "False Consensus Effect—Egocentric Bias in Social-perception and Attribution Processes." *Journal of Experimental Social Psychology* 13 (3): 279–301.

Rottinghaus, Brandon, and Kent L. Tedin. 2012. "Presidential 'Going Bipartisan' and the Consequences for Institutional Approval." *American Behavioral Scientist* 56 (12): 1696–717.

Rozin, P., and E. B. Royzman. 2001. "Negativity Bias, Negativity Dominance, and Contagion." *Personality and Social Psychology Review* 5 (4): 296–320.

Russell, Annelise. 2018. "U.S. Senators on Twitter: Asymmetric Polarization in 140 Characters." *American Politics Research* 46 (4): 695–723.

Russell, Annelise. 2020. "Minority Opposition and Asymmetric Parties? Senators' Partisan Rhetoric on Twitter." *Political Research Quarterly* 74 (3): 615–27.

Russell, Annelise. 2021. *Tweeting Is Leading: How Senators Communicate and Represent in the Age of Twitter*. Oxford: Oxford University Press.

Sabl, Andrew. 2015. "The Two Cultures of Democratic Theory: Responsiveness, Democratic Quality, and the Empirical-Normative Divide." *Perspectives on Politics* 13 (2): 345–65.

References 263

Santos, L. R., and T. Gendler. 2014. "Knowing Is Half the Battle." Response to 2014 Annual Question: What Scientific Idea Is Ready for Retirement? Edge. https://www.edge.org/response-detail/25436.

Santos, Luiza A., Jan G. Voelkel, Robb Willer, and Jamil Zaki. 2022. "Belief in the Utility of Cross-partisan Empathy Reduces Partisan Animosity and Facilitates Political Persuasion." *Psychological Science* 33 (9): 1557–73.

Schaeffer, Katherine. 2020. "Far More Americans See 'Very Strong' Partisan Conflicts Now than in the Last Two Presidential Election Years." Pew Research Center, March 4. https://www.pewresearch.org/fact-tank/2020/03/04/far-more-americans-see-very-strong-partisan-conflicts-now-than-in-the-last-two-presidential-election-years/.

Schaffner, Brian F. 2020. *The Acceptance and Expression of Prejudice during the Trump Era.* Cambridge: Cambridge University Press.

Schaffner, Brian F., Matthew Streb, and Gerald Wright. 2001. "Teams without Uniforms: The Nonpartisan Ballot in State and Local Elections." *Political Research Quarterly* 54 (1): 7–30.

Scharrer, Erica. 2008. "Media Exposure and Sensitivity to Violence in News Reports: Evidence of Desensitization?" *Journalism & Mass Communication Quarterly* 85 (2): 291–310.

Schattschneider, E. E. 1960. *The Semisovereign People: A Realist's View of Democracy in America.* New York: Holt, Rinehart and Winston.

Schiffer, Adam J. 2000. "I'm Not THAT Liberal: Explaining Conservative Democratic Identification." *Political Behavior* 22: 293–310.

Schneider, Monica C., and Angela L. Bos. 2011. "An Exploration of the Content of Stereotypes of Black Politicians." *Political Psychology* 32 (2): 205–33.

Schneider, Monica C., and Angela L. Bos. 2014. "Measuring Stereotypes of Female Politicians." *Political Psychology* 35 (2): 245–66.

Schöne, Jonas Paul, Brian Parkinson, and Amit Goldenberg. 2021. "Negativity Spreads More than Positivity on Twitter after Both Positive and Negative Political Situations." *Affective Science* 2 (4): 379–90.

Sheffer, Lior, and Peter Loewen. 2019. "Electoral Confidence, Overconfidence, and Risky Behavior: Evidence from a Study with Elected Politicians." *Political Behavior* 41: 31–51.

Sheffer, Lior, Peter John Loewen, Stefaan Walgrave, Stefanie Bailer, Christian Breunig, Luzia Helfer, Jean-Benoit Pilet, Frédéric Varone, and Rens Vliegenthart. 2023. "How Do Politicians Bargain? Evidence from Ultimatum Games with Legislators in Five Countries." *American Political Science Review* 117 (4): 1429–47.

Sheffield, Matthew. 2019. "Dem Voters Care More about Beating Trump Than Any One Policy Issue." The Hill, May 17. https://thehill.com/hilltv/what-americas-thinking/444295-poll-democratic-voters-prioritize-defeating-trump-over-their/.

Sherman, David K., Leif D. Nelson, and Lee D. Ross. 2003. "Naïve Realism and Affirmative Action: Adversaries Are More Similar Than They Think." *Basic and Applied Social Psychology* 25 (4): 275–89.

Simas, Elizabeth N., Scott Clifford, and Justin H. Kirkland. 2020. "How Empathic Concern Fuels Political Polarization." *American Political Science Review* 114 (1): 258–69.

Simon, Herbert A. 1971. *Designing Organizations for an Information-rich World.* Baltimore, MD: Johns Hopkins University Press.

Soroka, Stuart N. 2012. "The Gatekeeping Function: Distributions of Information in Media and the Real World." *Journal of Politics* 74 (2): 514–28.

Soroka, Stuart, Patrick Fournier, and Lilach Nir. 2019. "Cross-national Evidence of a Negativity Bias in Psychophysiological Reactions to News." *Proceedings of the National Academy of Sciences* 116 (38): 18888–92.

Soroka, Stuart, and Stephen McAdams. 2015. "News, Politics, and Negativity." *Political Communication* 32 (1): 1–22.

Stapleton, Carey E., and Ryan Dawkins. 2022. "Catching My Anger: How Political Elites Create Angrier Citizens." *Political Research Quarterly* 75 (3): 754–65.

Stefonek, Jonathan. 2021. "National Politics Seeps into Local Races." *DeForest Times-Tribune*, March 25. https://www.hngnews.com/deforest_times/national-politics-seeps-into-local-races/article_c77a2ad0-c49d-5ed3-8842-cb3e8d54014f.html.

Stimson, James, Michael MacKuen, and Robert Erikson. 1995. "Dynamic Representation." *American Political Science Review* 89 (3): 543–65.

Stone, Daniel F. 2020. "Just a Big Misunderstanding? Bias and Bayesian Affective Polarization." International Economic Review 61 (1): 189–217.

Swers, Michele L. 2002. *The Difference Women Make: The Policy Impact of Women in Congress*. Chicago: University of Chicago Press.

Tajfel, Henri. 1970. "Experiments in Intergroup Discrimination." *Scientific American* 223 (5): 96–102.

Tajfel, Henri. 1982. "Social Psychology of Intergroup Relations." *Annual Review of Psychology* 33 (1): 1–39.

Tausanovitch, Chris, and Christopher Warshaw. 2013. "Measuring Constituent Policy Preferences in Congress, State Legislatures, and Cities." *Journal of Politics* 75 (2): 330–42.

Tausanovitch, Chris, and Christopher Warshaw. 2014. "Representation in Municipal Government." *American Political Science Review* 108 (3): 605–41.

Theriault, Sean M. 2006. "Party Polarization in the US Congress: Member Replacement and Member Adaptation." *Party Politics* 12 (4): 483–503.

Theriault, Sean M. 2008. *Party Polarization in Congress*. Cambridge: Cambridge University Press.

Theriault, Sean M. 2013. *The Gingrich Senators: The Roots of Partisan Warfare in Congress*. New York: Oxford University Press.

Thomsen, Danielle M. 2017. *Opting Out of Congress: Partisan Polarization and the Decline of Moderate Candidates*. Cambridge: Cambridge University Press.

Tillery, Alvin B. 2019. "Tweeting Racial Representation: How the Congressional Black Caucus Used Twitter in the 113th Congress." *Politics, Groups, and Identities* 9 (2): 219–38.

Tomz, Michael, and Robert P. Van Houweling. 2009. "The Electoral Implications of Candidate Ambiguity." *American Political Science Review* 103 (1): 83–98.

Treul, Sarah, Danielle M. Thomsen, Craig Volden, and Alan E. Wiseman. 2022. "The Primary Path for Turning Legislative Effectiveness into Electoral Success." *Journal of Politics* 84 (3): 1714–26.

Tromble, R., and S. C. McGregor. 2019. "You Break It, You Buy It: The Naiveté of Social Engineering in Tech—and How to Fix It." *Political Communication* 36 (2): 324–32.

Trubowitz, Peter, and Nicole Mellow. 2005. "'Going Bipartisan': Politics by Other Means." *Political Science Quarterly* 120 (3): 433–53.

Tyson, Alec. 2019. "Partisans Say Respect and Compromise Are Important in Politics—Particularly from Their Opponents." Pew Research Center, June 19. https://www.pewresearch.org/fact-tank/2019/06/19/partisans-say-respect-and-compromise-are-important-in-politics-particularly-from-their-opponents/.

Valentino, Nicholas A., Ted Brader, Eric W. Groenendyk, Krysha Gregorowicz, and Vincent L. Hutchings. 2011. "Election Night's Alright for Fighting: The Role of Emotions in Political Participation." *Journal of Politics* 73 (1): 156–70.

Ventresca, Rachel. 2018. "Clinton: 'You Cannot Be Civil with a Political Party That Wants to Destroy What You Stand For.'" CNN, October 9. https://www.cnn.com/2018/10/09/politics/hillary-clinton-civility-congress-cnntv/index.html.

Vesoulis, Abby. 2021. "'He's Saying One Thing and Then He's Doing Another.' Rep. Madison Cawthorn Peddles a Different Kind of Trumpism in a Post-Trump World." *Time*, January 27. https://time.com/5931815/madison-cawthorn-post-trump/.

Voelkel, Jan G., Michael N. Stagnaro, James Chu, Sophia Pink, Joseph S. Mernyk, Chrystal Redekopp, Matthew Cashman, James N. Druckman, David G. Rand, and Robb Willer. n.d. "Megastudy Identifying Successful Interventions to Strengthen Americans' Democratic Attitudes." Institute for Policy Research Working Paper WP-22-38, Northwestern University. Accessed July 2, 2024. https://www.ipr.northwestern.edu/our-work/working-papers/2022/wp-22-38.html.

Volden, Craig, and Alan E. Wiseman. 2014. *Legislative Effectiveness in the United States Congress: The Lawmakers*. Cambridge: Cambridge University Press.

Volden, Craig, and Alan E. Wiseman. 2018. "Legislative Effectiveness in the United States Senate." *Journal of Politics* 80 (2): 731–35.

Volden, Craig, Alan E. Wiseman, and Dana E. Wittmer. 2013. "When Are Women More Effective Lawmakers than Men?" *American Journal of Political Science* 57 (2): 326–41.

Wallander, Lisa. 2009. "25 Years of Factorial Surveys in Sociology: A Review." *Social Science Research* 38 (3): 505–20.

Ward, Dalston G., and Margit Tavits. 2019. "How Partisan Affect Shapes Citizens' Perception of the Political World." *Electoral Studies* 60: 102045.

Webster, Steven W. 2020. *American Rage: How Anger Shapes Our Politics*. Cambridge: Cambridge University Press.

Webster, Steven W., and Alan I. Abramowitz. 2017. "The Ideological Foundations of Affective Polarization in the U.S. Electorate." *American Politics Research* 45: 621–47.

Westfall, Jacob, Leaf Van Boven, John R. Chambers, and Charles M. Judd. 2015. "Perceiving Political Polarization in the United States: Party Identity Strength and Attitude Extremity Exacerbate the Perceived Partisan Divide." *Perspectives on Psychological Science* 10 (2): 145–58.

Westwood, S. J. 2021. "The Partisanship of Bipartisanship: How Representatives Use Bipartisan Assertions to Cultivate Support." *Political Behavior* 44 (3): 1–25.

Whyman, Melissa. 2019. "Which Congress Is the Most Productive?" *Extensions: A Journal of the Carl Albert Congressional Research and Studies Center*, November 6. https://extensionscac.com/news/which-congress-is-the-most-productive/.

Winberg, Oscar. 2017. "Insult Politics: Donald Trump, Right-Wing Populism, and Incendiary Language." *European Journal of American Studies* 12 (2): 4–5.

Wlezien, Christopher. 2004. "Patterns of Representation: Dynamics of Public Preferences and Policy." *Journal of Politics* 66 (1): 1–24.

Wojcieszak, M. E., and V. Price. 2012. "Perceived versus Actual Disagreement: Which Influences Deliberative Experiences?" *Journal of Communication* 62 (3): 418–36.

Yang, JungHwan, Hernando Rojas, Magdalena Wojcieszak, Toril Aalberg, Sharon Coen, James Curran, Kaori Hayashi, Shanto Iyengar, Paul K. Jones, Gianpietro Mazzoleni, Stylianos Papathanassopoulos, June Woong Rhee, David Rowe, Stuart Soroka, and Rodney Tiffen. 2016. "Why Are 'Others' So Polarized? Perceived Political Polarization and Media Use in 10 Countries." *Journal of Computer-Mediated Communication* 21 (5): 349–67. https://doi.org/10.1111/jcc4.12166.

Yates, Frank, Carolyn Jagacinski, and Mark Faber. 1978. "Evaluation of Partially Described Multiattribute Options." *Organizational Behavior and Human Performance* 21 (2): 240–51.

Yiannakis, D. E. 1982. "House Members' Communication Styles: Newsletters and Press Releases." *Journal of Politics* 44 (4): 1049–71.

Young, Dannagal G. 2020. *Irony and Outrage: The Polarized Landscape of Rage, Fear, and Laughter in the United States.* Oxford: Oxford University Press.

Zaller, John R. 1992. *The Nature and Origins of Mass Opinion.* Cambridge: Cambridge University Press.

Zhong, Chen-Bo, et al. 2008. "Negational Categorization and Intergroup Behavior." *Personality and Social Psychology Bulletin* 34 (6): 793–806.

Zhong, Chen-Bo, Adam D. Galinsky, and Miguel M. Unzueta. 2008. "Negational Racial Identity and Presidential Voting Preferences." *Journal of Experimental Social Psychology* 44 (6): 1563–66.

INDEX

Page numbers in italics refer to figures and tables.

Abramowitz, Alan, 20
Abrams, Samuel A., 20
Achen, Christopher, 36
affective forms of representation, 8
affective partisan polarization: consequences of, 23–24, 184; definition of, 4, 21, 22; demographics and, 175–76; elite animosity and, 115–17; hypothesis of, 30–35; ideology and, 71, 108, 192; incivility and, 154; measure of, 21–23, 22; media and, 138; misperceptions and, 196–97, 202–4, 204; political candidates' perceptions about, 89–91, 91, 95; possible future benefits of, 213–14; rhetoric and, 51, 72, 102; substantive representation and, 67. *See also* partisanship; polarization; rhetoric
Akerlof, George, 39
American National Election Studies (ANES), 21–22, 118, 175
Augoustinos, Martha, 43

Barber, Michael, 154
Bartels, Larry, 36
Beyond Ideology (Lee), 19
Biden, Joe, 206–8, 207
Binder, Sarah, 79
bipartisan language: electoral safety and, 69–71; elite communication and, 43–44; ideology and, 71–75, 73, 74; in newsletters and tweets, 49, 50, 54, 58,

59, 87–89, 88; research findings on, 4, 47–55. *See also* rhetoric
bipartisanship: as appeal to voters, 30–31, 44; within contemporary Congress, 68; legislative effectiveness and, 75–79, 77, 78; people's preference for, 24, 213
"Blue Wave," 172
Broockman, David E., 173

campaigning: negative, 7, 90, 127–30, 128, 154; negative advertisements in, 63–64; perceptions about changes in, 127–30, 128
Capuano, Michael, 52
Cawthorn, Madison, 36
censures, 1–2, 243n2 (chap. 1)
Center for Effective Lawmaking, 76
Citizens United v. Federal Election Commission, 142
CivicPulse, 92
civility, in relation to negativity, 7. *See also* incivility
Clinton, Hillary, 43, 58, 60
CNN, 139, 205
Cole, Tom, 41
conjoint experimental approach: to compare subgroups and negative representation, 182; experiment design for effect of negative partisanship, 97–103, 98, 101, 102; for negative

conjoint experimental approach (*cont.*)
partisanship and policy congruence,
162–63, 246n4 (chap. 8); for policy
congruence and negative rhetoric,
158–59; on politician's level of partisan
animosity, 121–25, *122–23, 124*; "rating-
based conjoint," 163; to study perceptions of representation, 155; to test
issue importance and electoral-based
rhetoric, 166
Cooperative Congressional Election
Study (CCES), 97, 162, 182, 185,
244n5
Cooperative Election Study (2020), 26,
244n5
Curry, James M., 68

DCInbox project, 45
De Garis, Stephanie, 43
Democracy for Realists (Achen and Bar-
tels), 36
descriptive representation, 27–28
Dickson, Eric S., 30–31
Disch, Lisa, 9
Downs, Anthony, 25
Druckman, James, 169
DW-nominate score, 17–18, 72–75

"egocentric bias," 121
electoral rewards, research findings on, 5
electoral safety: negative representation and, 69–71, *70*; research findings
on, 4–5
electoral success: ideological distance on
perceived, 108–10, *109*; partisan rhetoric and ideological distance on, 103–
8, *105, 106, 107*
elite-driven hypothesis, of negative representation, 31–33, 116
Enders, Adam M., 115
exposure hypothesis, of negative representation, 33–35, 116, 133

Facebook, *205*
false consensus effect, 32, 38, 121, 125,
197, 202
false uniqueness effect, 38, 197, 202

feeling thermometer, to measure partisan affect, 117–18, *118*, 181–82
Feinstein, Dianne, 132
Fenno, Richard, 17, 26–27, 82
Ferguson, Andrew, 67, 79
Fine, Jeffrey A., 34, 133
Fiorina, Morris, 9, 20
"folk theory of democracy," 36
Fox News, *139, 140*, 204, *205*
future, of politics: keeping perspective
about, 213; questions about, 210–12;
reducing partisan animosity and, 215;
role of media in, 216–17

Gaetz, Matt, 67
Geer, John, 34
Gingrich, Newt, 172
Goldenberg, Amit, 34
Gosar, Paul, 1
Greene, Marjorie Taylor, 2, 67, 114
Grimmer, Justin, 42
group dynamics, rhetoric and, 43–44

Hainmueller, Jens, 155
Hall, Richard, 173
Hangartner, Dominik, 155
Harden, Jeffrey J., 26
Holder, Eric, 114, 126
homestyle, 26–27, 82
Hoyer, Steny, 52
Hu, Minqing, 61
Hunt, Megan F., 34, 133

identity: negational, 81, 151; political, 3,
23; social, appeals, 31, 43, 197; social-
psychological theories of, 2–3, 8, 152,
171. *See also* negative representation;
partisanship
ideological consistency, 20
ideological extremity, 175; partisan affect
and, 117; penalties for, 244n6; rhetoric
and, 71–75, *73, 74*, 124, 124–25
ideological representation, 156
ideological sorting, 114–15
implicit partisan bias, 22–23
incentives, media and fundraising:
negative representation and, 34–35,

132–33; research findings on, 5; rhetoric and, 143–48, *145*, *147*; roll call votes and, 173; social media and, 142–43. *See also* exposure hypothesis, of negative representation; social media

incivility: effects of, 154; and future implications, 214–15; rhetoric of Trump and, 58, 60, 83; on social media, 137, 158, 188; as type of negative partisanship, 102, 165; use of uncivil language, 7

Internet Archive's Television News Archive Explorer, 138

Iyengar, Shanto, 22–23, 82–83, 156

Kalla, Joshua L., 173
Klar, Samara, 23, 188–89
Klein, Ezra, 10–11
Krupenkin, Masha, 82–83
Krupnikov, Yanna, 23–24, 188–89

La Raja, Raymond, 214
Lau, Richard R., 7
Lee, Barbara, 132
Lee, Frances, 19, 68
legislative effectiveness scores, 76
legislative responsiveness, 26
Lelkes, Yphtach, 156
Levendusky, Matthew, 20, 169, 198, 200, 205
Liu, Bing, 61
Lucas, Jack, 115
Lucid, 157, 166, 246n3 (chap. 8)

Making Constituencies (Disch), 9
Malhotra, Neil, 198, 200, 205
Mayhew, David, 26, 42, 48, 81
McGregor, Shannon C., 216
media, news: negativity bias and, 33–34; perception gap and, 204–5, *205*; role in future politics, 216–17; role in relation to negativity and coverage, 138–41, *139*, *140*
median voter model, 25
Meuser, Dan, 52
Miller, Warren E., 25

misperceptions: affective polarization and, 202–4, *204*; about desires for negative representation, 199–202, *201*, *202*; education level and, *206*; media sources and, 204–5, *205*; about others' beliefs, 197–99; voting behaviors and, 206–7, *207*

More in Common, 201, 205
MSNBC, *139*, *140*, 204–5
Muirhead, Russ, 214

negative attention cycle, 138, 188
negative campaigning, 7, 90, 127–30, *128*, 154. *See also* campaigning
negative partisanship, *95*; activists and, 186; causes of, 29–35; consequences of, 35–39; across different constituency groups, 175–81, *177*, *179*; effective lawmaking and, 75–79, *77*, *78*; electoral strategy changes and, 165; electoral success and, 104–8, *105*, *106*, *107*, 130–31; elite perceptions about, 89–91, *91*, 94–97, *96*, 111, 130–31; negative partisans and, 182–84, *183*; other groups with partisan animosity and, 184–88, *187*; political donors and, 186, *187*; political hobbyists and, 188; primary voters and, 185–86, *187*; reaction across different parties to, 189–91, *190*; reasons politicians engage in, 112–13; research findings on elite-driven, 5, 23, *92*, 92–94. *See also* political representation
negative representation: definition of, 6–7; electoral safety and, 69–71, *70*; explanation of, 3–4; factors that allow for, 194; feedback loop of, 38, 79–80, 131, 209–10; misperceptions about, 38–39, 197–202, *201*, *202*; research findings on, 4; research findings on penalties for, 5; research findings on perception gaps and, 6; substantive representation and, 27, 35–39, 68, 130–31; theory of, 8–9. *See also* political representation
negativity bias, in media, 33–34, 140–41, 216

newsletters: communication changes over time in, 55–61, *56*, *59*; as form of congressional communication, 44–45; fundraising and, 143–48, *145*, *147*; most common political words in, *49*; negativity and out-partisan rhetoric in, 61–65, *62*, *64*; study data on, 45–46. *See also* vote share

Newsmax, 204, *205*

New York Times, *205*

NPR, *205*

OANN, 204, *205*

Obama, Barack, 43

Obama, Michelle, 114, 126

Ocasio-Cortez, Alexandria, 39

OpenSecrets report, 142

Other Divide, The (Krupnikov and Ryan), 23–24

Palazzo, Steven, 4

Parkinson, Brian, 34

partisan antipathy, 117–21, *118*, 131

partisanship: agenda-setting and, 19; benefits of, 213–15; across different constituency groups, 175–81, *177*, *179*, *180*; identities and, 3–4, 82–83, 188; reactions to negative, 189–91, *190*; reduction of partisan animosity, 215. *See also* affective partisan polarization

Pascrell, Bill, 63

Pelosi, Nancy, 8

perception gap: education level and, *206*; of favorability of other party, 203, *204*; media sources and, 204–5, *205*; of negative representation, 200–202, *201*, *202*; of polarization, 196–97; voting behavior and, 206–7, *207*

Pew Research Center, 199

Pitkin, Hanna, 2, 6, 25, 29

polarization: benefits of, 213–15; cycle of, 40, 209–10; ideological, 20–21; perception of, 196–97; study of contemporary political, 10–11; in US Congress, *18*, 19–20. *See also* affective partisan polarization

political representation: constructivist perspective of, 9; effects of legislator traits on preferences for, 159–61, *160*; future of, 211–18; party identification and, *161*, 161–62; perceptions about, 152–53, 155–57, *156*; polarization within, 2, 9–10, 24; policy agreement vs. partisan rhetoric and, 163–65, *164*; politician leeway and, 172–74; research insights on contemporary, 4–5, 171–72; style of, 9; theory of, 2–3. *See also* descriptive representation; negative partisanship; negative representation; polarization; substantive representation; symbolic representation

Pomper, Gerald M., 7

Poole, Keith T., 17–18

Pope, Jeremy C., 20, 154

Porter, Katie, 132, 142, 245n2 (chap. 7)

Pressler, Larry, 196, 208

Pressley, Ayanna, 67, 79

Price, David, 8

Promise of Party in a Polarized Age, The (Muirhead), 214

"race to the bottom," 39–40

"Republican Revolution," 172

rhetoric: based on winning and losing elections, 8; conclusions about, 65–66; elite, 42–44, 55–61, *56*, *59*; fundraising and, 143–48, *145*, *147*; ideological extremity and, 71–75, *73*, *74*, *124*, 124–25; legislative effectiveness and, 75–79, *77*, *78*; negativity and out-partisan, 61–65, *62*, *64*, 244n7 (chap. 3); overlap of, 53, *54–55*; partisan, 43–44, 47–48, 51–53, *105*, *106*, *107*; partisan, and policy congruence, 191–94, *192*, *193*; policy, 51–52; prevalence of partisan and policy, *50*, 57–61; in relation to other party's rhetoric, *126*, 126–30; as tool to appeal to voters, 30; when discussing out-partisans, 119–21, *120*, *122*, 122–25, *123*, *124*. *See also* affective partisan polarization; bipartisan language; negative partisanship; vote share

Robinson, Robert J., 198
"role model effect," 212
roll call voting, 18, 173
Rosenthal, Howard, 17-18
Ross, Lee, 198
Ryan, John Barry, 23-24

Saunders, Kyle L., 20
Schaffner, Brian, 214
Schattschneider, E. E., 214
Scheve, Kenneth, 30-31
Schiff, Adam, 1, 132
Schöne, Jonas Paul, 34
Sheffer, Lior, 115
Shimkus, John, 52
social desirability bias, 112, 208
social distance (interpersonal relationships), 23-24
social media, 133-38, *135*, *136*, 142-43, 216. *See also* incentives, media and fundraising
Social Research Surveys, 200
Sood, Gaurav, 156
Stahl, Lesley, 114
Stanbery, William, 1-2
Stanford University, 215
Stevenson, Andrew, 1
Stokes, Donald E., 25
"Strengthening Democracy Challenge" (Stanford University), 215
substantive representation: affective partisan polarization and, 67; explanation of, 25; negative representation and, 27, 68; and perceived electoral success, 108-11, *109*, 130-31; research findings on, 5, 25-27; research findings on citizen preference for, 5; rhetoric and, 75-79, *77*, *78*; study of issue priorities over electoral wins, 166-70, *167*, *168*
symbolic representation: communication and, 43-44; explanation of, 28-29

Tavits, Margit, 24
Tlaib, Rashida, 67, 243n2 (chap. 1)
Tromble, Rebekah, 216

Trump, Donald: censures and, 1; partisan affiliation and support of, 177-78, *179*, *180*; party identification and, 188-91, *190*; perception gaps and, 206-8, *207*; rhetoric and, 43, 58, 60-61, 83; study effects of being supporter of, 119, *192*; Twitter and, 140, 158
Twitter, *62*; communication changes over time, 55-61, *56*, *59*; effect of party identification on, *161*, 161-62; as form of Congressional communication, 45; fundraising and, 143-48, *145*, *147*; misperceptions and, 204-5, *205*; most common political words used on, *49*; negativity and out-partisan rhetoric on, 52-53, 61-65, *62*, *64*; partisan incivility and, 158; popularity of congressional tweets with partisan language, 134-37, *135*, *136*; study data on, 46-47; study of emotional language on, 34. *See also* vote share

"US House Members in Their Constituencies" (Fenno), 17

Volden, Craig, 76
voter "blind spots," 173
voter-driven hypothesis, of negative representation, 29-31, 82, 104
vote share: negative partisanship and, 171; rhetoric effect on, 85-89, *86*, *88*, 156; voter-driven hypothesis and, 31; as way to categorize districts, 69. *See also* rhetoric
Voting Rights Act (1965), 19

Ward, Dalston G., 24
Wayman, Frank W., 173
Westwood, Sean J., 22
"white identity politics," 175
Why We're Polarized (Klein), 10
Wiseman, Alan E., 76
Witherspoon, Rebecca, 90

Yamamoto, Teppei, 155
YouGov, 97, 162

CHICAGO STUDIES IN AMERICAN POLITICS

A series edited by Susan Herbst, Lawrence R. Jacobs, Adam J. Berinsky, and Frances Lee; Benjamin I. Page, editor emeritus

SERIES TITLES, CONTINUED FROM FRONT MATTER:

Prisms of the People: Power and Organizing in Twenty-First-Century America by Hahrie Han, Elizabeth McKenna, and Michelle Oyakawa

Democracy Declined: The Failed Politics of Consumer Financial Protection by Mallory E. SoRelle

Race to the Bottom: How Racial Appeals Work in American Politics by LaFleur Stephens-Dougan

The Limits of Party: Congress and Lawmaking in a Polarized Era by James M. Curry and Frances E. Lee

America's Inequality Trap by Nathan J. Kelly

Good Enough for Government Work: The Public Reputation Crisis in America (And What We Can Do to Fix It) by Amy E. Lerman

Who Wants to Run? How the Devaluing of Political Office Drives Polarization by Andrew B. Hall

From Politics to the Pews: How Partisanship and the Political Environment Shape Religious Identity by Michele F. Margolis

The Increasingly United States: How and Why American Political Behavior Nationalized by Daniel J. Hopkins

Legacies of Losing in American Politics by Jeffrey K. Tulis and Nicole Mellow

Legislative Style by William Bernhard and Tracy Sulkin

Why Parties Matter: Political Competition and Democracy in the American South by John H. Aldrich and John D. Griffin

Neither Liberal nor Conservative: Ideological Innocence in the American Public by Donald R. Kinder and Nathan P. Kalmoe

Strategic Party Government: Why Winning Trumps Ideology by Gregory Koger and Matthew J. Lebo

Post-Racial or Most-Racial? Race and Politics in the Obama Era by Michael Tesler

The Politics of Resentment: Rural Consciousness in Wisconsin and the Rise of Scott Walker by Katherine J. Cramer

Legislating in the Dark: Information and Power in the House of Representatives by James M. Curry

Why Washington Won't Work: Polarization, Political Trust, and the Governing Crisis by Marc J. Hetherington and Thomas J. Rudolph

Who Governs? Presidents, Public Opinion, and Manipulation by James N. Druckman and Lawrence R. Jacobs

Trapped in America's Safety Net: One Family's Struggle by Andrea Louise Campbell

Arresting Citizenship: The Democratic Consequences of American Crime Control by Amy E. Lerman and Vesla M. Weaver

How the States Shaped the Nation: American Electoral Institutions and Voter Turnout, 1920–2000 by Melanie Jean Springer

White-Collar Government: The Hidden Role of Class in Economic Policy Making by Nicholas Carnes

How Partisan Media Polarize America by Matthew Levendusky

Changing Minds or Changing Channels? Partisan News in an Age of Choice by Kevin Arceneaux and Martin Johnson

The Politics of Belonging: Race, Public Opinion, and Immigration by Natalie Masuoka and Jane Junn

Trading Democracy for Justice: Criminal Convictions and the Decline of Neighborhood Political Participation by Traci Burch

Political Tone: How Leaders Talk and Why by Roderick P. Hart, Jay P. Childers, and Colene J. Lind

Learning While Governing: Expertise and Accountability in the Executive Branch by Sean Gailmard and John W. Patty

The Social Citizen: Peer Networks and Political Behavior by Betsy Sinclair

Follow the Leader? How Voters Respond to Politicians' Policies and Performance by Gabriel S. Lenz

The Timeline of Presidential Elections: How Campaigns Do (and Do Not) Matter by Robert S, Erikson and Christopher Wlezien

Electing Judges: The Surprising Effects of Campaigning on Judicial Legitimacy by James L. Gibson

Disciplining the Poor: Neoliberal Paternalism and the Persistent Power of Race by Joe Soss, Richard C. Fording, and Sanford F. Schram

The Submerged State: How Invisible Government Policies Undermine American Democracy by Suzanne Mettler

Selling Fear: Counterterrorism, the Media, and Public Opinion by Brigitte L. Nacos, Yaeli Bloch-Elkon, and Robert Y. Shapiro

Why Parties? A Second Look by John H. Aldrich

Obama's Race: The 2008 Election and the Dream of a Post-Racial America by Michael Tesler and David O. Sears

News That Matters: Television and American Opinion, Updated Edition by Shanto Iyengar and Donald R. Kinder

Filibustering: A Political History of Obstruction in the House and Senate by Gregory Koger

Us Against Them: Ethnocentric Foundations of American Opinion by Donald R. Kinder and Cindy D. Kam

The Partisan Sort: How Liberals Became Democrats and Conservatives Became Republicans by Matthew Levendusky

Democracy at Risk: How Terrorist Threats Affect the Public by Jennifer L. Merolla and Elizabeth J. Zechmeister

In Time of War: Understanding American Public Opinion from World War II to Iraq by Adam J. Berinsky

Agendas and Instability in American Politics, Second Edition by Frank R. Baumgartner and Bryan D. Jones

The Party Decides: Presidential Nominations Before and After Reform by Marty Cohen, David Karol, Hans Noel, and John Zaller

The Private Abuse of the Public Interest: Market Myths and Policy Muddles by Lawrence D. Brown and Lawrence R. Jacobs

Same Sex, Different Politics: Success and Failure in the Struggles over Gay Rights by Gary Mucciaroni